G. L. BROOK is Professor of English Language and of Medieval English Literature at the University of Manchester, England. He was educated at the University of Leeds and won the Ripon English Literature Prize in 1931. Professor Brook is interested in the study of dialect and was the founder of the Lancashire Dialect Society and first editor of its *Journal*. His publications include *An English Phonetic Reader, English Sound Changes, An Introduction to Old English,* and *Glossary to the Works of Sir Thomas Malory.*

G. L. BROOK

A History of
The English Language

The Norton Library
W · W · NORTON & COMPANY · INC ·
NEW YORK

W. W. Norton & Company, Inc. also publishes *The Norton Anthology of English Literature*, edited by M. H. Abrams et al; *The Norton Anthology of Poetry*, edited by Arthur M. Eastman et al; *World Masterpieces*, edited by Maynard Mack et al; *The Norton Reader*, edited by Arthur M. Eastman et al; *The Norton Facsimile of the First Folio of Shakespeare*, prepared by Charlton Hinman; and the Norton Critical Editions.

SBN   393   00248   9

PRINTED IN THE UNITED STATES OF AMERICA

6 7 8 9 0

CONTENTS

PREFACE

AN APOLOGY is needed for the addition of yet another *History of the English Language* to the large number of existing books on that subject. My defence is that the subject has so many different aspects that there is room for many different books, each approaching it from a different point of view. Although the synchronic study of language is so much to the fore at present, I have written this book in the firm belief that the historical approach can still provide valuable help in the understanding of a language like English, of which we are fortunate in possessing records from very early times. I have deliberately avoided saying much about the history of the English vocabulary, because this aspect of the history of the language has been fully treated elsewhere, notably in Otto Jespersen's *Growth and Structure of the English Language*, Dr Mary S. Serjeantson's *A History of Foreign Words in English*, and Dr J. A. Sheard's *The Words We Use*. I have tried to meet the needs of university students and of the general reader who is willing to seek in the past history of our language for some explanation of the puzzling features of present-day English. I have not assumed a previous knowledge of Old English or of phonetics, and in Chapter III I have tried to give a brief description of the way in which speech-sounds are made and a definition of such phonetic terms as are necessary for the understanding of Chapter IV. Chapter IV thus presupposes a knowledge of Chapter III, and parts of Chapter V presuppose a knowledge of Chapters III and IV, but the remaining chapters can be read independently of each other.

I am indebted to Professor Simeon Potter, Dr Randolph Quirk and Professor R. M. Wilson, who read the book in typescript and who made many valuable suggestions for its improvement, to my colleague Dr R. F. Leslie for his help in reading the proofs and in preparing the index, to Miss P. C. Horne and Mrs E. Levine, who showed great patience in typing the book and in removing inconsistencies of presentation, to my wife

for her ungrudging help at every stage, and to Mr Eric Partridge for his very friendly encouragement and advice.

G. L. BROOK

May 1957

TABLE OF ABBREVIATIONS

AN	Anglo-Norman
Gmc	Common Germanic
IE	Indo-European
JEGP	*Journal of English and Germanic Philology*
ME	Middle English
MnE	Modern English
NED	*The New English Dictionary* (see p. 212)
OE	Old English
OF	Old French
ON	Old Norse
ONF	Old Northern French
PMLA	*Publications of the Modern Language Association of America*
SPE	Society for Pure English
WS	The West Saxon dialect of Old English

Phonetic symbols are for the most part those of the International Phonetic Association and are explained in Chapter III. They are given in square brackets.

An asterisk preceding a form indicates that the form is hypothetical, and not recorded in the extant texts.

CHAPTER I

The Nature of Language

THE study of one's mother tongue has an importance different in kind from that which attaches to other branches of study. One can do with or without most other subjects, but one's own language is inescapable. It can be studied for its own sake, as all subjects can, but it has the added importance that it is the medium through which knowledge of any other subject is normally acquired. It does not follow that a detailed knowledge of the nature and history of one's own language is indispensable, or that the historical approach is the only one possible, but such knowledge has some importance for everyone and not merely for professed students of the history of the English language.

The study of language cannot be isolated from other branches of study. For example, some philosophical problems can be shown to be merely disputes about words; when the meaning of the words used is examined, the problem disappears. An example of such a problem is the old question: 'What happens when an irresistible cannon-ball strikes an immovable post?' The contingency is an impossible one because an irresistible force and an immovable object cannot exist simultaneously. It is sometimes said that thought cannot exist without language. Whether we accept this view or not will depend to some extent on our definition of the two words 'thought' and 'language', but it is certainly true to say that most of our thinking involves the use of words. Students of literature must devote much of their time to what are in effect linguistic problems, and literature can have no existence without language. The study of language can throw light on social history, and it has something to contribute to psychology, anthropology and sociology, just as in its turn it has much to gain from these studies. But, quite apart from the help that it can give to other studies, the study of language is a branch of knowledge of interest for its own sake, since it is the study of an important aspect of human behaviour.

Language has been defined as 'a purely human and non-instinctive method of communicating ideas, emotions, and desires by means of a system of voluntarily produced symbols'.[1] One feature of language that is emphasized in this definition is that it must be deliberate. An involuntary and inarticulate cry of pleasure or pain cannot properly be regarded as language, because it is not the purpose of the cry to express ideas or emotions to someone else, although it may have that result. How far language must be regarded as purely human is debatable. Some of the more highly organized insect communities, such as those of bees and ants, may make use of arbitrary symbolic movements to express elementary ideas, but in the present state of our knowledge it is hard to say how far such actions are instinctive. Animals such as the horse and the dog, which have come into contact with man, can be taught to react to some of the simpler features of human language, but they do not imitate them, and it is reasonable to regard language as an essentially human activity. Metaphors are often used with reference to language, as when we speak of a family of languages or of a liquid consonant. Such metaphors are often convenient, but it is well continually to remind ourselves what are the literal facts that these metaphors describe or conceal. Although some writers refer to language as if it were an organism having an independent life of its own, it is necessary to remember that language is a series of habits formed by human beings and that it has no independent existence.

It may be noted that language may communicate ideas, emotions and desires in an indirect way. We have all had experience of people who cause a good deal of social embarrassment by maintaining a grim silence for what seems to them the sufficient reason that they have nothing to say. They are ignoring one of the functions of language, which is to make it clear to the person addressed that the speaker is well disposed towards him, even if he does not wish to say anything more specific than that. This is the purpose of such greetings as *Good morning* and *How do you do?*

The word 'system' in Sapir's definition calls attention to a distinction which often has to be made: that between speech

---

[1] Edward Sapir, *Language, An Introduction to the Study of Speech*, p. 7.

and language. Speech is the action of an individual or the isolated actions of a number of individuals; language is an organized system of means of communication employed by a group of people who can understand one another. This distinction between speech and language is often associated with the name of De Saussure, who, in his *Cours de Linguistique générale* (published posthumously in 1916), made a distinction between *parole* and *langue* which corresponds in some respects with that made by English scholars between speech and language. The distinction, however, was recognized in England at least as early as the sixteenth century, when Puttenham wrote, 'After a speach is fully fashioned to the common vnderstanding, and accepted by consent of a whole countrey and nation, it is called a language'. (*The Arte of English Poesie* (1589) ed. Arber, p. 156.) One branch of the study of language, known as linguistic analysis, deals with the methods by which millions of separate utterances can be reduced to a system which can be regarded as a language. The study of speech can throw light on the study of language. The advantage of the study of speech is the precision with which a single utterance can be described, whereas there must always be a certain vagueness about any statement about language. On the other hand, knowledge of the language of a community is for most purposes more useful than knowledge of the speech of an individual. Language presupposes a hearer as well as a speaker, and a hearer can understand the meaning of what he hears only by relating it to the language of which it forms a part.

No two speakers of a language speak in exactly the same way, and a language does not exactly correspond with the speech of any one speaker of the language. It may therefore seem that a language is a rather unreal abstraction, like the 'average man'. In fact, however, the lack of exact identity of speech-sounds is unimportant, since no ear is able to distinguish them with perfect accuracy. All that is necessary is that the speech-sounds used by different speakers of a language in pronouncing a particular word shall resemble each other so closely that most hearers think that the sounds are identical. A similar test may be used to define that much discussed abstraction Standard English. Standard English is that form of English speech which so closely resembles the average pronunciation of most educated speakers as to seem identical with it to a hearer with a reasonably good ear. This definition abounds in expressions that cannot be exactly measured, and those who are made unhappy by such expressions would be wise to avoid the use of a term like Standard English altogether.

Speakers whose deviations from Standard English are considerable are said to speak a dialect, but it is well to remember that Standard English is itself a dialect which has acquired greater importance than the other English dialects for reasons which are in the main non-linguistic. Dialects are of two kinds: they may be regional or they may depend on the social class to which the speaker belongs. The two kinds of dialect are not mutually exclusive, and some linguistic features are characteristic of both regional and class dialects. In the course of the history of the English language regional dialects have become less important as more and more speakers have learned to speak Standard English, but class dialects have, for good or ill, become more important. Regional dialects are important for the student of the history of a language because they often preserve older forms which have been lost in the standard language. Many words which are obsolete in Standard English are still in frequent use in dialects, and dialects preserve forms unaffected by sound-changes which have taken place in the standard language.

The symbols which constitute a language may be spoken or written or they may consist of gestures. Gestures do not as a rule play a very important part in the language of civilized peoples, and from the point of view of the development of a language the spoken language is much more important than the written. We are probably more bookish today than our ancestors were at any time in the past, and even the most bookish person speaks very much more than he writes, even though he may read more than he listens. As far as the average user of any language is concerned, the disproportion between speech and writing is even greater, and in the earlier periods of the history of English, as of most other languages, a large number of the speakers who shared in the task of transmitting the language from one generation to another were illiterate.

One advantage which speech enjoys as compared with

writing or gesture is that while we are speaking or listening the hands and eyes are left free. It is sometimes said that a further advantage of speech is that it is capable of a much wider range of expressiveness than either writing or gesture. It is true that a speaker can express subtle shades of meaning which cannot easily be expressed by means of writing or gesture, but it is doubtful whether speech can do this by reason of any inherent advantage which it possesses over other forms of expression. It is more likely that the subtle meaningful variations of which speech is capable are the result of the use of speech as a medium of expression by countless generations of speakers. Writing and gesture are, like speech, capable of infinite variation, but these variations have not come to be associated with particular meanings.

Writing has some advantages which are not shared by speech. The chief of these is the ease with which it can be preserved and reproduced. It may be noticed that comparatively recent scientific inventions, the gramophone, the wireless and the tape recording machine, have done something to give to speech the advantages which writing has enjoyed for several centuries, but so far no invention has provided compensation for the fact that, whereas the ear can detect sounds only in succession, the eye can see a number of different objects at a single glance. As everyone who has listened to a lecture or a news bulletin knows to his cost, the listener has to accept the speed chosen by the speaker whereas the reader can go at his own speed, lingering over difficult passages and skipping very quickly over the passages of less interest or importance.

Whatever may be the position of future historians of the English language, who will be able to listen to gramophone records of the spoken English of the nineteenth and twentieth centuries, one problem that confronts a student of the history of a language is that his knowledge of the history of the spoken language has to be obtained in the main from written or printed records. One of his chief tasks, therefore, is to find out how far written records present an accurate picture of the spoken language. It is often assumed that the sole function of the written language is to represent the spoken language, and this assumption underlies many of the arguments of the advocates of spelling reform, but Henry Bradley has shown in a famous paper[1] that for most readers today there has developed a direct association between the written symbol and the idea to be expressed. In earlier times, however, before English spelling became stabilized in the seventeenth century, it is probable that most English writers were striving, however imperfectly, to record what they believed to be the pronunciation of the words they used, and spelling can be used, with reservations, as evidence of pronunciation.

The differences between spoken and written language are not confined to the representation of individual words; they extend also to syntax. Conversations in Victorian novels often seem to readers of today to be stilted and unreal. One reason for this unreality sometimes lies in the choice of words, but the most frequent cause is that the author has not realized how great is the difference between the syntax of speech and that of the written language. There are many constructions which are perfectly well established in the written language but which are out of place in conversation, and, on the other hand, the spoken language develops a syntax of its own which has rules quite different from those of the written language. The practice of reading aloud, once much more common than it is today, presents special problems since the reader has to express by means of the spoken word sentences which were meant for a different medium. One reason for the differences between speech and writing is that in speech we can make use of many devices for the expression of meaning which cannot be used in writing, such devices as variation of intonation, speed or loudness of the voice, a shrug of the shoulders or a smile, all of which can have a profound influence on meaning.

The difference between the syntax of spoken English and that of the written language has to be borne constantly in mind when we are dealing with the history of English syntax. The most obvious difficulty is that we have little means of knowing what was the syntax of the spoken language in Early English. During the last few hundred years we have rather more evidence from

[1] 'On the Relations between Spoken and Written Language, with special Reference to English' in the *Proceedings of the British Academy* 1913–1914, pp. 211–232.

plays, conversations in novels and such books as Swift's *Polite Conversations*, but such evidence has to be used with caution. One cannot feel sure that an author has achieved, or even aimed at, realism in his record of spoken English.

It may be that advantages would result from lessening the differences between spoken and written English. The tape recording machine has enabled many people to realize for the first time how great these differences are. It is sometimes said that a newspaper reporter with a grudge against a public speaker has an easy way of getting his own back by recording exactly what the speaker says without smoothing away the repetitions and examples of faulty grammar. No one wants to hear people 'talking like a book', but many of us are too ready to rely on inarticulate grunts as a substitute for speech. Many people are reluctant even to say 'Yes', but substitute for the word a noise, or succession of two noises, made in the throat. Conversely, something might well be done to improve upon the very clumsy devices which we use in writing to represent such aspects of speech as loudness or intonation. Italics and punctuation marks are some of the devices that are used for this purpose at present. The written language has some features, such as quotation marks, for which there is no recognized equivalent in speech.

Few questions connected with language have aroused so much discussion as its origin. Much of the discussion has been mere speculation, and there is a frequent tendency to dismiss the subject as unprofitable. As long ago as 1866, when La Société de Linguistique was founded in Paris, it was laid down that papers and discussions on this subject were not to be allowed.[1] Although certainty cannot be achieved, however, the question of origins is closely bound up with any investigation of the nature of language.

One theory is that words imitated natural sounds, such as the cries of animals or the noises made by rapidly moving or colliding objects. Words that had this origin are sometimes said to be *onomatopoetic*, but the term *echoic* is to be preferred as being shorter, easier to spell, and more obviously descriptive of what is intended. The test of a genuinely echoic word is its

---

[1] Jespersen, *Language, its Nature, Development and Origin*, p. 96.

intelligibility to a foreigner who has no knowledge whatever of the language in question, and the number of such words in any language is very small, though it must be remembered that words which were originally echoic may have become less so because of the effects of sound-change. A process which has a good deal in common with echoism is the symbolism by which certain sounds are associated with particular ideas. Opinions differ considerably about the part which such symbolism plays in linguistic development; some scholars go so far as to say that it plays no part at all, whereas others see it everywhere. Examples that are often quoted are the use of words containing a short *i* to express smallness and the use of the initial group *sl-* to express dislike, *fl-* to describe movement and *st-* to express stability. It is, of course, easy to find exceptions to all these tendencies, but they may provide an explanation of some of the changes that have taken place in the meanings of English words. The meaning of the word *sly* (ON *slœgr* 'skilful') could have degenerated without assistance, but the associations of the initial *sl-* group may have contributed to the process. Some examples of the association of certain sounds with particular ideas may well have resulted from the accident that particular groups of sounds happen to occur in a large number of related words that have been preserved; the association of *st-* with stability no doubt had this origin. A speaker or a writer resorting to echoism is not greatly concerned whether the words that he uses are new coinages or words that already exist, but it is sometimes possible by its use to achieve very expressive effects, as in Mr P. G. Wodehouse's description of the noise made by a pig feeding as 'a sort of gulpy, gurgly, plobby, squishy, wofflesome sound'.[1]

Another theory is that language had its origin in unthinking exclamations called forth by various emotions. Such exclamations are not themselves language, since their purpose is not to communicate with others, but they can easily develop into language. A cry of pain may be at first involuntary, but it produces certain effects when heard by others, and when it is deliberately used to achieve those effects, for example when it is used as a protest or a warning, it becomes language. Theories

[1] *Blandings Castle*, Chapter 3.

that do not carry immediate conviction are that language had its origin in the expulsion of breath accompanying strong muscular effort, and that words originated in the movements of the tongue in imitating natural gestures such as beckoning.

In so far as such theories are acceptable at all, they explain only small parts of language; it is hard to see how they can be extended to account for all language. Something may probably be learnt about the origin and development of language by observing the way in which a child learns to speak. Although not all philologists are agreed about the value of such investigation, it may well be that a good deal of language had its origin in a process parallel to that by which a child first pronounces meaningless groups of sounds to which meanings are afterwards attached either by the child itself or by its hearers. A notable stage in the history of language was reached when significant sounds began to be handed down from one generation to another, and then imitation came to play an important part in the development of language.

By tracing the history of existing languages, it is possible to notice certain trends of development that will allow us to draw inferences about the state of languages many centuries earlier than the date of the earliest written records, although many thousands of years later than the origin of language. Some of these conclusions are rather unexpected. We might expect language in the distant past to have been simpler than in more recent times, but it is clear that in many respects, notably in accidence, the parent language from which most of the languages of Europe have developed was much more complicated than any of the modern languages that are descended from it. Although new linguistic irregularities can arise at any time as a result of sound-change, a more common tendency has been that towards the smoothing away of irregularities. Variations like that between *father* and *mother*, or between *be, am, is* and *was*, where related ideas are expressed by different root-words, are characteristic of the older stages of language development; variations like that between *actor* and *actress* or between *walk* and *walked* are characteristic of a later stage. Jespersen has summed up his impression of the general trend of the development of language: 'The evolution of language shows a progressive

tendency from inseparable irregular conglomeration to freely
and regularly combinable short elements'.[1] This change results
in an improvement in the efficiency of language as a medium
of expression in that subtle shades of meaning can be expressed
with the use of a smaller amount of speech-material with a
consequent lessening of the strain on the memory.

The very great diversity of languages at the present day is
due in part to the splitting up of earlier languages. With our
present knowledge it is not possible to show that all the languages of the world are descended from a single original language, but it is possible to distinguish large groups of languages
which are related to each other in this way. This splitting up
has resulted from one of the most strongly marked characteristics of spoken language: the tendency to change. Since the
written language usually lags some way behind the spoken
language, these changes are not always recorded in writing, but
many of them are so recorded. The changes that have affected
the English language can be classified according to the main
divisions of linguistic study, and these changes form the main
part of the subject-matter of this book.

One of the most important processes in the building up of a
language is known as analogy. We divide the words that we use
into groups according to the function they perform, and we feel
free to replace a word by another word belonging to the same
group in order to express a different meaning. We learn to in-
flect words in particular ways in order to express various shades
of meaning or syntactic relations, but we do not as a rule
remember each inflected form separately. The forms that we
construct out of familiar linguistic elements are nearly always
identical with the traditional forms because other speakers
have used the same elements in the same way as ourselves, and
the labour of learning and using a language is considerably
lessened by this process of building up words. If we learn new
words we make them conform to the pattern of words that we
already know; that is to say, we form them on the analogy of
existing words. Similarly we learn that certain spellings correspond to particular sounds in some words and we assume that a

---

[1] *Language, its Nature, Development and Origin*, p. 429.

similar correspondence will hold good in words with which we
are unfamiliar. The irregularities of English spelling are such
that analogy often leads to variations of pronunciation or spelling. Thus, some people pronounce the *ei* of *inveigle* like the *ei* of
receive; some people pronounce it like the *ei* of *eight*.

The result of the operation of linguistic analogy is usually to
make more complete the partial resemblance between two words.
Unless there is some resemblance, either in form or in meaning,
between two words, analogy is not likely to take place. The conservative attitude to language which results from widespread
literacy is hostile to analogical change, just as it is hostile to other
kinds of linguistic change, and children are corrected when they
indulge in analogical changes that are exactly parallel to changes
which are now accepted as a normal part of our language.

Analogy may operate in any of the divisions of language
which are discussed in this book: spelling, phonology, morphology, syntax and semantics. Analogy has influenced spelling in
the word *rhyme*, which occurs side by side with *rime*. *Rime* is the
historically correct spelling (OE *rīm*); *rhyme* is due to the influence of *rhythm*. Similarly the *g* in *sovereign* is due to the influence of *reign*. More often analogy affects pronunciation as
well as spelling. For example, *sorry* (OE *sārig*) has a short vowel
on the analogy of *sorrow* (OE *sorg*). An example of analogical
interference with the regular operation of sound-changes is
provided by the word *staff*, with its plural *staves*. The differences
between the two forms arise from sound-changes of which more
will be said later. We have here the conditions requisite for the
operation of analogy: close resemblance in meaning and a
rather less close resemblance in form. Analogy takes place in
both directions to increase the resemblance in form: the plural
staves is re-formed as *staffs* to make it more like the singular, and
from the plural *staves* a new singular *stave* is formed. The result
here has been the creation of a new word, and the two words
staff and *stave* have had an independent semantic development.
Similarly *shade* is from the Old English nominative *sceadu*, while
shadow is from inflected forms such as the dative *sceadwe*, but the
two forms have developed as independent words. *Clothes* is the
regular development of the Old English plural *clāþas*; *cloths* is
an analogical new formation from the singular.

Sometimes sound-changes cause pairs of related words to diverge in form and, when this happens, analogy often restores the resemblance between the two forms. For example, the adjective *ghastly* is closely related to the noun *ghost*. Sound-changes led to the divergence between the stem-vowels of the two words, and speakers felt the need for a new adjective whose connexion with *ghost* should be more obvious. They therefore coined the adjective *ghostly* as an analogical new formation with *o* from the noun. Similarly the adjective *cool* formed the basis of a verb which by the time of Shakespeare had become *to keel*. The verb *to cool* is a new formation from the adjective and the verb *to keel* has become obsolete.

Analogy has played a large part in the simplification of English accidence. The nominative plural of *lamb* in Old English was *lambru*, but the Modern English plural has been re-formed on the analogy of the very large declension of nouns which had the ending *-as* in the nominative plural in Old English. The infinitive of the verb *to lay* was in Old English *lecgan*, and the regular development of this infinitive in Modern English would have been *ledge*; the form *lay* is due to the analogy of forms like the third person singular of the present indicative which had the medial consonant *g* instead of *cg* in Old English. Analogy has here introduced a possibility of confusion, since the new infinitive happens to be identical in form with the preterite of the verb *to lie* (OE *licgan*, pret. *læg*).

An example of analogy in syntax may be taken from the use of prepositions. The original meaning of *averse* was 'turned away' and it was therefore followed by the preposition *from*, as was the adjective *different*, but on the analogy of other adjectives, such as *partial* and *similar*, which were followed by the preposition *to*, the adjectives *averse* and *different* are often followed by *to*, and many people now regard an insistence on the use of *from* after these adjectives as pedantic. We also occasionally find *differ with* on the analogy of *agree with*. These examples serve to illustrate a further point: the association of ideas which serves as the starting point of analogy may be one of contrast rather than one of similarity. By a process similar to analogy two different ways of expressing the same idea are sometimes confused to produce an idiom which will not stand up to investigation. One not infrequently hears it said that the importance of something or other cannot be underestimated. The remark may be true, but it is not as a rule what the speaker intends. Such a statement results from confusion between two different ways of emphasizing the importance of a statement: we can say that its importance 'should not be underestimated' or that it 'cannot be overemphasized', but the two constructions should be kept apart.

The effect of analogy on the development of meaning is probably more widespread than is generally recognized, since it accounts for many undetected misunderstandings on the part of individuals. We all understand, or think we understand, many more words than we ourselves have occasion to use, and it is only by chance that misunderstandings are revealed. It is sometimes possible to explain these misunderstandings by assuming association with other words, and such associations account for malapropisms, frequent in literature long before the time of Sheridan and sometimes, though less often, met with in real life. A surprisingly large number of those who took part in one experiment defined the word *panoply* as 'pomp, splendour' and a few gave it the meaning 'some sort of awning'. It is probable that unconscious association with *canopy* accounts for some of these mistakes. Another example of such confusion is *impertinent* which used to mean 'irrelevant', but which has probably been influenced by *pert* and has consequently come to mean 'impudent'.

Analogy is a very powerful tendency working towards the smoothing out of the irregularities in a language. The words which are most likely to resist its operation are everyday words, such as the parts of the verb *to be* or irregular plurals like *children*, *mice* and *men*, which are used so frequently that they are not likely to be forgotten.

One kind of substitution that can be regarded as a variety of analogy is the sound-substitution that often takes place in words borrowed from other languages. When we borrow a foreign word containing a sound that does not exist in English, there are three possible ways of dealing with it. We may, if we happen to speak the language from which the word is borrowed, use the foreign pronunciation, as many people do when they use French words like *ingénue*. A second way of dealing with the loan-word is by sound-substitution: we replace the foreign sound by the

English sound or group of sounds which seems to be nearest to it. Thus in the word *fête* some English speakers use the diphthong which they use in *fate*, and in the first syllable of *envelope* many speakers substitute *on* for the French nasalized vowel. A third way is to ignore the original pronunciation and resort to a spelling pronunciation based on the analogy of native English words. This is most likely to happen in words which are not of recent introduction; it is illustrated by the other current pronunciation of the word *envelope*.

Language may be studied from several different points of view. Two quite different approaches are known as the synchronic and the diachronic. Synchronic linguistics deals with the state of a language at a given time; diachronic linguistics deals with the historical development of a language. The great achievements in linguistic study during the nineteenth century were in the historical field, whereas today synchronic study is attracting an increasing amount of attention. One reason for this increased attention is that in recent years more attention has been paid to languages of whose history little or nothing is known. These languages have in the past been neglected because they are spoken by peoples who have not played a prominent part in world history, but they have considerable linguistic interest. In the study of many of these languages synchronic study is the only approach possible, and there has been a tendency on the part of students of these languages to assume that only the synchronic study of a language can be regarded as truly 'scientific' and to disparage the diachronic approach even to languages like English for the historical study of which there are ample materials. There is, however, no reason why the two approaches to language should conflict with each other. When De Saussure made his now famous distinction between these two approaches to language study, he insisted that the two methods should always be kept distinct, but historical and descriptive linguistics can help each other: the history of a language provides an explanation of many of the puzzling features of the language today, and, by observing the linguistic habits of living people, it is possible to form a better idea of the true nature of linguistic change.

With the exception of etymology, which is a purely historical study, any of the main branches of linguistic study may be approached either synchronically or diachronically; these branches themselves result from different ways of regarding a language. We may examine its sounds or its word-formation, the way in which the words are arranged or their meaning. It may be well at this stage to define the terms that are used to describe the broad divisions of linguistic study.

Phonetics deals with the properties of speech-sounds, how they are made and combined with each other, and the acoustic effect that they produce.

Phonology deals with the sounds found in any one language or group of related languages. If the approach is diachronic, phonology deals with the changes that those speech-sounds have undergone, and that is the sense in which the word is used in this book. If the approach is synchronic, phonology is a systematic study of the sounds found in a given language at a given time.

Morphology deals with the grouping of sounds into words. It is concerned with the forms and the formation of words and it includes the study of inflexional endings and of word-formation.

Syntax deals with the relation of words to each other and with the arrangement of words in sentences.

Semantics deals with the meanings of words and with the reasons for their survival or disappearance.

Etymology deals with the history of words and their relationship to other words.

Etymology helps to provide the material for the other branches of the study of language. Opinions differ about its importance to the user of language. One view is that meaning is all-important, and that the etymology of a word is of no importance unless both speaker and hearer are conscious of it. Another view, which is implied more often than it is explicitly stated, is that words must always be used in their etymological sense. The truth probably lies between these two extreme views. It may be noticed that the etymology of a word can affect its meaning even though a speaker is not aware of the etymology. The meaning which speakers or hearers attach to a particular word depends in the main upon the contexts in which they have previously heard or seen the word used, and it is fairly certain that in some of those contexts, especially the literary ones, the meaning of the word was influenced by its etymology. A knowledge of etymology is necessary to the student of literature. There are very many words in the works of Shakespeare and Milton which are used in a sense closer to the etymological sense than that current today.

Until the second half of the nineteenth century etymological methods were very haphazard, but with the growth of the historical study of languages a reaction against unscientific theorizing set in, and it came to be realized that, before an etymology can be regarded as established, every sound in the word must be accounted for. This cautious approach to etymology is reasonable, since etymology is a branch of linguistic study upon which many other branches depend. It is of no use to discuss the semantic or phonological development of a word until we are sure whether we are dealing with one word or two. For example, in discussing the semantic development of the word *queen* it is necessary to remember that there are in English two distinct, though related words, *queen* and *quean*, which have had a different semantic history. It must be remembered, however, that confusion between the two words is as much a fact of linguistic history as their separate origin, and etymology is only one of the factors that have to be taken into account.

Vocabulary is the aspect of language study whose interest is most obvious, but from the point of view of the structure of a language, it is not the most important, because words can be borrowed from one language into another in very large numbers, whereas phonology and morphology are concerned with essential features of a language that are much less likely to be borrowed. It is true that foreign plurals such as *phenomena* or *indices* are borrowed, but these are not instances of the borrowing of inflexional endings as such. The plural endings have been borrowed along with the words to which they belong, but they have not been attached to other words.

It is important to remember that in the mind of a speaker of a language at any one time all the different aspects of language are present together and one can influence another, but historically they follow different lines of development, and, when we are studying the history of a language, it is convenient to examine them separately.

This method of studying a language by isolating the variables is not free from dangers, which have been described by W. J. Entwistle: 'The historical investigation of single elements seen in isolation did not produce a picture of a language as it is or was. The language itself—the almost complete pattern of correspondences which makes communication possible—died on the operating table'.[1] The image is graphic, but misleading. The patient does not die unless the surgeon loses interest half way through the operation and fails to complete his task. It is the business of the student of language, after analysing the development of the various strands of which a language is composed, to bring them together again. The procedure of a court of law offers a parallel. To decide whether an offence has been committed and, if so, what is the appropriate punishment is too complicated a question to be answered all at once. It is necessary for the jury to decide whether a particular action has been committed; the judge has to decide whether that action is contrary to the law. While these questions are under consideration, any previous convictions of the accused must not be taken into account, but, if the accused is found to be guilty, the judge has the task of re-assembling all the variable factors in the case in order to decide what punishment to impose.

The student of language has a task similar to that of the judge: when the variables have been isolated, he has to bring them together again in order to see how the various aspects of language interact on each other at any one time. Instances of this interaction are to be seen at many stages in the history of the English language: the decay of inflexional endings is an aspect of accidence, but it had a phonetic cause in the light stress carried by such endings, and it is closely bound up with problems of syntax because of the devices, such as auxiliary verbs and prepositional phrases, which were used to replace the old inflexions and which may sometimes have contributed to their decay. The auxiliary verbs and prepositions which were used in this way were not newly coined for the purpose; they were existing words whose meanings were extended, and so the development can be discussed from the point of view of semantics.

[1] *Aspects of Language*, p. 72.

CHAPTER II

The Development of English

W HEN an Englishman learns another European language, he is usually struck by a number of resemblances between the foreign language and his own. He takes some of the resemblances for granted, and it may well happen that the existence of some common characteristics in all the languages that he knows will mislead him into thinking that these characteristics are necessarily shared by all the languages of the world. Common linguistic characteristics may have many different explanations. First of all, they may arise from some fundamental characteristic of human nature or of natural phenomena independent of language. The second of these causes is the explanation of the few genuinely echoic words in any language. Again, the resemblance may be purely accidental. The number of sounds used for the expression of meaning is comparatively small, although the number of possible combinations of those sounds is large. On the other hand the number of ideas to be expressed and the number of languages in the world are large, and it is not surprising that there should be some accidental coincidence; such coincidences in the same language provide the basis of puns. To explain a single resemblance the possibility of accident can never be ruled out, but the explanations mentioned so far can account for only a very small proportion of the resemblances between two languages. Another reason for resemblance, which applies especially to resemblance of vocabulary, is borrowing from one language into another. The borrowing may have taken place in either direction, or it may be that the two languages have borrowed a word from a third language. Since sound-changes may have taken place in all the languages concerned both before and after the borrowing, it is often possible to tell from the form of a word whether it has been borrowed and, if so, from what source and approximately at what time. Borrowing can account for a very large number of resemblances, as a glance at any page of an etymological dictionary of English will show, but it cannot account for resemblances in phonology or inflexional endings, and the likelihood of borrowing is often ruled out by the known facts of general or linguistic history. Borrowing cannot take place unless there is some sort of contact between the speakers of two languages, and the sound-changes which a word has undergone often show that it must have existed in a particular language from very early times. Yet another possible explanation of linguistic resemblances is that the two languages concerned have developed from a common source and have both preserved some of the characteristics of their common ancestor. Resemblances of this kind, when the other possibilities have been eliminated, form the basis of the classification of the languages of the world into families of related languages. Confirmation of the view that two languages, such as English and German, are derived from a common source may be obtained when we see that the farther back we go in tracing the history of these languages the closer becomes the resemblance between them.

If we compare English with German, Dutch and the Scandinavian languages, we find that all these languages have certain features in common. There are resemblances in vocabulary, especially in simple, everyday words such as numerals and nouns of relationship, words that are less often borrowed than more out-of-the-way words. Even more significant are the resemblances in accidence. In each of these languages there are two large groups of verbs: strong verbs, which form their past tense by changing the vowel of the stem, and weak verbs, which form their past tense by the addition of a suffix containing a dental consonant. On the basis of such resemblances we are able to say that English, German, Dutch and the Scandinavian languages are all descended from a single earlier language, and that they represent the various forms into which a parent language has been differentiated by divergent development. No texts written in this parent language, known as Common Germanic or Germanic, have survived, but it is possible, by comparing the languages composing the group, to reconstruct forms which must have occurred in the parent language. When such forms are quoted in grammars they are usually marked with an asterisk, a conventional sign to show that the forms are hypothetical.

By applying similar methods to other groups of languages we obtain similar results. The Romance languages, such as French, Spanish and Italian, can be shown to go back to a common source, which was a form of Latin, although it was not identical with Classical Latin. The languages of the Romance group stand in a close relationship to each other and in a less close relationship to the Germanic languages. The explanation is that Common Germanic and the language from which the Romance languages are derived both belong to a larger group of related languages, known as Indo-European, to which belong most of the languages of Europe and some of the languages of Asia. There is a limit to this process of discovering relationships. Indo-European is only one of several large language groups which have not so far been shown to have any relation with one another. Two of these families of languages whose speakers have come into contact with the speakers of Indo-European languages are the Semitic and the Finno-Ugrian groups. To the first group belong Arabic and Hebrew, at one time assumed to be the ancestor of all other languages because it was thought to be the language spoken in the Garden of Eden. To the Finno-Ugrian group belong Magyar, which is the language of Hungary, and Finnish.

INDO-EUROPEAN

The Indo-European family of languages is the most widespread group of languages in the world and is used by a very large number of speakers, but there is little or no connexion between the number of speakers of a language and its linguistic interest or its efficiency as a medium of expression. The wide extension of Indo-European languages in every continent of the world is due to the accident that speakers of those languages have been conquerors and colonizers who have taken their language with them. They have been able to do this because they have settled in regions of the world which had not already achieved a settled government and because they have often been reinforced by subsequent waves of settlers speaking the same language. If the country colonized already has a settled government or if the colonizers fail to keep in constant touch with their mother country, the original language of the colony is usually the one to survive. Thus, neither the Scandinavians nor the Normans succeeded in permanently imposing their language on the English, although they contributed many loan-words to the English language, and most of the immigrants who made their homes in the United States in the nineteenth century were content to learn English, though there are still pockets in various parts of the United States where foreign languages are spoken. It is important to remember that there is no necessary connexion between race and language. The speakers of the original Indo-European language may have belonged to several different races, and there is no reason to suppose that any of the peoples who speak Indo-European languages today are racially descended from the original speakers of Indo-European.

Although it is sometimes convenient to use words like 'origin' and 'original' in speaking of a language the use of these words is not free from danger, and the senses in which they are used should perhaps be defined. When we speak of Indo-European as the origin of languages like English, French and German, we simply mean that Indo-European is the earliest form of the language that we can reconstruct. It is unlikely that Indo-European was any more static than the languages that are descended from it, and it is safe to assume that it had a long earlier history the details of which are unknown to us. It is generally assumed that the dispersal of the speakers of Indo-European, which led to the splitting up into groups, took place somewhere between 3000 and 2000 B.C. When we speak of the original home of the speakers of Indo-European, we mean the part of the world where they lived shortly before their dispersal. Until the middle of the nineteenth century it was usual to assume an Asiatic origin for the speakers of Indo-European. Europe had suffered from the later invasions of the Huns and the Turks and other Asiatic hordes, and it therefore seemed natural to think of movements of population from east to west. This idea was encouraged by the discovery that Sanskrit was an Indo-European language and that in many ways it was closer than the languages of Europe to the parent speech. Later it came to be realized that the accident of the preservation of early records of Sanskrit was enough to account for its closeness to Indo-European, and that in some respects, such as its vowel system, it was less close than some European languages such as Greek. Moreover most of the languages of the Indo-European family have been spoken in Europe from the earliest times of which we have any knowledge, and it seemed more natural to suppose that the original home was fairly near the centre of the area occupied by speakers of Indo-European languages rather than on its eastern fringe.

The evidence of language has been used to throw light on the problem. If a word occurs in nearly all the branches of the family or in two or three branches sufficiently remote from each other to make borrowing unlikely, it is likely that it formed a part of the vocabulary of the parent language. This kind of evidence has to be used with caution because of the possibility of changes of meaning and of widespread borrowing. As an example of its dangers we may instance the occurrence of modern scientific words like *telephone* in most European languages today. Moreover deductions from negative evidence are particularly dangerous in view of the observed tendency of words to pass out of use and to be replaced by other words without any easily discernible reason. The evidence of single words would be of little value, but cumulatively the evidence of common vocabulary does help to build up a picture which can be used to test the validity of information obtained from other sources. The Indo-European languages have fairly widely spread common words for winter, snow, freezing, cold, honey, and for animals such as the wolf, the horse and the bear and plants such as the pine tree which are characteristic of a fairly cold climate. The absence of survivals of a common word for the sea has led to the guess that the original home was inland. On the whole the most likely region seems to be somewhere on the steppes of south-western Russia.

The problem of how differences which characterize the various Indo-European languages came into being has aroused much discussion. The oldest view is that of August Schleicher, who in 1866 put forward the *pedigree theory* that the differences among Indo-European languages developed as the result of a series of successive bifurcations. He expressed the relations of the various Indo-European languages to each other by means of a genealogical tree. This theory is no longer generally accepted, but it has had its influence on the terminology of linguists which is still in use, as, for example, when one speaks of the Indo-European family of languages or when one says that a language is descended from another. Such terms enable those who are sceptical about the value of comparative philology to secure a debater's point by saying that to speak of one language as descended from another is like saying that a man is his own father.

A more serious objection to Schleicher's theory is that there are resemblances, like those between Germanic and Celtic, which cut across any such classification. To explain these, Johannes Schmidt in 1872 propounded his *wave theory*. He assumed an original speech spread over a wide area in which dialect differences gradually arose. These differences developed among the speakers of what had once been a homogeneous language, and eventually became so marked that they led to the creation of distinct languages. The dialect areas overlapped and it is thus possible to explain the resemblances which are shared by some Indo-European languages but not by all. This theory does not explain all the problems involved, but it provides a working hypothesis which can be modified in the light of supplementary theories. If has, for example, been suggested that differences would tend to develop more quickly if they were encouraged by early migrations. A further point of some importance is that theories about the splitting up of the Indo-European languages tend to assume the homogeneity of the parent Indo-European language, but it has been pointed out that there were probably dialectal variations within the Indo-European parent language, and there is a danger that our ignorance of the exact nature of Indo-European may lead us to over-simplify the problems involved.

However the differences arose, it is possible to use them as the basis of a classification of the Indo-European languages. The classification is based upon linguistic features which are shared by some of the languages of the family but not by all. One such feature is the development of the Indo-European palatal plosives, which in some languages fell in with the velar plosives but in other languages became alveolar fricatives.[1] Broadly speaking the former development took place in the western Indo-European languages while the latter development took place in the eastern languages. The word meaning 'hundred' occurs in most of the Indo-European languages, and its initial consonant was affected by the changes in question. The two broad divisions of the Indo-European family are therefore generally called the *centum* and the *satem* branches respectively from the form of the word meaning 'hundred' in Latin and Avestan, which have for this purpose been regarded as representative languages of the two branches. By applying similar tests it is possible to divide the Indo-European family of languages into about ten groups. When we consider what a large part accident has played in the preservation of records of some of the 'dead' Indo-European languages, it becomes clear that many languages or whole groups of languages may have disappeared. This view has been confirmed by the discovery during the present century of languages the existence of which was not suspected when the main features of the classification of the Indo-European languages were discovered, but which throw light on some of the problems connected with the origin and classification of these languages. These languages, both of them 'dead', are Hittite and Tocharian. It is probable that several different languages were current among the Hittites, and inscriptions discovered at the ancient capital of the Hittites in Asia Minor suggest that at least one of these languages had affinities with Indo-European. One important result of the discovery of Hittite has been to suggest that Indo-European may have been less homogeneous than was at one time supposed. The name Tocharian is given to two languages or dialects used in manuscripts, belonging to the first seven centuries of the Christian era, which have been discovered in Eastern Turkestan. The most interesting feature of Tocharian is that it is a *centum* language preserved in an area where we should expect to find either a *satem* language or one not belonging to the Indo-European family at all.

---

[1] For an explanation of these terms see Chapter III.

The following are the main groups into which the remaining Indo-European languages have been divided:

Indian. The oldest literary texts written in languages belonging to this group are the Vedas or sacred books of India consisting of hymns which may have been written about 1000 B.C., though it is difficult to date them exactly. The language in which they are written is known as Vedic Sanskrit to distinguish it from Classical Sanskrit, a later form of the language which was given a fixed literary form by Indian grammarians in the fourth century B.C. Sanskrit formerly held a place in India similar to that held by Latin in medieval Europe, and it is still studied as a learned literary language, but it has long ceased to be a spoken language. Side by side with Sanskrit there existed a large number of spoken dialects known as Prākrits, many of which developed into literary languages. From these Prākrit dialects have developed many, but not all, of the languages of present-day India, such as Hindī, Panjābī, and Bengālī. The Gypsy languages, sometimes called Romany, which are still spoken in many countries, are developed from a dialect of north-west or central India which was carried to Persia early in the Christian era.

Iranian. The earliest records of this group fall into two divisions known respectively as Avestan and Old Persian. Avestan is the language of the Avesta, the sacred writings of the Zoroastrians, some of which may go back as far as 1000 B.C. Old Persian is preserved only in rock inscriptions chiefly recording the achievements of the kings Darius and Xerxes. A later form of this language is Middle Iranian or Pehlevi, from which Modern Persian is descended, although Modern Persian has greatly simplified the inflexional system and introduced many loan-words from Arabic. Beside Persian there are many languages, such as Kurdish and Afghan, which belong to the Iranian group.

Armenian. Records of Armenian are preserved from the fifth century A.D., the earliest being a translation of the Bible. Modern Armenian has absorbed a large number of loan-words from neighbouring languages, especially Iranian, and it was once thought to belong to the Iranian group, but it has distinctive features which require it to be regarded as an independent group. One of these features is a shifting of certain consonants in some ways similar to the consonant shift which forms the most distinctive feature of the Germanic languages.

Albanian, except for a few words, is recorded only from the seventeenth century A.D. and contains a very large proportion of loan-words from neighbouring languages. It may be descended from ancient Illyrian but the evidence is insufficient for certainty.

Balto-Slavonic. The two groups, the Baltic and the Slavonic, have some features in common, and may be said to form sub-divisions of a single group. The Baltic languages include Lithuanian and Lettish. Lithuanian is of importance to the student of Indo-European because it is very conservative and preserves some old features which have disappeared in nearly all the other Indo-European languages. The Slavonic group includes Russian, Czech, Polish, Serbo-Croatian, and other languages. The earliest recorded form of Slavonic is known as Church Slavonic or Old Bulgarian and is the language into which the missionaries Cyril and Methodius translated part of the Bible in the ninth century.

Hellenic. This branch consists of the Greek dialects, which were spoken on the mainland of Greece and in the islands of the Ægean and in Asia Minor. For some time records dating back to the ninth century B.C. have been known, but recent discoveries of clay tablets at Pylos have laid bare records that may date from the thirteenth century B.C. The most important of the various dialects was Attic, the dialect of the city of Athens, which owed its supremacy to the dominant political and cultural position of Athens in the fifth century B.C. The Attic dialect became the basis of a common literary language which from the fourth century superseded the other dialects and became the general language of the eastern Mediterranean. The dialects of modern Greece are descended from this language.

Italic. As early as the sixth century B.C. we have evidence of a number of languages being spoken in Italy. One of these languages, Etruscan, was non-Indo-European; some of the other languages were Indo-European and belonged to the Italic group. Latin was the language of Rome and, as a result of the political supremacy of Rome, it drove out the other languages, chief of which were Oscan and Umbrian, known today only from inscriptions and place-names. The growth of the Roman Empire carried Latin into many parts of Europe, and the Romance languages are descended from spoken Latin, often known as Vulgar Latin to distinguish it from the literary language, Classical Latin. The chief Romance languages are French, Provençal, Italian, Spanish, Catalan, Portuguese, and Rumanian. As a result of conquest and colonization some of these languages have been carried very far from their original home: Portuguese to Brazil, Spanish to the rest of South America and French to many parts of the world.

Celtic. At the beginning of the Christian era languages of this group were spoken over a large part of western Europe, but today they are spoken only by comparatively small minorities of the populations of France and the British Isles. The Celtic languages fall into two groups distinguished by their manner of treating the Indo-European labio-velar consonants. In the Brittonic or *p*-group these consonants became labials; in the Goedelic or *q*-group they became velar consonants. Thus we have Welsh *pedwar* 'four' beside Old Irish *cethir*. The Brittonic group includes Cornish (which passed out of use as a spoken language in the eighteenth century), Breton and Welsh. The Goedelic group includes Irish, Scots Gaelic and Manx.

The remaining group is Germanic. Since this is the group to which English belongs, it merits fuller treatment here.

GERMANIC

The name Germani is first used by Caesar in his *Gallic War* (between 52 and 50 B.C.) and is later used by Tacitus in his *Germania* (A.D. 98). The origin of the name is still disputed. One theory connects the name with the Celtic stem *germo* 'hot' (cognate with the English adjective *warm*), referring to hot springs near Aachen; another theory regards it as derived from Latin *germānus* 'genuine'. It is probable that Latin historians did not distinguish very clearly between Celtic and Germanic tribes, but the two groups of languages are quite distinct. The term Germanic is the one generally used to describe the group of languages to which both English and German belong.

One of the most striking differences between Indo-European

and Germanic was in the position of the accent. In Indo-European accent depended on both pitch and stress, and the chief accent of a word was sometimes on a suffix or ending, whereas in Germanic the accent was mainly stress accent and the chief stress was on the first syllable of each word, except in verbs with separate prefixes and in some nouns derived from them. The most important result of the strong stress-accent has been the weakening of the vowels of lightly stressed syllables in the Germanic languages. In lightly stressed syllables long vowels are shortened and short vowels tend to be weakened or to disappear.

The Germanic languages share other characteristics which justify us in regarding them as a group. The most noticeable of these results from a series of changes which affected consonants in Common Germanic, generally known as the First Consonant Shift or Grimm's Law; details of this change are given in Chapter IV. Another characteristic of Germanic was a simplification of the verbal system, which retained only the present and the preterite tenses. This simplification went too far, and the separate Germanic languages have had to develop new ways of expressing differences of tense. A further characteristic of Germanic was the rise of a new class of verbs, known as weak verbs, which express the past tense by the use of a suffix containing a dental or alveolar consonant. There are also many resemblances in vocabulary, but these are comparatively unimportant as a basis for classification because they may be due to borrowing or to the accident of survival.

Before the beginning of the Christian era Common Germanic began to split up. It is usual to distinguish three sub-divisions: East, West and North Germanic.

The only East Germanic language of which substantial records survive is Gothic. At the beginning of the Christian era the Goths occupied the region of the Lower Vistula. From that region they migrated in a south-easterly direction, and by the middle of the third century they reached the Black Sea. As a result of persecution, in A.D. 348 a band of Goths crossed the Danube into Lower Moesia (now Bulgaria) and they were allowed by Constantius to settle there. For their use Bishop Wulfila (whose name means 'little wolf') translated parts of the

Bible into Gothic, and this fourth-century translation is the earliest literary work that has survived in any Germanic language. It is preserved in the *Codex Argenteus* at Uppsala and in fragments of other manuscripts written chiefly in Northern Italy, where the Goths established an empire towards the end of the fifth century. There are no other extant records of Gothic of any consequence, but as late as the sixteenth century a Fleming named Busbecq collected a number of words in the Crimea from two Goths whose language struck him as being remarkably like his own.

The North Germanic group comprises the languages of Scandinavia. Remains of very early date survive in runic inscriptions dating from the third or fourth century A.D. The North Germanic group in its turn split up into West Norse and East Norse. To the former division belongs Icelandic; to the latter belong Danish and Swedish. The linguistic situation in Norway is complex. Two languages are in use: *bokmål*, a literary language used mainly in towns, and *nynorsk*, a synthetic language based on country dialects and used mainly in the country. The Scandinavian languages are important to the student of English partly because of the parallels between Old Icelandic and Early English literature and partly for linguistic reasons. As a result of the Danish invasions before the Norman Conquest, Scandinavian languages were at one time spoken over a large part of England, and they have left their mark on the language in many loan-words.

The West Germanic group can be subdivided into three divisions: (1) High German, (2) Low German and Low Franconian, (3) Anglo-Frisian. High German is distinguished from the other West Germanic languages by a distinctive development of its consonant system. It was first spoken in the mountainous country of South Germany and it is now the official language of Germany, Austria, and a large part of Switzerland. Low Franconian has developed into the national languages Dutch and Flemish, and Low German has formed the basis of many dialects current in North Germany. English and Frisian, which together form the Anglo-Frisian group, have many features in common. The Frisians were at one time a great seafaring people, but their power declined and today their language is represented only by dialects spoken and written in Friesland (now a province of the Netherlands), along the Schleswig coast, and in the islands off the coast.

OLD ENGLISH

The inhabitants of Britain at the time of the Roman invasions spoke a Celtic language of which no literary texts remain. This language has had remarkably little permanent effect on the English language which afterwards replaced it; Celtic forms survive in English chiefly in place-names such as *Dover* and river names such as *Avon* and *Ouse*. Since records are so scanty, we cannot say to what extent the Roman invasions led to the use of Latin in Britain between the landing of Julius Caesar in 55 B.C. and the withdrawal of the Roman troops in the fifth century. Probably Latin was used by Roman soldiers and those town-dwelling Britons who came into frequent contact with them; Celtic was probably spoken in country places, and Celtic languages have survived until today in parts of Wales and the Highlands of Scotland, where the mountainous country has enabled the inhabitants to resist foreign influence.

The history of the English language in England begins with the settlement of the Angles, Saxons and Jutes in Britain. The settlement attained significant proportions by the middle of the fifth century, though it may have begun before then. These three Germanic tribes came from the North German plain near to the district which is now known as Schleswig-Holstein. The Angles settled in the area extending northward from the Thames over the greater part of what is now England and the Lowlands of Scotland. The Jutes settled in Kent, the Isle of Wight and along part of the Hampshire coast. The Saxons settled in the rest of England south of the Thames with the exception of the South-West, which was still held by the Celts. The invaders had to encounter varying degrees of hostility from the Celts, and for mutual protection various tribes combined to produce small kingdoms. The grouping of tribes was not very permanent, since a vigorous ruler sometimes succeeded for a short time in uniting two or more kingdoms, but seven kingdoms can be distinguished as having a fairly stable existence, and these are described as the Anglo-Saxon Heptarchy. They are Northumbria, Mercia, East Anglia, Wessex, Sussex, Essex and Kent. The relative importance of these kingdoms fluctuated. In the seventh century Northumbria enjoyed political supremacy as well as leadership in literature and learning. During the eighth century the leadership passed to Mercia, and in the ninth century it passed to Wessex. In 830 all England acknowledged the overlordship of Egbert, King of Wessex, and under Alfred (871–899) Wessex enjoyed the leadership in learning that had once belonged to Northumbria. These historical facts have had their influence on the language. The lack of political unity encouraged the existence of a number of dialects. The four chief dialects represented by texts which have come down to us from England before the Norman Conquest are West Saxon, Kentish, Mercian and Northumbrian, and it will be seen that these correspond to four of the kingdoms of the Heptarchy, although the scarcity of accurately localized texts prevents us from knowing how closely linguistic boundaries corresponded with political ones. The same scarcity of texts prevents us from saying whether the other kingdoms of the Heptarchy had distinctive dialects. The political supremacy of Wessex during the ninth and tenth centuries and its comparative freedom from Scandinavian inroads had linguistic and literary consequences, since these conditions led to the preservation of many more manuscripts in this dialect than in any other. Our knowledge of Old English is therefore derived mainly from West Saxon sources, whereas other dialects were more important in forming the basis of the English language of today.

Since language is constantly changing, it is not always easy or profitable to divide the history of a language into periods. Yet it is sometimes convenient to make such a division, and it is possible to divide the history of the English language as spoken in England into three periods, known respectively as Old English, Middle English and Modern English. The Old English period extends from the time of the earliest surviving written documents in the eighth century until the end of the eleventh century; the Middle English period extends from the middle of the twelfth until the middle of the fifteenth century; the Modern English period extends from the end of the fifteenth century until the present day. The first half of the twelfth and the second half of the fifteenth century may be regarded as periods of transition, the existence of which emphasizes the gradual nature of the change. The Norman Conquest did not suddenly put an end to the Old English period, but to it may be attributed directly or indirectly many of the characteristic differences between Old and Middle English. The mingling together of people speaking different languages is one of the causes of linguistic change, but from this point of view the Scandinavian inroads were probably more influential than the Norman, because Scandinavian and English resembled each other enough for it to be possible for the speakers of the two languages to understand one another approximately without learning a new language. A further result of the Scandinavian and French invasions was the introduction of large numbers of loan-words, which form one of the chief differences between Old and Middle English. In some ways the effect of the Norman Conquest has been to make the difference between Old and Middle English seem greater than it really was. The disturbed political conditions which accompanied the Conquest did not favour the production or preservation of literary works, and when texts again become common in the thirteenth century, changes are recorded in writing which had really been spread over several centuries. Moreover, the Norman Conquest led to a break in the Old English scribal tradition, and some changes which had already begun to take place in pronunciation in Old English are first found in manuscripts some centuries later when, because of the loss of the Old English literary language, French or Norman scribes recorded them by using their own spellings, which were more phonetic than those current in late Old English.

The form of English in use before the Norman Conquest is sometimes called 'Anglo-Saxon', but the term is rather old-fashioned, and the more usual term is now 'Old English', a description which has the advantage of emphasizing the essential continuity of the English language before the Conquest and after. The word 'Anglo-Saxon' was not applied to the language until the late seventeenth century, but the name *Anglo-Saxones* had been in use as early as the ninth century by writers in Latin, who used it to distinguish the Saxons who came to Britain from those who remained on the Continent. It is sometimes convenient to use the term to describe the people, but it is better to use the term 'Old English' to describe their language. When it is necessary to refer to both Old and Middle English without distinguishing between them, the less precise term 'Early English' is sometimes used.

The chief characteristics of Old English may be illustrated by a specimen. The following extract is the Lord's Prayer in the West Saxon dialect of the tenth century:

Fæder ūre þū þe eart on heofonum, sī þīn nama gehālgod. Tō becume þīn rīce. Geweorþe ðīn willa on eorðan swā swā on heofenum. Ūrne dæghwāmlīcan hlāf syle ūs tō dæg. And forgyf ūs ūre gyltas, swā swā wē forgyfað ūrum gyltendum. And ne gelæd þū ūs on costnunge, ac ālȳs ūs of yfele. Sōþlīce.

Many of the letters used in Old English manuscripts differ in shape from their modern equivalents. The old shapes of letters are not generally reproduced in editions of Old English texts, but there are three letters used in this passage, as elsewhere in Old English, which have no single letters corresponding to them in Modern English, with the result that the Old English letters are still used in modern editions. The letters 'þ' and 'ð' are both used to represent the sounds which are today spelt 'th' occurring in the words *thin* and *then*; the letter 'æ' represented a sound nearly like the 'a' in the Southern English pronunciation of *had*. The horizontal lines above certain vowels indicate that they are to be pronounced long; they are not as a rule marked long in Old English manuscripts.

The first thing that strikes us about this passage is that a large proportion of the words are recognizably the same words as those that we use today, although nearly every word has undergone some change. Of the 54 words in the passage, 43 are still in use today and about half the remainder have partial cognates today or survive as archaisms. For example, *rīce* 'kingdom' survives in *bishopric*, and *gyltendum* (dative plural) 'offenders' is related to 'guilt'; *dæghwāmlīcan* includes the elements found in *daily*, and *sōþlīce* is made up of the archaic word *sooth* and the suffix *-ly*. The words in the passage which have survived have for the most part remained unchanged in meaning, although *syle*, from *sellan*, now means 'sell' whereas in Old English it meant 'give'. It is notable that the prepositions have changed in meaning quite considerably: *on* means 'in' and 'into' as well as 'on', and *of* means 'from'. Changes in form have been more frequent than changes in meaning. Nearly every word in the passage differs in form from its modern equivalent, and further investigation shows that the differences are due in part to changes in pronunciation and in part merely to changes in spelling: the 'æ' and the 'd' of *fæder* represent different sounds from the 'a' and the 'th' of *father*, but the 'f' of *heofonum* represents the same sound as the 'v' of *heaven*. There are differences in syntax between the Old English passage and the corresponding passage in the Authorized Version of 1611, and that version in its turn differs in syntax from the usage of today. The chief points of syntactic interest in the Old English passage are in word-order, but we may notice also the use of the pronoun 'thou' in two sentences from which it would be omitted in Modern English. One characteristic of the Old English passage is the frequent occurrence of inflexional endings. For example, the word 'our' occurs in the three different forms *ūre*, *ūrne*, and *ūrum*, according to the case and number of the noun with which it agrees. A comparison of the Old English passage with its Modern English equivalent thus illustrates some of the main trends in the development of the English language: the continuity in essentials from Old English to the present day, a continuity which is quite compatible with considerable changes in spelling, pronunciation and syntax and with the weakening or disappearance of many inflexional endings.

Because of the simplicity of its diction, the Lord's Prayer does not illustrate one very marked difference between Old English and Modern English: the very considerable extension of the English vocabulary that has been brought about by the borrowing of words from other languages. There were in Old English many loan-words from Latin, and in late Old English a few words were borrowed from Scandinavian and French, but in comparison with Modern English, Old English is remarkable for the small number of loan-words which its vocabulary includes. To make up for the shortage of words of foreign origin, the speakers of Old English showed great resourcefulness in adapting to new uses the store of words at their disposal. One way of doing this was by changing the meanings of existing words; another was by means of word-formation. The various methods of enriching the language may be illustrated by examining the linguistic results of the conversion of the English to Christianity, which introduced a large number of new ideas for which words had to be found. This is the sort of situation which normally leads to the borrowing of words from other languages, and this way of coping with the situation was sometimes adopted in Old English. Several words which were borrowed from Latin at this time have remained in the language to the present day and have become so familiar that we no longer think of them as loan-words. Examples are *bishop* (OE *biscop* from Latin *episcopus*), *monk* (OE *munuc* from Latin *monachus*), and *priest* (OE *prēost* from Latin *presbyter*). These three words are ultimately of Greek origin. The adaptation of the meanings of native words may be illustrated by *bless* (OE *bletsian*, originally meaning 'to sprinkle with blood'), *Easter* (OE *Ēastron*, originally a spring festival in honour of a pagan goddess of the dawn), and *Yule* (OE *geōl* 'Christmas', but probably originally a pagan festival to celebrate the passing of the shortest day). Word-formation was based upon both the native word-stock and Latin loan-words. To describe the scribes and Pharisees of the New Testament the Anglo-Saxons used the words *bōceras* and *sundorhālgan*. The first word is derived from *bōc* 'book' by the addition of the common suffix -*ere* (Modern English -*er*), and the second word is a compound of *sundor* 'apart' and *hālga* 'saint', 'holy one', related to the adjective *hālig* 'holy'. The two words illustrate the two chief methods of word-formation in Old English: the addition of suffixes and 'compounding' or 'composition'. Similar methods could be applied to loan-words. When *biscop* was borrowed, other words were formed from it: *biscoplīc* 'episcopal', *biscopscīr* 'diocese', and *biscopian* 'to confirm'. One is impressed by the ingenuity shown in many of these coinages. Sometimes a hint for the formation of a compound word was provided by a Greek or Latin compound. The two elements of the foreign word were translated separately into Old English, and the resulting compound is sometimes described as a *calque* or 'translation loan-word'. The best-known example of this process is *gospel*. Greek ἐυαγγέλιον 'good tidings' was expressed in Old English as *gōdspell*. Later the ō was shortened and the word was misunderstood as 'message of God', a misunderstanding which accounts for the form in which the word was borrowed from English into Icelandic, *guðspjall*. Other examples are *heathen* (OE *hǣþ* 'heath', as Latin *paganus* is derived from *pagus* 'a country district') and some words which have not survived, such as *prīnes* (literally 'threeness') 'Trinity', and the grammatical term *dǣlnimend* 'participle'.

One characteristic of Old English is the existence of a special poetic vocabulary. The leisurely movement of Old English poetry, where a single idea was driven home by being expressed in several different ways, called for an extensive stock of synonyms or near-synonyms. One way in which these were provided was by the use of *kennings*. A kenning has been well defined by Professor Kemp Malone as 'a two-member (or two-term) circumlocution for an ordinary noun: such a circumlocution might take the form of a compound, like *hronrād* 'sea' (literally 'riding-place of the whale'), or of a phrase, like *fugles wynn* 'feather' (literally 'bird's joy')[1]. A single kenning was capable of producing a large number of variations. For example, once the description of a ship as a sea-horse was accepted, any word meaning 'sea' could be combined with any word meaning 'horse' to provide a slightly different image. To express ideas of frequent occurrence in Old English poetry, such as 'battle' or 'sea' or 'hero', there were therefore very many words available. It is misleading to call these words synonyms, because each word stressed a different aspect of the thing described. For example, a prince might be described by such words as *ēþelweard* 'protector of his native land', or *bēaggiefa* 'giver of rings', stressing his generosity, or *beadorinc* 'warrior', stressing his valour. Most of these words were used only in poetry, and their existence was very useful to Anglo-Saxon poets when they had to satisfy the exacting demands of alliteration. Alliteration has frequently been used as an ornament in English poetry of all periods, but in Old English it was structural and an essential part of the system of versification. The Old English poetic vocabulary has not had much permanent influence on the

[1] *A Literary History of England* ed. by A. C. Baugh, p. 29.

language, but the alliterative poetry which flourished in both Old English and Middle English may well be the origin of some of the alliterative phrases, such as 'friend or foe', 'a labour of love', and 'might and main', which are common in both rhetorical and colloquial language today.

MIDDLE ENGLISH

Norman influence on English did not begin in 1066. In the year 1002 King Æthelred had married a Norman wife, and when he was driven into exile by the Danes he took refuge in Normandy. His son Edward the Confessor was brought up in France and, when he came to the throne in 1042, he brought with him many Normans and gave them positions of importance in the government. As a result of this Norman influence, several French loan-words, such as *proud* and *castle*, are recorded in English before the Norman Conquest. For several generations after the Conquest all the important positions in church and state were held by Normans or men of foreign blood, and as a result the influence of the foreigners was out of all proportion to their number. One result of the thoroughness with which the Normans ousted the English from important positions was that the invaders had little inducement to learn English. For about two centuries after the Conquest Norman French was freely used by the upper classes in England. Numerically the speakers of English were no doubt in a large majority, and it was through them that the continuity of the English language from the Old English period was preserved, but the class to which the writers and readers of books belonged spoke Norman French. Throughout the Middle Ages in England there was competition between Latin and English as a literary medium; during the two hundred years following the Conquest there was in addition competition with Norman French. So firm was the foothold which French had gained in this country that special dialectal features of Norman French began to develop on English soil. The resulting dialect is known as Anglo-Norman, and many important literary works written in this dialect have been preserved.

The chief reason why French continued to be used by the upper classes in England from the Conquest until the beginning of the thirteenth century was that all the time there was a close connexion between England and the Continent. William the Conqueror and his sons spent about as much time in France as in England, and most of the powerful English nobles had possessions in France. The loss of Normandy by King John in 1204 had important results. Nobles who had estates on both sides of the Channel were compelled to give up either their English or their French lands. At about the same time the links between England and the south of France began to be strengthened. In 1200 King John married Isabel of Angoulême, who came from the neighbourhood of Poitou, and in 1236 King Henry III married Eleanor of Provence. Both these marriages led to a great influx of Frenchmen into England. The chief linguistic result of the loss of Normandy was that English began to gain ground among the ruling classes in England. The chief result of the new links with the more southerly parts of France was that Norman influence on the English language was replaced by the influence of Central French, and the difference between the two dialects of French is reflected in loan-words into Middle English. Such words as *catch*, *cattle* and *warden* are from the Norman dialect; *chase*, *chattel* and *guardian* are from their Central French cognates.

In the course of the fourteenth century French gradually gave place to English. Some writers were bilingual or trilingual, like the poet Gower, who wrote long poems in each of the three languages Latin, French and English, and there are macaronic lyrics in which poets pass with ease from one language to another in the middle of a sentence. One sign of the trend from French to English was the decision of Parliament in 1362 that henceforth all lawsuits should be conducted in English. Another was the change from French to English as the medium of instruction in schools. Ranulph Higden, writing his *Polychronicon*, a universal history, about 1327, complains that English children do not learn English properly because at school they are forced to speak in French rather than in English. John of Trevisa, translating Higden's book about 1385, adds a comment of his own to the effect that all this is now changed and that English is now the medium of instruction in all grammar schools. A quotation from Trevisa will serve the double purpose of provid-

ing contemporary evidence of the attitude towards French and
of giving a specimen of English prose of the latter half of the
fourteenth century. Trevisa's translation of Higden runs:

> This apayrynge of þe burþe tunge is bycause of tweie þinges:
> oon is for children in scole aȝenst þe vsage and manere of alle
> oþere naciouns beeþ compelled for to leue hire owne lan-
> gage, and for to construe hir lessouns and here þynges in
> Frensche, and so þey haueþ seþ þe Normans come first in to
> Engelond. Also gentil men children beeþ itauȝt to speke
> Frensche from þe tyme þat þey beeþ irokked in here cradel,
> and kunneþ speke andp layewiþ a childes broche; and vplond-
> isshe men wil likne hym self to gentil men, and fondeþ wiþ
> greet besynesse for to speke Frensce, for to be [more] itolde of.

Trevisa's comment is:

> Þis manere was moche ivsed tofore þe firste moreyn and is
> siþþe sumdel ichaunged; for Iohn Cornwaile, a maister of
> grammer, chaunged þe lore in gramer scole and construc-
> cioun of Frensche in to Englische; and Richard Pencriche
> lerned þat manere techynge of hym and oþere men of
> Pencrich; so þat now, þe ȝere of oure Lorde a þowsand þre
> hundred and foure score and fyue, and of þe secounde kyng
> Richard after þe conquest nyne, in alle þe gramere scoles of
> Engelond, children leueþ Frensche and construeþ and
> lerneþ an Englische, and haueþ þerby auauntage in oon side
> and disauauntage in anoþer side; here auauntage is, þat þey
> lerneþ her gramer in lasse tyme þan children were iwoned
> to doo; disauauntage is þat now children of gramer scole
> conneþ na more Frensche þan can hir lift heele, and þat is
> harme for hem and þey schulle passe þe see and trauaille in
> straunge landes and in many oþer places. Also gentil men
> haueþ now moche ileft for to teche here children Frensche.[1]

When we compare this passage with Modern English we are
struck first of all by the fact that nearly all the words used have
survived until the present day, although with quite considerable
changes of form and meaning. Some of the words have survived

[1] Higden's *Polychronicon* II. 159–161 (Rolls Series).

with a different prefix, as *apayrynge*, which means the same as Modern English *impairing*, or *tofore*, which means *before*. Sometimes the difference is one of accidence, as in *tweie* (from the Old English masculine whereas *two* is from the feminine and neuter), or *kunneþ* (which is the plural form whereas *can* is from the singular of the verb), or past participles like *irokked* and *iwoned* (which have *i-* from the Old English prefix *ge-*, sometimes attached to words borrowed from French, as in *ichaunged*). Some words have changed their meaning, like *lore*, which is used in its original sense of 'teaching', and *construccioun*, which means 'construing'. The form *vplondisshe* (made up of *up*, *land*, and *-ish*) 'country, provincial', shows that English still had the power of making expressive compound words from native elements. In syntax we may notice the long and involved sentences, which do not make for easy reading but which do not preclude the occasional use of a vigorous and expressive colloquial expression like 'they know no more French than their left heel'.

The opening sentence of G. K. Chesterton's *Chaucer*[1] begins: 'If I were writing this in French, as I should be if Chaucer had not chosen to write in English. . . .' This is one of many instances which could be quoted of a tendency to attribute most of the important stages in the development of medieval English language and literature to the influence of the greatest medieval English poet, but the statement is not true. The battle between French and English in England had already been won when Chaucer wrote, and his use of English may be said to be the result rather than the cause of the victory of the English language. But the victory was not gained without lasting marks of French influence being left on the English language. One of these marks was the introduction of large numbers of French loan-words into English; another was the drastic modification of English spelling to make it conform to the practice of French scribes. These two are among the more striking differences between Old and Middle English.

One change that brought about important differences between Old and Middle English was in part due to foreign influence. This was the decay of the Old English inflexional system. The weakening of the vowels of lightly stressed syllables had begun in the Old English period, and it is probable that the confusion of inflexional endings was increased by the presence in England of large numbers of Scandinavians and, to a lesser extent, by the presence of speakers of French. Many words had identical stem-syllables in English and Scandinavian, differing only in the inflexional endings. It is natural that, when the speakers of the two languages intermingled, inflexional endings should suffer.

The decay of inflexional endings had an influence on syntax. So long as inflexions served to indicate the cases of nouns, word-order was comparatively unimportant, but when nominative and accusative came to be identical in form, a fixed word-order was necessary in order to make clear the important distinction between 'The man killed the lion' and 'The lion killed the man'. One of the devices used to replace inflexional endings was the greater use of prepositions, and this development became even more marked in the Modern English period.

Another important change which took place in early Middle English was the loss of grammatical gender. In Old English, as in Modern French and German, the gender of nouns had no connexion with their meaning and was sometimes in direct contradiction to it. Thus, *wīfmann* 'woman' was masculine, while *wīf* 'woman' and *cild* 'child' were neuter. Already in Old English we find the beginnings of natural gender, as in King Alfred's Preface to the translation of Gregory's *Pastoral*, where the neuter pronoun *hit* is used to refer to the masculine noun *wīsdōm*. The gender of an Old English noun was often indicated by the form of an adjective or pronoun agreeing with it. When the decay of inflexions made it impossible to distinguish the gender of a noun in this way, the tendency to replace grammatical gender by natural gender was accelerated.

One difference between Old English and Middle English is the apparent greater diversity of dialects in Middle English. So far as the surviving manuscripts are concerned, the difference is a real one, but there are two circumstances which make it unwise to conclude that the spoken dialects of Middle English were more varied than those of Old English. The chief reason why Middle English dialects seem more varied is that the number of manuscripts that have been preserved from the

Middle English period is much larger than the number of surviving Old English manuscripts. A second reason for the greater dialectal homogeneity of Old English manuscripts is the strength of the West Saxon scribal tradition, which caused the written documents to give a misleading picture of the contemporary spoken language. The French scribes and the English scribes trained in French schools who wrote the Middle English manuscripts were free from any such limitation: they recorded the sounds they heard by whatever spellings seemed to them most appropriate.

The greater freedom enjoyed by Middle English scribes has had the result that there is no lack of evidence for the study of Middle English pronunciation, but it has had further results which have greatly increased the difficulty, as well as the interest, of the study of Middle English dialects. The scribe felt under no obligation to preserve the forms of his original. He would modernize forms which he regarded as archaic. If, as often happened, his own dialect differed from that of the text he was copying, he would not hesitate to rewrite forms in his own dialect. If scribes had modernized texts or altered dialectal forms with consistent thoroughness, we should have been able to feel confident that, whatever may have been the dialect of the original, the manuscript presented a true picture of the dialect of the scribe at the time when he was writing. But scribes showed no such consistency; in the same manuscript they modernized some forms while leaving others unchanged and left some forms in the dialect of the original or of an earlier scribe while they rewrote others in their own dialect. All this is clear from an examination of texts which have been preserved in several manuscripts.

It may seem that there are such possibilities of error and confusion that it is impossible to make any statement about Middle English dialects that will be both precise and accurate, but the problems presented, though often difficult, are not as a rule insoluble. Occasionally we find a manuscript, such as that containing the only known version of Dan Michael of Northgate's *Ayenbyte of Inwyt*, which is in the author's own handwriting and which is exactly dated and localized. The spelling of place-names can sometimes be used as evidence, although we have to remember that place-names may be mentioned in a document written by a scribe from another part of the country who would not hesitate to alter the spelling to make it accord with his own dialect. It is unfortunate that it is just those legal documents which provide accurately dated and localized evidence that are most likely to be written in Latin or Anglo-Norman. Something can be learnt by comparing Middle English forms with those occurring in Old English or Modern English dialects. A careful examination of the language of each surviving manuscript will often yield valuable results. Very often scribes have spoilt a rhyme by modernizing one of the rhyming words, and by restoring the rhyme it is possible to draw conclusions about the original dialect of the text in question. Sometimes unwillingness to spoil a rhyme causes a scribe to leave the forms of his original when they occur in rhyme while altering them when they occur in the middle of a line. It is thus possible to say that certain Middle English forms are characteristic of particular dialects and to say very approximately what were the boundaries which separated one feature from another. These boundaries were not lines but belts of land or border areas within which either of the two variant forms might be used. They did not remain fixed throughout the Middle English period. For example, the ending -*es* in the third person singular of the present indicative of verbs began by being a feature of Northern dialect, but it spread South until it became general over the whole country.

In spite of the confused nature of much of the evidence and the complicated nature of the linguistic reality which lies behind this evidence, it is possible for the student of Middle English dialects to speak of dialect areas and boundaries, whereas the number of non-West-Saxon texts in Old English is so small that the only practicable method of study is to compile a grammar of each text with only the vaguest attempt at localization. The method of drawing the boundaries between Middle English dialects is to prepare a series of maps showing the distribution of the various dialectal features.[1] By superimposing these maps on each other it is sometimes possible to see that the boundaries of

[1] Such maps are to be found in J. P. Oakden, *Alliterative Poetry in Middle English: The Dialectal and Metrical Survey* (Manchester, 1930) and in S. Moore, S. B. Meech and H. Whitehall, *Middle English Dialect Characteristics and Dialect Boundaries*, Michigan Essays and Studies XIII, 1935.

certain features approximately coincide with each other. Whenever a number of boundaries of separate dialectal features thus coincide, it is reasonable to regard the belt of land where they occur as a boundary between two dialect areas. The main Middle English dialect areas are Northern, East Midland, West Midland, South-Eastern and South-Western. The Northern area includes the area north of the Ribble and the Aire, and it can be subdivided into Scottish and the dialect of the North of England. East Midland and West Midland cover the area between the Humber and the Thames, except that there is a tendency for the South-Western dialect to encroach into the Southern part of the West Midland area.

MODERN ENGLISH

Between the Middle English and the Modern English periods there is no such convenient division as that which the Norman Conquest provides between Old and Middle English. The invention of printing, which was introduced into England by Caxton about 1476, undoubtedly affected the development of the English language, but its influence was slow to take effect and it became important only when the gradual spread of education increased the number of people who could read. Moreover its influence was exerted primarily on the written language, whereas in linguistic history the spoken language is always more important. Another important event in the early Modern English period was the Renaissance, the influence of which is most clearly to be seen in the introduction of a large number of Latin loan-words into English.

Linguistically the most important features of the early Modern English period are the Great Vowel Shift and the rise of Standard English. Most of the English long vowels were affected by the Great Vowel Shift, and this series of changes brought about the most characteristic differences between Chaucerian pronunciation and that of the present day. The changes began to take place in the fourteenth century and were probably spread over some centuries. The consequences of the shift were that the long vowels, which in the fourteenth century were pronounced approximately like the vowels in *calm, fête, seen, go, saw* and *shoe* have today come to be pronounced like the vowels or diphthongs in *name, see, fine, shoe, go,* and *house* respectively. The rise of Standard English in the fifteenth century began a movement, which is not yet and probably never will be completed, towards the adoption of a uniform type of speech over the whole of England. Towards the end of the Old English period, West Saxon was beginning to occupy a position of greater prestige than the other Old English dialects, but the Norman Conquest put an end to this tendency. During the Middle English period important literary works were written in each of the main dialects, but towards the end of that period there were signs that the dialect of London was coming to be regarded as something of a standard and was sometimes used by writers coming from other parts of England, for example by the poet Gower, who came from Kent. This tendency became stronger during the fifteenth century, and was encouraged by Caxton's use of the London dialect, although the tendency had begun well before the time of Caxton.

The rise of Standard English led to a decline in the literary importance of the various English regional dialects, although they have continued to be used to the present day as spoken dialects and, to a lesser extent, for literary works. The only dialect, apart from Standard English, which has remained in constant literary use since the Middle English period is Lowland Scots. The London English which formed the basis of Standard English was in the main an East Midland dialect, but it incorporated a few forms from other dialects. The chief reason for the importance of the East Midland dialect in the development of Standard English is that it was the dialect of London and the Court, but the existence of the universities of Oxford and Cambridge in or near that dialect area undoubtedly increased its importance.

Side by side with the decline in importance of the regional dialects of Middle English, we find a new kind of dialect beginning to assume importance: class dialect. In the sixteenth century to speak a regional dialect was no bar to advancement, even at Court, and we learn from Aubrey[1] that Sir Walter

---

[1] *Aubrey's Brief Lives,* ed. O. L. Dick (1949), p. 255.

Raleigh all his life kept traces of the dialect of his native county of Devonshire. But we find Sir Thomas Elyot in Chapter V of his *Gouernour* (1531) complaining that the sons of noblemen and gentlemen 'haue attained corrupte and foule pronuntiation' from their nurses and other foolish women. We here have the beginnings of an attitude towards language which becomes increasingly important during the Modern English period: the recognition of the existence of dialects which owe their variation from each other primarily to social rather than to geographical causes.

One kind of evidence is available to the student of the early Modern English period which is not available to the student of earlier periods: that of contemporary grammarians. Some of these grammarians describe English pronunciation for the benefit of foreigners who wish to learn English; some of them write for Englishmen and aim at correcting what they believe to be errors in pronunciation or spelling. The evidence of these early grammarians is useful when it is considered in relation to other kinds of evidence, but it has to be used with caution. The grammarians vary a good deal in reliability, but in general they have two important faults: they are often unskilled in noticing and describing subtle variations of pronunciation, and in describing sounds they nearly all attach too much importance to the spelling. The evidence of early grammarians is of most value when they condemn some form of speech. Grammarians tend to be conservative in their attitude to language, and pronunciations condemned by grammarians are often the early stages of sound-changes.

The other sources of our information about English pronunciation during the early Modern period are similar to the sources of our knowledge of Middle English pronunciation: spelling, rhymes, and such general considerations as the historical development of words down to the present day interpreted in the light of phonetic probability.

The evidence of spelling is less valuable in the study of Modern English than in the study of Middle English because spelling has become more conventional. Nevertheless, until about the middle of the seventeenth century there was still a good deal of variation in spelling in printed books. The student of the history of the English language can learn a good deal from the spellings used in the early quartos and folios of Shakespeare, and the textual critic can profit from a knowledge of the history of the English language. During the Modern English period, too, we have a new source of evidence in the collections of letters written in English by private persons, many of them by their own hands. The most famous collection of such letters is that written by members of the Paston family in the fifteenth century, but many other collections have been preserved. The importance of these letters is that the writers, not being professional scribes, were not very much influenced by scribal tradition, and their spellings are therefore much more likely to represent contemporary pronunciation. It should be added that there is much difference of opinion about the value that can be attached to occasional variations of spelling. It is unsafe to draw conclusions about pronunciation from single occasional spellings, but when a particular spelling occurs in several independent documents it is reasonable to use it as evidence.

The evidence provided by rhymes can best be used in conjunction with other kinds of evidence. The first thing necessary is to make sure that the poet whose work we are using as evidence was careful in his use of rhymes and was not content with traditional eye-rhymes. A second safeguard is not to pay too much attention to a single rhyme but to consider the normal practice of several poets who were at work at about the same time. The necessity for supporting evidence is clear when we remember that a rhyme merely indicates that two words contained the same sound: it does not indicate what that sound was.

General historical considerations can sometimes throw light on a problem by preventing us from interpreting evidence too superficially. For example, the spelling might lead us to suppose that the word *son* was pronounced with an *o* at the time of Shakespeare, but we know that in Old English it was spelt with *u*, at the present day it is pronounced with the sound [ʌ], which is normally derived from earlier [u], and we know too that in Middle English the sound [u] was often spelt *o* as a result of French influence. It is therefore safe to conclude that the *o* of *son* at the time of Shakespeare represented [u] or [ʌ] or some intermediate sound.

One of the characteristic features of the Modern English period has been the enlargement of the vocabulary. At the time of the Renaissance, many English writers deliberately set out to enrich the language by borrowing words from Latin and Greek, but opinion in the sixteenth century was divided on the value of such borrowings, and some well-known Englishmen, who were themselves classical scholars, protested against the introduction into English of so-called 'ink-horn terms' from Latin and Greek. Among those who protested were Sir John Cheke, first Regius Professor of Greek at Cambridge, and Roger Ascham, whose *Scholemaster* was published in 1570, two years after his death. The influence of Italian literature, together with the growing fondness shown by young Englishmen for travel in Italy, led to an increase in the number of Italian loan-words, and this influence in its turn met with some hostility from those who disliked the 'Englishman Italianate', who brought back from his travels many Italian habits of speech, dress and manners.

Since the sixteenth century there has been a very considerable increase in the number of languages from which English has adopted words. The chief reason for these adoptions has been the increase of trade with all parts of the world, and many of our loan-words are the names of foreign products which have been borrowed along with the products they describe. Such words are *tea* from China, *potato* from Haiti through Spanish, and *shawl* from Persia. Many of these words have passed through several different languages on their way to English, and these languages have often left their mark on the form of the borrowed word; many of them have been borrowed into most of the languages of Europe and so constitute a common European vocabulary. Later in the Modern English period science began to exert a good deal of influence on the English vocabulary. Many of these scientific terms, too, belong to the common European vocabulary. Because of the richness of Greek in word-forming elements, and because some knowledge of Greek has formed part of the heritage of most European countries, many of these scientific words are made up from Greek elements. It is interesting to note that we have found it necessary to go back to Latin and Greek to find words to describe an *aeroplane* and *television*.

CHAPTER III

The Sounds of Speech

PHONETICS is the name given to the scientific study of speech-sounds, and some knowledge of general phonetics is an indispensable preliminary to the study of the history of the pronunciation of any language. The first step is to discover how speech-sounds are made, and the most satisfactory way of doing this is to analyse and describe the movements of one's own organs of speech in the pronunciation of the sounds of Modern English. It is important from the outset to guard against being misled by the spelling. For example to say that the word *fin* contains short *i* while *fine* contains long *i* may have been true several centuries ago but it is not true of English speech today, which pronounces the *i* of *fine* as a diphthong. If one disregards the spelling, it is easy to notice that the sound begins like the *a* in *cat* and finishes like the *i* in *fin*. It is often desirable to record pronunciation in some less clumsy way than this, and phonetic symbols have been devised for this purpose. The essential characteristic of any system of phonetic transcription is that a given sound shall always be represented by the same symbol. Different symbols are used to record pronunciation with varying degrees of accuracy. Those which aim at recording fairly subtle distinctions between sounds are known as 'narrow' symbols; those which record only the more obvious differences are known as 'broad'. In recording contemporary speech there is a lot to be said for using narrow symbols, but broad symbols are more suitable for recording the pronunciation of earlier periods, since the available evidence does not allow us to describe the pronunciation in past centuries with the precision that is possible when we are dealing with contemporary speech. The phonetic symbols used in this book are for the most part the broad symbols of the International Phonetic Association, and they are given in this chapter along with the detailed descriptions of the English speech-sounds.

The organs of speech that are most important when we are describing the formation of speech-sounds are those that are movable, namely the vocal cords, the soft palate, the tongue and the lips.

The vocal cords or vocal lips are stretched across the larynx from front to back. The larynx is the upper extremity of the windpipe and is popularly known as the Adam's apple. The space between the vocal cords is known as the glottis. The vocal cords can take up a number of positions. When they are apart, leaving space for the breath to pass through without obstruction, any speech-sounds that are produced are said to be voiceless; when the vocal cords vibrate, the accompanying speech-sounds are said to be voiced. To the first group belong such consonants as *p, t, k* and *f*; to the second group belong all vowels and such consonants as *b, d, g* and *v*. English nasal consonants are usually voiced, but it is possible to pronounce them without voice. Voiced sounds have much greater carrying power than voiceless sounds, and therefore in order to make voiceless sounds audible it is necessary to pronounce them with greater breath force. When the glottis is completely closed and then opened suddenly to release air that has been compressed by pressure from the lungs, the resultant sound is known as the glottal stop [?]. It is not normally used in Standard English, but it is sometimes heard before initial vowels in words pronounced with special emphasis.

The soft palate. If the tip of the tongue is pressed against various parts of the roof of the mouth, it is clear that the palate is hard near the front of the mouth but becomes soft further back. The soft palate is called the *velum*, and sounds made by pressing the tongue against it are said to be *velar*. The soft palate is used to open or close the passage leading from the throat to the nose. When it is lowered, the passage to the nose is open and the resultant sound is said to be nasal. If a speaker, while opening the passage to the nose, closes the passage of air through the mouth, the sound is a nasal consonant; if air is allowed to pass through the mouth as well as the nose, the sound is a nasalized vowel. Such vowels do not occur in Standard English, though they are common in French, and some English speakers use them.

The tongue is the most important of the movable organs of speech. It plays the chief part in the formation of vowel sounds, and it plays an important part in the formation of most English consonants. The names of the parts of the tongue, which cannot be rigidly distinguished, are, beginning from the back of the mouth, the root, the back, the front, the blade and the tip. The back of the tongue is the part opposite the soft palate and the front of the tongue is opposite the hard palate.

The lips can be used to assist in the formation of both vowels and consonants. In the articulation of vowels the lips always act in conjunction with the tongue; when the lips are brought close together and rounded they modify the quality of a vowel-sound. The consonants in the pronunciation of which the lips play a part are called labials, and they form a convenient group with which to begin the study of speech-sounds because the movements of the lips are very easy to observe.

The fixed organs of speech call for little comment. All English speech-sounds, if we exclude the clicks by which we express annoyance, are made by expelling a column of air through the mouth or nose, and this column of air comes from the lungs, which may thus be included among the organs of speech. The teeth play a part in the pronunciation of certain consonants, and so do the gums or the teeth-ridge immediately behind the upper teeth. The gums of the lower teeth are comparatively unimportant in the production of speech-sounds but they provide a resting-place for the tip of the tongue in the pronunciation of vowels. The gums are sometimes called the *alveoli* and consonants in the production of which they play a part are said to be *alveolar*.

Each of the movable organs of speech can act independently of the others, and one of them, the tongue, is capable of taking up a very large number of different positions. The number of theoretically possible different speech-sounds is therefore very large indeed. Any one language, such as English, contains only a small proportion of the total number of possible sounds.

Speech-sounds are generally classified as vowels and consonants, but the distinction between the two is not rigid. The initial consonants of *you* and *will* are called semivowels because they have some of the characteristics of vowels but are in other respects like consonants, and the sounds *l* and *n* can be regarded as consonants in *look* and *not* but as vowels in *bottle* and *hidden*. The distinction between vowels and consonants depends upon the amount of obstruction offered to the current of air as it passes through the mouth. A vowel is a voiced sound in the pronunciation of which there is no obstruction or narrowing of the current of air of such a kind as to cause audible plosion or friction. A consonant is a sound, which may be either voiced or voiceless, in the pronunciation of which there is either a complete or partial obstruction of the current of air of such a kind as to cause audible plosion or friction. A diphthong may be defined as two successive vowels pronounced with only one peak of energy or stress so that they constitute a single syllable. Hence a diphthong consists of an infinite number of vowel-sounds produced as the tongue moves from the position required for the first vowel to that required for the final vowel of the diphthong. Diphthongs are usually represented phonetically by two symbols, the first of which represents the starting point of the tongue while the second represents the direction in which the tongue moves, although the tongue does not always reach the position indicated by the second phonetic symbol. If the chief stress of a diphthong is on the first element, the diphthong is said to be 'falling'; if the chief stress is on the second element the diphthong is said to be 'rising'. Most English diphthongs today are falling, but there is evidence that some of them were once rising, and the sound represented by *ew* in *few* can be regarded as a rising diphthong.

Complete precision in the articulation of speech-sounds is unattainable. No two speakers pronounce a given sound in exactly the same way, and the same speaker may pronounce the sound differently on different occasions. The different pronunciations heard from different people when they try to reproduce a particular sound are known as *variant pronunciations*. The different varieties of a sound heard in the speech of one person which owe their variety to differences of phonetic context are said to constitute a *phoneme*. Thus, in the speech of many people the second vowel of *city* is rather more open than the first because it is final, although both vowels are represented by the same phonetic symbol [i], and most speakers would make a distinction between the two *l*-sounds in *little*. The differences among the various sounds which constitute a phoneme are so slight that they do not affect the significance which a hearer attaches to the phoneme. Habit plays a large part in determining which differences between sounds are considered to be slight, and two sounds may belong to the same phoneme in one language but to different phonemes in another.

In order to describe the pronunciation of any consonant, it is necessary to answer three questions about it: How is it made? Where is it made? Is it voiced or voiceless? Each of these questions can be answered by one word, and the three words answering these questions can be combined to form a brief description of the consonant in question, which serves to identify it. In the following account of English consonants, when pairs of similar consonants are mentioned, the first is voiceless and the second voiced; when a single consonant is mentioned, it is voiced unless otherwise described. When no phonetic symbol is given, the usual printed form of the letter can be used without ambiguity as a phonetic symbol.

Plosive consonants are formed by completely stopping the passage of air at some point. Air accumulates under pressure behind the stoppage and, when the stoppage is released, the air escapes with a slight explosion. In the pronunciation of *p* and *b* the stoppage is made by the two lips, and these consonants are therefore called labial plosives; in *t* and *d* it is made by pressing the tip of the tongue against the upper teeth-ridge, and these consonants are therefore called post-dental or alveolar plosives; in *k* and *g* it is made by pressing the back of the tongue against the velum, or soft palate, and these consonants are therefore called velar plosives. Plosives may be pronounced with or without aspiration. An aspirated plosive is one in the pronunciation of which an *h*-sound accompanies the release of the current of air. Aspirated plosives are common in pronunciation, though not in spelling, in Standard English of today. In Southern English voiceless plosives are generally pronounced with some aspiration when they occur in strongly stressed syllables. Thus, the *t* in *ten* is slightly aspirated, whereas the *t* in *letter* is not. Voiced plosives are less strongly aspirated than voiceless plosives in English.

Fricative consonants are formed by narrowing the mouth passage at some point, without completely closing it, so that the air from the lungs makes a noise as it passes through. In the pronunciation of *f* and *v* the narrowing is between the upper teeth and the lower lip, and these consonants are therefore called labio-dental fricatives. The spelling *th* is used in English to represent both a voiceless consonant, as in *thin*, and a voiced consonant, as in *then*. The phonetic symbols for these sounds are respectively [θ] and [ð]. They are pronounced either by allowing the tip of the tongue to protrude slightly between the teeth or to touch the back of the upper teeth while air is forced between the tongue and the teeth. They are called pre-dental fricatives. The post-dental fricatives *s* and *z* are made by narrowing the space between the tongue and the teeth-ridge. In the palato-alveolar fricatives the narrowing is rather further back in the mouth and produces the initial consonant of *shoe* and the medial consonant of *pleasure*, for which the phonetic symbols are [ʃ] and [ʒ] respectively. The aspirate *h* is a voiceless glottal fricative, which is pronounced by expelling air from the lungs in such a way that slight friction occurs as the air passes between the open vocal cords. The tongue is left free to take up the position for the following vowel, and as a rule the articulation of the *h* accompanies that of the vowel instead of preceding it.

A rolled *r* is made by a rapid succession of taps by the tip of the tongue against the teeth-ridge. This is the usual variety of *r* in Scots speech, but most English speakers today use a voiced post-dental fricative, of which the phonetic symbol is [ɹ]

Lateral consonants are made by pressing the centre of the tip of the tongue against the upper teeth-ridge and allowing the air to escape along one or both sides of the tongue. English lateral consonants are all spelt *l*, but the tongue is so flexible that it is possible to pronounce many different varieties of *l*-sound, all of which satisfy this description. The consonant *l* can be pronounced with the resonance of any vowel, and two varieties are particularly noteworthy. When English *l* occurs before vowels, it has a resonance nearly like that of the vowel *i*, achieved by raising the front of the tongue, and the *l* is said to be *clear*; when it occurs before consonants or finally, *l* has a *u*-resonance, achieved by slightly hollowing the front of the tongue and raising the back, and it is said to be *dark*. English *l* is normally voiced, but a voiceless *l* occurs in Welsh, where it is spelt *ll*. It is of frequent occurrence in Welsh place-names, where it causes difficulty to English speakers, who often use a voiced *l* either alone or preceded by a [θ] or [k], apparently in the hope that a preceding voiceless consonant will cause the *l* to become unvoiced by assimilation. The simplest way of pronouncing voiceless *l* is to put the tongue in the position for *l* and then blow.

Nasal consonants are formed by closing the passage of air through the mouth at some point and at the same time lowering the soft palate so that air can escape through the nose. If the stoppage is caused by the lips the consonant is the labial nasal *m*; if the stoppage is caused by pressing the tip of the tongue against the teeth-ridge the consonant is the post-dental nasal *n*; if the stoppage is caused by pressing the back of the tongue against the soft palate, the consonant is the velar nasal [ŋ], which is sometimes spelt *ng*, as in *sing*, and sometimes *n*, as in *ink*. The spelling *ng* is also used to represent [ŋg], as in *finger*, and it is probable that this was the pronunciation represented by *ng* in Old English.

Semivowels are sounds in the pronunciation of which the tongue is raised very slightly above the position requisite for a close vowel. If the front of the tongue is raised as high as this the resultant sound is the palatal semivowel [j], usually spelt *y* as in *you*. If the back of the tongue is raised while the lips are rounded and pushed forward, the sound produced is the velar semivowel, which occurs both unvoiced [ʍ] and voiced [w]. Most speakers in the South of England use only the voiced sound, but most Scots and Irish speakers and some speakers elsewhere use [ʍ] for *wh* in words like *which* and *what*.

Affricate consonants can best be regarded as plosives pronounced with slow separation of the organs of speech, with the result that the plosive is followed by the corresponding fricative. An affricate consonant can therefore always be regarded as a group of two consonants. The two affricate consonants that are most important for the study of the history of English are the palato-alveolar affricates [tʃ] and [dʒ], which occur initially in the words *charm* and *gem*.

In describing the pronunciation of vowels it is necessary to say which part of the tongue is raised and how high it is raised. The terms 'front' and 'back', as applied to vowels, describe the part of the tongue which is highest in the mouth; in the pronunciation of central vowels the tongue is flat without being arched either at the front or the back. The terms 'close', 'half-close', 'half-open', and 'open' are used to describe the four approximately equidistant levels to which the tongue can be raised. In the pronunciation of some vowels the muscles of the tongue are tense and rigid; in the pronunciation of others the muscles are slack, making the tongue soft. These differences affect the quality of the vowel, but, in English, differences in the tenseness of the tongue are accompanied by differences in its height, which form a more satisfactory basis of classification. To illustrate the effect of tenseness one may compare the tense vowel-sound of the second syllable of *machine* with the slack vowel-sound of *hit*. If the lips are rounded, the fact is normally mentioned when the vowel is described; in the absence of any comment on the lips it may be assumed that they are in a neutral position. In the pronunciation of all English vowels the vocal cords vibrate and the soft palate is pressed back to close the passage to the nose.

It happens that in Modern English the front vowels are unrounded whereas most of the back vowels are rounded, but in Early English there were front rounded vowels. Two such vowels, which have not survived into Modern English, were the front close rounded vowel [y], pronounced like the *u* in French *tu*, which was spelt *y* in Old English and *u* in Middle English, and the half-close front rounded vowel [ø], pronounced like the *eu* in French *peu* and spelt *œ* in Old English and usually *eo* or *ue* in Middle English. The vowels of Modern English may be described thus:

Front close: [i], which occurs short in *bit* and long in *machine*. The short vowel in English speech is rather more open than the long, and in narrow phonetic transcription different symbols are used to represent the two sounds.

Front half-open: [ɛ], which occurs short in *set*.

Front between half-open and open: [æ], which occurs short in *cat*.

Back close rounded: [u], which occurs short in *put* and long in *fool*. Like the corresponding front vowel [i], the short vowel is rather more open than the long and is represented by a different symbol in narrow phonetic transcription. The sound represented by *u* in *run* and many other words is represented by the phonetic symbol [ʌ]. In the articulation of this sound the highest part of the tongue is between the centre and the back, and it is raised to a level rather more open than the half-open position.

Back half-open rounded: [ɔ], which occurs long in *saw*. A rather more open back vowel is [ɒ], which occurs short in *got*.

Back open: [ɑ], which occurs long in *father*.

Lastly there is the extremely common central vowel [ə], which is pronounced by allowing the tongue to remain flat about half-way between the close and open positions. This is the initial sound of *about* and the final vowel of *father*. A lengthened form of this vowel, which differs slightly from it in quality, is the vowel-sound of *bird*. It is the noise made unconsciously by most of us when we are wondering what to say next.

Some of the vowels which occur as the first elements of diphthongs do not occur in English except in diphthongs. The first element of the diphthong heard in *gate* [geit] is more close than the *e* in *get* [gɛt], and the first element of the diphthong heard in *go* [gou] is more close than the *o* in *got* [gɒt]. The first element of the diphthongs heard in *find* [faind] and *found* [faund] respectively is a front open vowel rather more open than the *a* in *cat* [kæt]. The other English diphthongs are made up of vowels which also occur as monophthongs. Examples are the diphthongs heard in *here* [hiə], *fair* [fɛə], and *four* [fɔə].

Apart from the quality of the sound, there are three attributes of speech-sounds which are only very imperfectly recorded in writing but which play an important part in speech and its development. These are length, stress, and intonation.

The length of a vowel-sound is its duration in time. It is possible to continue the articulation of a vowel-sound as long as the breath holds out, and the number of different degrees of length is infinite, but it is usually necessary to distinguish only two or three different degrees. In phonetic transcription short vowels are left without any indication of length whereas a symbol followed by a colon represents a long vowel. The upper point of a colon is used to represent an intermediate degree of length, and vowels so marked are said to be half-long. The length of vowels in Old and Middle English forms is usually indicated in grammars by a horizontal line above the vowel-symbol. This method has the advantage of making it possible to record both spelling and vowel-length by a single set of symbols. The length of vowels is important for the study of the historical development of English because long and short vowels have often had a different development. Thus in Old English the difference between the stem-vowel of *scafan* 'to shave' and that of *stān* 'stone' was purely one of length whereas the difference between the diphthongs of *shave* and *stone*, which are descended from these Old English forms, is one of quality.

Most consonants can be prolonged in the same way as vowels. Such consonants are known as continuants, and this term can be applied to all the groups of English consonants with the exception of plosives. It is an essential characteristic of plosives that when they are pronounced the organs of speech concerned are separated suddenly, and it may therefore seem that plosives cannot be lengthened, but the effect of lengthening a plosive consonant is achieved by allowing a slight pause to intervene between the bringing together of the organs of speech and their separation. Long consonants occur in Old English and they are indicated in spelling by the doubling of the letter, but in Modern English the long or double consonants have for the most part come to be pronounced as though they were single, with the result that there is now no difference of pronunciation between *in* and *inn*. Double or long consonants may be heard in present-day English speech in compound words, like *book-case*, in which the final consonant of the first element is identical with the initial consonant of the second element.

Stress depends upon the force with which breath is expelled. Strongly stressed syllables are pronounced more loudly than lightly stressed syllables, the vowels of which tend to lose their distinctive quality or to disappear. Stress has been an important factor in the development of English from the earliest times. It was probably one of the chief causes of the variation of vowels in Indo-European, and in Germanic voiceless fricatives were voiced when the preceding syllable was lightly stressed but not when it was strongly stressed. In more recent times variation of stress has led to a similar variation between voiced and voiceless consonants in pairs of words such as *of* and *off*. There are many pairs of words identical in origin which have diverged because of differences of stress. Examples are *to* and *too*, *as* and *also*, *of* and *off*. It may be that some of the sound-changes for which no good explanation has yet been found, such as the shortening of the vowel in words like *blood* and *death*, were due originally to variations of sentence-stress.

Intonation is the name given to variations in the pitch of the voice, which are due to changes in the rate of vibration of the vocal cords. Intonation is extremely important in the spoken language, where it is used to express shades of meaning which cannot easily be translated into writing, but it has had less influence than stress upon the development of English.

CHAPTER IV

Phonology

MANY attempts have been made to explain why sounds change, but these attempts have not been completely successful. It is quite likely that several distinct causes have contributed to the development of sound-changes in various languages. We can often point to contributory causes of change, but we cannot feel certain that we have discovered the primary cause.

One explanation that has often been given to explain sound-changes is that they take place 'for the sake of euphony'. If we give to 'euphony' its literal meaning 'pleasing sound', this explanation has little to recommend it, for as a rule the sound that results from a change is not demonstrably more pleasing than the sound it has replaced. But the word euphony is often used in this connexion to describe a tendency to phonetic change for the sake of ease of pronunciation, and it seems fairly certain that an unconscious search for greater ease of pronunciation is sometimes a cause of sound-change. At the best, however, this is an incomplete explanation since it does not explain why certain changes take place only at particular times and in particular languages.

It has been suggested that sound-changes may be caused by differences of climate. Such an explanation can be applicable only when the speakers of a language have migrated to a region of different climatic conditions, whereas sounds go on changing when the people speaking the language continue to live in the same climatic conditions. No specific sound-change has yet been shown to have resulted from this cause.

Another explanation that can be applicable to only a very limited set of circumstances is that sound-change results from racial characteristics, such as thickness of the lips or the shape of the face. It is true that very slight variations in the structure of the organs of speech can cause considerable differences of sound, but many sound-changes have taken place without any racial differences. Another theory is that sound-change results from contact with foreign speakers who need not necessarily belong to a different race. The contact may take the form of conquest. Conquering or colonizing nations often impose their language on the people they conquer, and it has been suggested that the conquered people may modify their new language as a result of the influence of the speech-habits of their old language. In support of this view, it has been pointed out that languages which have had few foreign contacts tend to be conservative.

The mistakes made by children in learning to speak have sometimes been mentioned as a possible cause of sound-change. Opponents of this theory maintain that the mistakes made by children are corrected and have no permanent effect on the development of a language. No doubt many of them are, but it seems reasonable to look for the explanation of sound-change in mistakes made by the users of a language, and such mistakes are likely to be especially common among children who are learning to speak. As early as 1821 the Danish philologist J. H. Bredsdorff[1] mentioned a number of causes of linguistic change, and among them he included mishearing and misunderstanding, defective memory, and imperfect speech-organs.

When we consider the imperfections of the human ear and the extreme difficulty of repeating with exactness a particular position of the tongue, especially in the articulation of vowel-sounds, it is not surprising that the speech-sounds of any individual speaker should differ from those that he has heard. Each speaker is, to the best of his ability, trying to correct any divergence from what he believes to be the norm, but the divergence may be too slight for him to notice it. When another speaker uses his speech as a model, the divergence from the norm may be smoothed out or it may be increased until, by a series of successive inaccurate imitations, a new sound noticeably different from the original sound comes to be used. It may be noticed that sound-changes resulting from inaccurate imitation do not always take place gradually. It is especially true of consonant

[1] Quoted by O. Jespersen, *Language, its Nature, Development and Origin*, p. 70.

changes that they are liable to take place by a sudden leap or substitution rather than by gradual change. Many people have difficulty in distinguishing between one voiceless fricative and another. Hence the velar fricative [x] has become a labio-dental fricative in *laugh* and *cough*, and similarly many people, especially children and Cockneys, say *wiv* for *with* and *fru* for *through*. The difficulty of regarding inaccuracy of imitation as the cause of sound-change is that it does not explain why a new pronunciation comes to be shared by a large number of speakers. The explanation of this spread of sound-changes may be that the successive inaccurate imitations are reinforced by one of the other causes of sound-change, such as the desire to make pronunciation easier. Another explanation may be that certain speakers enjoy a prestige which causes their pronunciation to be imitated by a large number of other speakers. The speakers who exert an influence on the speech of others in this way may be either individuals or social groups, and the imitation may be either unconscious or deliberate. This kind of influence is described in *2 Henry IV* with reference to Hotspur:

> And speaking thick (which Nature made his blemish)
> Became the accents of the valiant,
> For those that could speak low and tardily
> Would turn their own perfection to abuse
> To seem like him.   (II. iii. 24ff.)

A more recent example of such imitation was to be noticed in the Second World War, when the very individual characteristics of Winston Churchill's speech were widely imitated by public speakers. The tendency of Standard English to spread over the whole country is due in part to the prestige enjoyed by speakers of that variety of English.

Two kinds of sound-change are to be distinguished. Independent or isolative sound-changes affect a given sound of a particular language or dialect whatever the neighbouring sounds may be; dependent or combinative changes take place only in the neighbourhood of particular sounds and are caused by them. Dependent changes can be further classified according to the result of the change. When successive sounds are pronounced in widely different parts of the mouth, there are two ways in which their pronunciation can be made easier: one sound may be wholly or partly assimilated to the other or an intermediate sound may develop as a glide between them. All these types of change are exemplified in the history of English pronunciation.

Side by side with the tendency of sounds to change, there are other tendencies which may have the effect either of preventing a change from taking place or of restoring the original sound. One of these tendencies is the desire to preserve intelligibility. The regular operation of sound-changes would have led to the loss or assimilation of many of the consonants in the consonant-groups which are among the characteristic features of English, but the desire for intelligibility through distinctness of speech has caused them to be retained.

Sound-changes have been taking place at every stage in the history of the English language. From the eighth century onwards these sound-changes are reflected in spellings found in manuscripts that have been preserved, but in the study of earlier periods we are less fortunate. It is likely that there were many sound-changes in Indo-European and Germanic of which no trace has been preserved, but there were other changes of which we can gain some knowledge by a comparison of the extant remains of the separate Indo-European languages. The safest way of describing these early sound-changes is by means of equations indicating the sounds in the various Indo-European languages which correspond with each other. Such equations are, however, cumbrous, and it is reasonable to draw inferences from them about the sounds in Indo-European or Germanic, provided that we realize that we are on less certain ground than we are in studying the later history of the separate Indo-European languages, and that we cannot be certain of the exact quality of the sounds whose past existence we assume.

The following account of phonology deals only with changes which have had an important effect upon present-day English, but it will be seen that some of these changes took place at a very early date. In each of the five chronological divisions changes affecting vowel quality are described first, then changes affecting the length of vowels, and finally changes affecting consonants.

INDO-EUROPEAN

Indo-European seems to have had the vowels *a*, *e*, and *o*, both long and short. In addition there were reduced vowels which probably occurred only in positions which were lightly accented in Indo-European. There was also a group of sounds known as sonants, which were intermediate between vowels and consonants and which developed differently according to the neighbouring sounds: between vowels they developed into consonants and between consonants they developed into vowels. They were *i̯*, *u̯*, *l*, *m*, *n*, *r*. Diphthongs were formed by combining any of the vowels *a*, *e* or *o*, whether long or short, with a sonant.

In all the Indo-European languages certain vowel-variations occur within groups of etymologically related words. Some of these variations, like that between the vowels in *mouse* and *mice*, were caused by sound-changes which took place within the separate languages; but many of them cannot be so explained, and the explanation of some of these must be sought in Indo-European. These vowel-variations in the parent language are included under the name *ablaut*, a term invented by Grimm for which English philologists sometimes use the name *gradation*. Ablaut variations are of several different kinds, both of vowel-length and quality, and they may have had several different causes, but it is probable that the most important cause was variation in the kind and amount of accent, a term which includes both pitch and stress. It seems probable that ablaut variations had at first no connexion with meaning, but once they had come into existence they were used to express differences of meaning.

The groups of vowels which stand in ablaut relationship to each other are known as series, and each vowel in an ablaut series is said to belong to a particular grade. The various grades may best be illustrated by an examination of the first, and most important, of the ablaut series, that in which *e* varies with *o*. In this series the vowel which normally occurred in fully accented positions was *e*, and this vowel is said to represent the full grade. In syllables which originally had a secondary accent the *e* was replaced by *o*, and *o* is said to represent the secondary grade. By reducing the stress on the syllable, the vowel could be further changed to an indeterminate vowel something like the first vowel of Modern English *potato*, and this is called reduced grade. Further reduction of stress could cause the vowel to disappear altogether, thus producing vanishing grade. Another grade was produced by lengthening the vowel of the full and secondary grades. This grade may have resulted from the loss of a following sound or syllable, and is called lengthened grade. Parallels to Indo-European ablaut variations could be cited from many languages. For example, Modern English shows a series of different pronunciations of the verb *can* according to the amount of stress: [kæn], [kən], [kn̩]. A parallel to the lengthened grade is provided by *can't* [kɑːnt], and the reasons for the lengthening in Indo-European and Modern English are very similar: the loss of a vowel in the following syllable.

The sonants stood outside the ablaut series, and when a sonant was added to a vowel to form a diphthong it could be added to each grade of the series. The long diphthongs which arose in this way were either monophthongized by the loss of their sonant element or shortened in nearly all of the Indo-European languages, including all those of the Germanic group.

It is clear that the number of theoretically possible ablaut variations is very large, but in any one Indo-European language we usually find that only a very small proportion of the possible variant forms of a word has survived. In English the variation is illustrated most clearly in the principal parts of strong verbs, but it is important to remember that it is not confined to them. The variation in the first class of strong verbs survives today in *ride, rode, ridden*. The stem-vowels of these forms may be traced back to IE *ei, oi,* and *i* and these represent respectively the full, secondary and vanishing grades of the first ablaut series followed by the sonant *i*. The nouns *road* and *raid* contain the same grade of vowel as the preterite *rode*, and all three forms are represented by *rād* in Old English. Similarly the second class of strong verbs may be traced back to the same three grades of the first ablaut series followed by the sonant *u*. The infinitive *seethe* (OE *sēoðan* 'to boil') is developed from a form with full grade; the past participle *sodden* is developed from a form with vanishing grade;

the secondary grade is not represented by any form of the verb *seethe* that has survived to the present day, but it gave the OE preterite singular *sēað*. Full illustration of the effects of ablaut variation on Modern English would involve a lengthy account of subsequent sound-changes which have diversified the variations, and such an account would be out of place here, but enough has been said to show that ablaut variations have had a lasting effect on the form of English words.

The Indo-European consonant system included the sonants *i̯*, *u̯*, *l*, *m*, *n*, *r*, when they developed as consonants, and the fricative consonant *s*, which sometimes became *z* by assimilation to a voiced consonant. The remaining Indo-European consonants fit into a symmetrical scheme, consisting of voiced and voiceless plosives either of which might be either unaspirated or aspirated. In each of these four groups there occurred consonants made in various parts of the mouth. Thus, there were the labial consonants *p*, *b*, *ph*, *bh*; the dentals or alveolars *t*, *d*, *th*, *dh*; the velars *k*, *g*, *kh*, *gh*; and the labio-velars k^w, g^w, k^wh, g^wh. A labio-velar consonant is one which is pronounced by raising the back of the tongue to the soft palate and at the same time rounding the lips. There was also a group of palatal consonants, but in all the languages belonging to the *centum* division of Indo-European this group fell in with the velars and need not be separately considered from the point of view of the history of the English language. In the separate Indo-European languages the labio-velars have generally had one of three developments: sometimes they have become velar consonants followed by the labial consonant *w*, sometimes they have lost their labial element, and sometimes they have lost their velar element. This varied development of the labio-velars, which depended in part on the neighbouring sounds and in part on the language or dialect in which the word occurred, has had some surprising results in increasing the differences between pairs of cognate words. Thus, *cow* and *beef* are cognates. The initial consonant was originally a labio-velar; *cow* (OE *cū*) has preserved the velar element while *beef* (OF *boef*) is descended from a Latin form which kept the labial element. Similarly the native English *wheel* and the Greek loan-word *cycle* are cognate with each other and show different developments of labio-velars.

GERMANIC

Some of the sound-changes which distinguished Common Germanic from Indo-European took place also in several of the other sub-divisions of the Indo-European family of languages; some of them took place only in Germanic. In order to illustrate Germanic sound-changes it is often useful to compare an English word with its Latin cognate. When such comparisons are made, it is important to remember that the English word is not derived from the Latin but that the English and Latin words go back to a common Indo-European source. Sometimes the Latin word has preserved unchanged the Indo-European sound in question, but sometimes it is necessary to take into account sound-changes in Latin as well as those in Germanic and English.

Many vowel-changes serve to distinguish Common Germanic from Indo-European. Some of these were independent changes, such as the development of the Indo-European *o* to Germanic *a* and that of Indo-European *ā* to Germanic *ō*. The first of these changes is illustrated by the comparison of Latin *quod* with its English cognate *what* and the second by the comparison of Latin *māter* with Old English *mōdor*, from which Modern English *mother* has been derived. Other changes are dependent; these include the raising of *e* to *i* before a nasal followed by another consonant, which accounts for the variation in vowel between Latin *ventus* and its English cognate *wind*.

The most striking differences between the Germanic languages and the other Indo-European languages are in the development of consonants. Most of the Indo-European consonants were changed in Germanic according to a series of clearly defined and very symmetrical changes generally grouped together under the name Grimm's Law. The changes are sometimes described as the First Consonant Shift in order to distinguish them from a later series of somewhat similar changes which took place in Old High German. The sonants and the fricative *s* were not affected by Grimm's Law. The changes which affected the other Indo-European consonants fall into three groups, and in each group the changes affect one sound from each of the phonetic categories: labial, dental or alveolar, and velar. The labio-velars share in the changes affecting the velars. The various changes may be classified as follow:

(1) The Indo-European voiced aspirated plosives *bh, dh, gh* lose their aspiration and become in Germanic the voiced fricatives [ƀ], [ð], [ɣ]. These voiced fricatives later become the corresponding voiced plosives in most positions. This series of changes is probably to be regarded as earlier than the other changes constituting Grimm's Law, since it is shared by many other groups of Indo-European languages, though it is not found in Sanskrit, Greek or Latin. Examples are OE *beran* 'to bear' compared with Greek φέρειν and Latin *ferre*, OE *dohtor* 'daughter' compared with Greek θυγάτηρ.

(2) The Indo-European voiceless plosives *p, t, k* become aspirated. They then fall in with the Indo-European voiceless aspirated plosives *ph, th, kh*, and, like them, become the voiceless fricatives [f], [θ], [x], respectively. Examples are OE *fōt* 'foot' beside Latin *ped-*, OE *þū* 'thou' beside Latin *tū*, OE *hund* 'hundred' beside Latin *centum*.

There are two notable exceptions to this series of changes: voiceless plosives remain unaffected when immediately preceded by *s*, and when two voiceless plosives occur next to each other only the first plosive of the group is affected. Thus OE *giest* 'guest' is cognate with Latin *hostis* 'stranger', and OE *eahta* 'eight' is cognate with Latin *octō*.

(3) The Indo-European plosives *b, d, g* become unvoiced to *p, t, k* respectively. Examples are OE *tōþ* 'tooth' beside Latin *dent-*, OE *cnēo* 'knee' beside Latin *genu*.

It is not possible to date the changes comprising Grimm's Law with any exactness, although some evidence is provided by the forms of Germanic loan-words in Finnish and by the treatment of Germanic proper names in the works of Greek and Latin writers. From such evidence we are able to say that the changes were probably completed before the beginning of the Christian era; they may have been spread over some centuries. It is possible to say something about the chronology of the changes in relation to each other and to other Germanic sound-changes. For example, it is clear that the Indo-European voiceless plosives had at any rate begun to be changed before the unvoicing of Indo-European voiced plosives was completed; otherwise the two groups of sounds would have fallen together. Again, we can be sure that the change of the voiceless plosives to fricatives was completed before the operation of another group of sound-changes known as Verner's Law, which affected voiceless fricatives in Germanic.

Verner's Law states that the voiceless fricatives [f], [s], [θ], and [x] became voiced in Germanic to [ƀ], [z], [ð], and [ɣ] when they occurred between voiced sounds unless they were immediately preceded by the chief stress of the word. This change affected a large number of words, but the effects of the change have sometimes been removed by analogy, and later changes have sometimes led to further divergent development, with the result that the variation is no longer one between a voiceless and a voiced fricative. Two of these later changes affecting voiced fricatives took place in West Germanic, where [z] became [r] and [ð] became [d] by independent changes. Hence the variation of consonants between *death* and *dead* and between *seethe* (OE *sēoðan*) and *sodden* (OE *soden*) results from Verner's Law. Similarly the differences between *arise* (OE *ārīsan*) and *rear* (OE *rǣran*) and that between *lose* (cf. OE *lēosan*) and *forlorn* (OE *forloren* pp. of *forlēosan*) arise from an earlier variation between *s* and *z*. Although Verner's Law was completed in Common Germanic, the connexion between voicing of consonants and lack of stress is one to which parallels can be quoted from later periods of the language. The words *of* and *off* were originally the same word, but *of* generally occurs in lightly stressed positions and therefore has a voiced consonant, whereas *off* occurs in strongly stressed positions and therefore has a voiceless consonant. Similarly we may compare the pronunciation of the *x* in *exert*, *exist* and *example*, where the stress is on the second syllable, with *exercise*, *execrate* and *execute*, where it is on the first.

OLD ENGLISH

Some of the sound-changes which took place in Old English have had little or no permanent effect on the language. It is therefore necessary to mention here only the most important.

If importance can be measured by the wide range of sounds affected and by the persistence in Modern English of the effects of the change, the most important of the Old English sound-changes was front mutation or *i/j*-mutation. This is the name given to the modification of a vowel or diphthong by an *ĭ* or *j* in the following syllable. By the time of the surviving Old English texts the *ĭ* or *j* which caused the change had generally either disappeared or been weakened to *e*, but the existence of the *ĭ* or *j* in primitive Old English can be deduced from its influence on the preceding vowel and by comparison with cognate languages. The effect of the change was to cause the vowel affected to approach *i* in its place of formation. Hence back vowels were fronted and front open vowels became more close. Most Old English vowels and diphthongs were affected by front mutation. Some of the changes are given below, with examples showing how the effects of the change are to be found in present-day English.

a before nasal consonants became *e*, as in *menn*, plural of *mann* 'man'.

u became *y*, as in *fyllan* 'to fill' beside the adjective *full*.

ā became *ǣ*, as in *hǣlan* 'to heal', beside *hāl* 'whole'.

ō became *ē*, as in *fēt* plural of *fōt* 'foot', *gēs* plural of *gōs* 'goose'.

ū became *ȳ*, as in *fȳlþ* 'filth' beside *fūl* 'foul', *mȳs* plural of *mūs* 'mouse'.

A number of Old English sound-changes affected the length of vowels. Short vowels were lengthened when they occurred in open monosyllables. This is the reason why the vowel in *who* (OE *hwā*) is long while that in *what* (OE *hwæt*) is short. In late Old English short vowels were often lengthened before a liquid or nasal followed by another voiced consonant. Lengthening before *r* + consonant was less widespread and less lasting in its effects than before the other groups; the effects of lengthening have been most lasting before *ld* and *nd*. No lengthening took place in lightly stressed words, such as *under* and *and*, or if a third consonant immediately followed the consonant group. Hence in Modern English we have diphthongs descended from Middle English long vowels in *hound* (OE *hund*), *find* (OE *findan*), and *child* (OE *cild*), but short vowels in *children* (OE *cildru*, pl.) and *hundred* (OE *hundred*).

There has been a tendency to shorten long vowels under varying conditions at many periods during the history of the English language. Long vowels were generally shortened in Old English before double consonants, before groups of two consonants in words of more than two syllables, and before groups of three consonants in all words. Examples are *met* (OE *mette*) beside *meet* (OE *mētan*), *fed* (OE *fedde*) beside *feed* (OE *fēdan*), *bless* (OE *bletsian*, related to *blōd* 'blood'), and *gospel* (OE *godspell*, related to *gōd* 'good'). Analogy often led to the restoration of a long vowel after shortening had taken place, especially in compound words which were still regarded as such. Thus, there is a long vowel in *cleanness* (OE *clǣnness*) because of the analogy of *clean* (OE *clǣne*). In *homestead* (OE *hāmstede*) the influence of *home* has preserved a long vowel, whereas the place-name *Hampstead* is from a form in which *ā* was shortened before a group of three consonants.

Many Old English sound-changes were not recorded in spelling until the Middle English period, when French scribes began to distinguish between sounds which had hitherto been represented by the same letter. This time-lag is particularly noticeable with regard to the fronting of the consonants *c* and *g*. When these consonants were followed by front vowels, they were fronted in primitive Old English, but it was not until the Middle English period that front *c* and *g* were spelt *ch* and *y* (*i*, *ȝ*) respectively. Examples of fronted *c* and *g* are *chin* (OE *cinn*), *choose* (OE *cēosan*), *yard* (OE *geard*), and *yield* (OE *gieldan*). Examples of the retention of a velar consonant are *come* (OE *cuman*) and *go* (OE *gān*). The *c* in the group *sc* was fronted, whatever the quality of the neighbouring vowels, and the group *sc* came to be pronounced [ʃ], although the spelling *sc* remained in use throughout the Old English period, to be replaced in Middle English by *sh*, a spelling which has remained to the present day. Examples are *should* (OE *sceolde*) and *fish* (OE *fisc*).

Another consonant change which was not generally recorded in spelling during the Old English period was the voicing of [f], [s] and [θ] to [v], [z] and [ð] respectively when they occurred between voiced sounds. It is because of this change that we find pairs of words today, one a noun and the other a verb, of which the noun has a voiceless fricative because the consonant was final in Old English, whereas the verb has a voiced fricative because it occurred between vowels. An example is *bath* (OE *bæþ*) beside *bathe* (OE *baþian*). Similarly many nouns ending in a voiceless fricative have a voiced fricative in the plural, as *wolf* (OE *wulf*) beside *wolves* (OE *wulfas*).

Some consonant changes arise from widespread phonetic tendencies and are liable to occur in any language at any time. One of the characteristics of English, resulting in part from the loss of lightly stressed vowels, is the large number of words containing heavy groups of consonants which are difficult to pronounce. For example, the word *strength* [stɹɛŋθ] contains six sounds, five of which are consonants. There are three ways of lessening the difficulty of pronouncing such groups, and already in Old English we find all three ways beginning to be used:

(1) A consonant may be omitted from a group. The middle consonant of a group of three often disappeared in Old English, as in *el(n)boga* 'elbow', *fæs(t)nian* 'to fasten'. The loss of a consonant was especially common when the group of three consonants included a double consonant, as in *sende* (earlier **sendde*) pret. of *sendan* 'to send'; *cyste* (earlier **cysste*) pret. of *cyssan* 'to kiss'. A similar loss of the middle consonant of a group has often taken place in pronunciation in Modern English, although the lost consonant has generally remained in spelling, as in *Christmas, postman, often.*

(2) A vowel may be inserted between two consonants. This is the origin of the *ou* in *borough* (OE *bur(u)h*) and *thorough* beside *through* (OE *þurh*). A similar glide before *r* is found in later English as a vulgarism, as in *umberella* and *Henery*. Sometimes unwillingness to have a heavy consonant group led to the retention of a vowel which would otherwise have disappeared, as in OE *hyngrede* 'was hungry', compared with OE *dēmde* 'judged'.

(3) The consonants may be assimilated to each other. Assimilation may be complete or partial and it may affect either or both of the two adjacent consonants. It may affect the place of formation of a consonant or it may have the effect of voicing or unvoicing a consonant. All these kinds of assimilation occurred in Old English. Complete assimilation occurred in *wimman* (earlier *wīfman*) 'woman', partial in *cīest* (earlier *cīesþ*) third person sing. pres. ind. of *cēosan* 'to choose'. In *wimman* the

first consonant of a group was affected; in *cīest* it was the second. In *bitt* (earlier *bid(e)þ*) third person sing. pres. ind. of *biddan* 'to pray', both consonants were affected: the *d* became unvoiced because it was followed by the voiceless consonant *þ* and the pre-dental consonant *þ* became the post-dental *t* because it was preceded by a post-dental. Similar assimilations have taken place in late Old English and are still going on.

Another consonant change which may take place at any time but which had begun to take place in Old English is *metathesis*, or the transposition of two consecutive sounds, one or both of which may be consonantal. When one of the sounds undergoing metathesis is a vowel, the consonant is usually *r*, and the transposition of *r* and the vowel is the result of the development of a glide vowel, which later takes the stress, while the original stressed vowel is reduced to a glide. Old English examples are *hors* 'horse', beside ON *hross*, and *berstan* 'to burst', beside ON *bresta*. It is likely that double forms of some words remained in existence side by side, one with and the other without metathesis. Thus OE *gærs* shows metathesis when compared with Gothic *gras*, but Modern English *grass* has developed from a form without metathesis. In *third* (OE *þridda*) metathesis has taken place since the Old English period. There are several Old English examples of the metathesis of *s* and a voiceless plosive, as *āscian* beside *ācsian* 'to ask', and *wæsp* beside *wæps* 'wasp'. The forms *ax* and *wopse* have survived in dialects.

MIDDLE ENGLISH

Dialectal differences play a more important part in Middle English than in either Old English or Modern English. They are less important in Old English because of the scarcity of non-West-Saxon texts; they are less important in Modern English because of the rise of Standard English, a single dialect which has acquired greater importance than the other dialects. Since our main concern in this book is with the rise of Modern Standard English, it is not necessary to give a detailed account of the differences between one Middle English dialect and another, but the broad differences must be mentioned, since Standard English has drawn on more than one Middle English dialect.

One of the most striking Middle English sound-changes is the development of OE *ā* to [ɔ:] at the beginning of the thirteenth century. Since OE short *a* remained unchanged in Middle English, the rounding of long *a* was the first step in the divergent development of OE short and long *a* which has continued to the present day. It also forms the basis of one of the most useful of the tests of dialect in Middle English, since the change did not take place in Northern dialects. Regular examples are *holy* (OE *hālig*), *road* (OE *rād*), and *home* (OE *hām*). A few Northern forms, in which the change has not taken place, have passed into Standard English during the Modern period, as *hale* beside *whole* (OE *hāl*), *raid* beside *road* (OE *rād*), and *laird* beside *lord* (OE *hlāford*). The *ai* in *raid* and *laird* is a Northern spelling used to represent Middle English *ā*.

Middle English sound-changes led to a divergent development of OE long and short *æ* as well as that of long and short *a*. OE *ĕ* became *a* in all dialects by the end of the Middle English period, as in *glad* (OE *glæd*), *apple* (OE *æppel*), although *e* is found in Southern and South-West Midland dialects in early Middle English. OE *ǣ* became open or close *ē* according to the dialect in which the form occurred. ME open and close *ē* have now fallen together, but they were distinct in early Modern English, and the difference in their development is recorded in the present-day spelling: the *ee* in *sleep* goes back to ME close *ē*, whereas the *ea* in *clean* goes back to ME open *ē*.

OE *y* whether long or short, had a threefold development in Middle English. In the Northern and East Midland dialects it was unrounded to *ĭ*; in South-Eastern dialects it had become *ĕ* in Old English and that development remained in Middle English; in the West Midlands and South-West the Old English sound remained, disguised by the French spelling *u*, until the end of the fourteenth century, after which it was gradually replaced by the Northern form. Modern English generally has *i*, as in *kiss* (OE *cyssan*) and *hide* (OE *hydan*), but a few words show the development of the dialects, as *knell* (OE *cnyll*), with South-Eastern *e*, and *cudgel* (OE *cycgel*) and *rush* 'water-side plant' (OE *rysc*), with South-Western *u*.

The Old English diphthongs became monophthongs in Middle English. Their development may be summed up in the statement that they lost their lightly stressed element while their strongly stressed element remained. In early Middle English the resulting monophthongs were sometimes rounded, but they lost their rounding in the course of the Middle English period. Most Old English diphthongs were falling diphthongs; that is to say, they had the chief stress on the first element. There were, however, some words with rising diphthongs, and the number of such words became larger in late Old English as the result of the tendency for the stress on a diphthong to shift from the first to the second element after a palatal consonant. Thus *shoot* (OE *sceotan*) and *choose* (OE *cēosan*) are from forms which underwent shift of stress. In some words it is uncertain whether the Old English digraph ever represented a genuine diphthong. The *e* in OE *sceolde* 'should' was probably merely a spelling device to show that the preceding consonant was palatal, and *young* seems to be derived rather from OE *iung* than from OE *geong*.

Diphthongs occur in many words in Middle English, as in Modern English, but they are not, for the most part, derived from Old English diphthongs. Many of them occur in loanwords from Scandinavian or French, as in *they* (ON *þeir*), *plain* (OF *plain*), *choice* (OF *chois*), and many of them arose in Middle English. There were two important sources of new diphthongs in native words in Middle English: vocalization of *g* and the development of a glide between a vowel and *h*.

The first of these changes began in late Old English, when *g* was vocalized to *i* when it occurred finally after front vowels. In Middle English this tendency was carried further, and by the end of the twelfth century it was usual for *g* to be vocalized to *i* (often spelt *y*) when it was preceded by a front vowel and to *u* (often spelt *w*) when it was preceded by a back vowel. The *i* or *u*, when not followed by a vowel, then combined with the preceding vowel to form a diphthong, as in *day* (OE *dæg*), *said* (OE *sægde*), *to fawn* (OE *fagnian*).

The development of a glide between a vowel and *h* took place during the thirteenth century. The glide was *i* after front vowels and *u* after back vowels, and the *i* or *u* combined with the preceding vowel to form a diphthong. Examples are *eight* (OE *eahta*) and *laughter* (OE *hleahtor*). Although this change and the vocalization of *g* both resulted in the rise of diphthongs whose second element was *i* or *u*, there is the important difference between them that the consonant *h* was preserved (spelt *h*, *gh* or *ʒ*) whereas *g* was not.

Several dependent changes affected Middle English vowels, and a few of them have had a permanent effect on the language. One of these was the fourteenth-century change of *e* to *a* before *r* belonging to the same syllable, as in *far* (earlier *ferre*), *star* (earlier *sterre*) and *dark* (earlier *derk*). There are several exceptions to this change: forms with *e* have been preserved or re-introduced later by the influence of the spelling in some words, especially in French and Latin loan ·words such as *serve*, *fervent*, and *certain*. Sometimes we have double forms at the present day, as in *person* and *parson*, where there has been a divergence of meaning, and a few words, such as *clerk* and *Derby*, have the spelling of one form and the pronunciation of another.

An important change affecting the length of vowels took place in the thirteenth century, when short vowels were lengthened in open stressed syllables of disyllabic words. This change is clearly later than the lengthening of short vowels before certain consonant groups described above, since short *a* lengthened in an open syllable did not undergo the change to [ɔː] described above, whereas short *a* lengthened before a consonant group did. It is reasonable to conclude that lengthening in open syllables was later than the change of *ā* to [ɔː]. Early ME *a*, *e*, *o*, were lengthened to [aː], [ɛː], [ɔː] in the first half of the century in all dialects, as in *hare* (OE *hara*), *bear* (OE *beran*), *throat* (OE *þrote*). Somewhat later in the century *i* and *u* were often lowered and lengthened, especially in northerly dialects, to [eː] and [oː] respectively. We find ME *cōme* (OE *cuman*) rhyming with *dōme* (OE *dōm*). From the second half of the fourteenth century forms with *ē*, *ō* began to spread South, and forms developed from them are found in the Standard English of the present day, as *week* (OE *wice*). Disyllabic forms often occurred in a paradigm side by side with monosyllabic or trisyllabic forms, as *staf* beside *stāves*, *hēven* beside *hevenes*. Analogy then took place, and some analogical forms have survived to the present day. Thus, Modern English *staff* and *staves* are regular, whereas *stave* and *heaven* are analogical.

A less common cause of lengthening of vowels in Middle English has something in common with the development of new diphthongs before *h*. When *i*, of whatever origin, was followed by *ht*, it was lengthened in southerly dialects in late Middle English, and Standard English generally has a development from a long vowel in words containing this group of sounds. Examples are *knight* (OE *cniht*), *night* (OE *niht*), *sight* (OE *(ge)-sihþ*).

The shortening of long vowels was extended in Middle English to groups of words which had not been affected in Old English. Shortening took place in Middle English in the first syllable of trisyllabic words even before single consonants, as in *holiday* (OE *hāligdæg*) and *errand* (OE *ærende*). Shortening took place also before groups of two or more consonants, whatever the number of syllables in the word, as in *dust* (OE *dūst*), *kept* (OE *cēpte*) and *fifth* (OE *fifta*). In words of more than one syllable, certain groups (such as *st* or a consonant followed by *l* or *r*) could form the beginning of the following syllable, and therefore did not cause shortening of a preceding long vowel. Hence, in a word like *priest* (OE *prēost*) there was shortening in the nominative singular but not in the oblique cases. The long vowel in *priest* is due to the analogy of the oblique cases, whereas *breast* (OE *brēost*) is from the nominative singular. In Middle English many of the vowels which had been lengthened before certain consonant groups in late Old English were shortened again. The only vowels which remained long were those which were lengthened before *ld* and *i* and *u* when lengthened before *nd*. We thus have *child*, *field*, *old*, *bind*, and *bound* beside *bring* and *send*.

Since the time of the earliest surviving records, the sound-changes affecting English consonants have been fewer and less important than those affecting vowels. In Middle English we find a continuation of some of the tendencies which had begun to operate in Old English, such as metathesis, as in *bird* (OE *brid*) and assimilation, as in *hemp* (OE *henep*). The most notable Middle English consonant changes are examples of the loss of consonants, especially in lightly stressed positions. Final *-n* had disappeared in Northumbrian during the Old English period in words of more than one syllable, and the tendency became more widespread in Middle English, although *-n* was sometimes re-introduced from inflected forms especially in the past participle of strong verbs in the North. In the indefinite article *a(n)* and the possessive adjectives *my(n)* and *thy(n)*, final *n* disappeared when the next word began with a consonant. Other examples of the disappearance of consonants include the loss of final *-ch* in lightly stressed positions, as in the pronoun *I* (OE *ic*) and the common suffix *-ly* (OE *-lic*), the loss of *l* before and after *ch*, as in *each* (OE *ǣlc*), *much* (OE *mycel*), and the loss of initial *h* before *l*, *n* or *r*, as in *leap* (OE *hlēapan*) and *raven* (OE *hræfn*).

One group of consonant changes which is difficult to date is the voicing of voiceless fricatives when they occurred initially or finally in lightly stressed positions. In words like *they*, *them* and *the*, the initial consonant is now voiced, and the voicing must have been fairly early because in the modern dialects of Kent and Sussex the resultant [ð] has undergone the further change to [d]. In lightly stressed final positions after voiced sounds [s] has become [z] as in *was* and in inflexional endings such as the *-es* of *bridges*. When the loss of lightly stressed *e* caused the final [z] to be immediately preceded by a voiceless consonant, the voiceless sound [s] was restored by assimilation, as in *eats* and *cats* beside *digs* and *dogs*.

Glide consonants were developed in a number of words especially after nasal consonants. The glide consonant was usually *b* or *p* next to *m*, and *d* or *t* next to *n*. Examples are *thumb* (OE *þūma*) and the related word *thimble* (OE *þȳmel*), *empty* (OE *ǣmetig*), *thunder* (OE *þunor*). In *listen* (OE *hlysnan*) and *glisten* (OE *glisnian*) the *t* has since been lost again in pronunciation, although it is kept in spelling. The development of these consonant glides may be explained as the result of faulty timing of the movements of the organs of speech. For example, in passing from *m* to *t* in the group *mt* it is necessary for three movements to take place simultaneously; the passage of air through the nose must be stopped, the vocal cords must cease to vibrate, and the stoppage caused by bringing the lips together must be replaced by one caused by pressing the tip of the tongue against the upper teeth-ridge. If the first of these movements is carried out a moment before the other two, the effect is to imprison air under pressure in the mouth with the result that the plosive *p* is heard when the lips are opened.

The normal Middle English development of Old English

palatal *c* was [tʃ], spelt *ch*, but forms with *k* occur frequently in Middle English especially in northerly dialects, and in some words *k* is the Standard English development. Examples are ME *þenken* beside *þenchen* 'to think' (OE *þencan*), ME *seken* beside *sechen* 'to seek' (OE *sēcan*), ME *wirken* beside *wirchen* 'to work' (OE *wyrcan*). It is probable that the forms with *k* are in large part due to Scandinavian influence, since Scandinavian speakers were unfamiliar with the palatal consonant, and they would tend to replace it by the *k*-sound which corresponded to it in cognate words in their own language. Another influence reinforcing that of Scandinavian speakers was that of analogy of native words in which palatalization and the subsequent change to [tʃ] did not take place. Thus, the *k* in *wirken* may be due to the influence of the noun *work* (OE *weorc*), and the *k* in *þenken* and *seken* may be due to the analogy of forms like the third person sing. pres. ind. *þencþ*, *sēcþ*, in which the *c*, being followed by another consonant, did not become [tʃ].

MODERN ENGLISH

As a rule Modern English sound-changes are not reflected in spelling, and it is therefore often difficult to date them. The most important of the independent sound-changes that have taken place since the Middle English period are those affecting the long vowels. All the long vowels have changed very considerably, but the distinction between one vowel and another has been preserved, except that ME open and close *ē* have fallen together. It is possible to detect two general tendencies in the development of the Middle English long vowels in Modern English: they have become more close and they have tended to become diphthongs. In the following account of the changes in detail, the Middle English long vowels have been arranged in an order to bring out the symmetry between front and back vowels.

ME *ā* was fronted to [æ:] in the fifteenth century, and this was raised to [ɛ:] in the sixteenth century and to [e:] in the seventeenth century. At the beginning of the eighteenth century this [e:] was diphthongized to [ei] and this diphthong has remained to the present day. Since OE *ā* had become [ɔ:] in

Middle English, the ā which underwent the series of changes here outlined was not developed from OE ā, but occurred in the main in French loan-words, such as *cage* and *fame*, or in words, such as *name* and *acre*, in which early ME short *a* had been lengthened in an open syllable.

ME [ɔ:] was raised to [o:] in the early sixteenth century, and this was diphthongized to [ou] at the beginning of the eighteenth century, as in *home*, *stone* and *oath*. ME [o:] was raised to [u:] in the fifteenth century. This has remained to the present day in the pronunciation of some speakers, but many speakers in the South diphthongize the vowel to a sound approximating to [uw], especially when it occurs in final positions. Examples are *goose*, *cool* and *do*.

ME [ɛ:] was raised to [e:] in the fifteenth or sixteenth century. In the second half of the seventeenth century this [e:] was further raised to [i:], which was diphthongized in the South to a sound approximating to [ij] before the end of the eighteenth century, as in *beat*, *leaf* and *eat*. ME [e:] was raised to [i:] in the fifteenth century, and this [i:] was diphthongized to [ij] in the South before the end of the eighteenth century, as in *grief*, *greet* and *fiend*. ME open and close ē thus differ from ME open and close ō in having fallen together in Modern English.

ME [u:] was diphthongized to [uw] in the fifteenth century, and this diphthong became [ou] in the sixteenth century, [eu] in the seventeenth, and [au] in the eighteenth, as in *loud*, *found* and *mouth*. The diphthongization of ME [u:] must have begun before ME [o:] became [u:] in the fifteenth century, since the two sounds have remained distinct.

The development of ME [i:] was parallel to that of ME [u:]. It was diphthongized to [ij] in the first half of the fifteenth century, and since that time the two elements of the diphthong have gradually become wider apart. Probably the stages were: [ij] became [ei] in the sixteenth century, and this became [əi] at the beginning of the seventeenth century and [ai] in the eighteenth century. Examples are *life*, *shine* and *child*.

Of the independent changes affecting short vowels only three need be mentioned:

The Middle English back open vowel [ɑ], spelt *a*, was fronted to [æ] about the end of the sixteenth century, but a back vowel has generally remained in the North until the present day, as in *glad* and *apple*.

At about the same time, ME [u] (which was often spelt *o*) became a more central vowel [ʌ] in most words, as in *begun*, *sun*, *son* and *some*. The influence of the spelling has often caused this sound to be replaced by [ɒ] or [ou], especially in words not in everyday use, as in *combat*, *coney*, and the adjective *wont*.

ME *o* has changed little since the Middle English period, though it has probably become somewhat more open. From the fifteenth to the eighteenth century there are spellings which suggest that *o* had been unrounded, and this unrounding is common in American speech and in some English dialects, but in Standard English [æ], resulting from the unrounding of ME *o*, is found in only a few words, such as *Egad*, *strap*, *sprat*, *nap* (of cloth).

The Middle English diphthongs *eu* and *iu* and Anglo-Norman [y:] spelt *u*, all fell together as [iu] in late Middle English. During the sixteenth century this [iu] became [ju:], and in most positions this is the usual pronunciation at the present day, although [iu] has remained in some dialects. Examples are *few*, *neuter*, *due* and *steward*.

ME *ai* has fallen in with ME *ā* although there is some difference of opinion about the date when the two sounds fell together. Some grammarians think that ME *ai* and *ā* fell together as [æ:] in the fifteenth century, but others think that ME *ai* never became a monophthong and that ME *ai* and *ā* remained distinct until they fell together as [ei] in the seventeenth century. Examples are *day*, *eight*, *raise*.

ME *au* became [ɔ:] through the intermediate stage [ɔu] by about the end of the sixteenth century. The first element of the diphthong was rounded by the influence of the second element, and the second element, being lightly stressed, then disappeared. Examples are *awe*, *hawk* and *autumn*.

In Middle English the spelling *oi* represents both [oi] and [ui]. The diphthong [oi] has generally become [ɔi] in Modern English, as in *joy*, *choice*, *avoid*. The first element of the diphthong [ui] had the same development as ME *u*, and in the seventeenth century it was therefore a central vowel. The diphthong then fell in with [əi], from ME *ī*. Owing to the influence of the spelling we get [ɔi] in pronunciation from the end of the eighteenth century, as in *boil, oil, joint, poison.*

Beside these independent changes, many dependent changes have affected Modern English vowels. The most important of these changes are those caused by a following *l* or *r*.

Between back vowels and a following *l* belonging to the same syllable (i.e. before final *-l* or *l* followed by a consonant) in late Middle English a glide was developed which became [u] and combined with the preceding vowel to form a diphthong. As a rule the [u] is not expressed in spelling, though it is found in a few words, such as *bowl* and *mould.* The changes in detail are:

(*a*) *a* became [au], probably in the second half of the fifteenth century. This [au], like [au] of other origins, has given [ɔ:] at the present day. The *l* was lost in pronunciation except when it occurred finally or before dentals, as in *talk, chalk* beside *all, tall* and *cauldron.* When the *l* was followed by a labial consonant, *f*, *v* or *m*, the [au] has developed to [ɑ:] instead of becoming [ɔ:]. Examples are *half, calf, calm.*

(*b*) ME *o* and [ɔ:] have become [ou] before *l*, as in *bolt, toll, bowl, bold, cold, old.*

(*c*) The development of *u* before *l* is less clear. Before *ld* or *lt*, *u* has become [ou], as in *shoulder, boulder, poultry, poultice.* Before other *l*-groups, *u* seems not to have been affected, as in *dull, wool, wolf.*

The influence of *r* on preceding vowels was even more marked than that of *l*. Short vowels have been lengthened and have generally also undergone a change in quality when followed by *r* belonging to the same syllable, but they have generally not been affected when the *r* (often spelt *rr*) was intervocalic. Hence we have *car* beside *carry* and *her* beside *herring*. The changes in detail are:

ME *a* became [æ] by an independent change, and in the seventeenth century this [æ], when followed by *r*, was lengthened to [æ:], which became [ɑ:] in the eighteenth century, as in *arm, sharp, garden.*

ME *e* generally became *a* before *r* in late Middle English and this became [ɑ:] like *ar* of other origins, as in *heart, dark, parson.* But *e* sometimes remained, or was reintroduced, before *r*, and this has given [ə:], as in *early, servant, person.*

ME *i* and *u* became [ə] before *r*, and this became [ə:] during the eighteenth century, as in *dirt*, *third*, *curse*, *turf*, *spurn*.

ME *o* became [ɔ:] before *r* in the seventeenth century, as in *for*, *horse*.

Between a long vowel or a diphthong and *r* [ə] was developed in the sixteenth and seventeenth centuries whether the *r* belonged to the same syllable or not. The [ə] is not usually expressed in spelling, though it is occasionally spelt *e*, as in *fiery*, *flower*, beside *fire*, *flour*. The changes in detail are:

ME *ā* before *r* has given [ɛə], as in *hare*, *spare*, *parent*.

ME [e:] has given [iə], as in *here*, *deer*, *dreary*.

ME [ɛ:], when not followed by a consonant, has become [ɛə] or [iə], as in *there*, *where*, *bear*, beside *ear*, *spear*, *besmear*.

ME *ī* has become [aiə], as in *fiery*, *admire*, *desire*.

ME [o:] has generally given [ɔə], as in *floor*, *swore*. When preceded by a labial the [ɔə] has generally become [uə], especially in the North, as in *poor*, *moor*.

ME [ɔ:] has become [ɔə], as in *boar*, *oar*, *score*.

ME *ū* has become [auə] before final *r*, as in *flower*, *hour*, *our*. Before *r* followed by a consonant, *ū* has become [ɔə], as in *course*.

ME *ai* has become [ɛə], as in *fair*, *chair*, *stair*.

ME *eu*, *iu*, and AN [y:] have generally given [juə], as in *ewer*, *sewer*, *cure*, *secure*.

ME *ou* has become [ɔə], as in *four*, *fourth*.

The development of the consonant *r* after it had modified a preceding vowel, is described below in the account of the consonants.

Some other dependent vowel-changes remain to be mentioned:

When ME *a* was preceded by *w*, it was rounded to [ɒ] before the sixteenth-century change of [ɑ] to [æ], as in *wash*, *swan* and *wan*. Apart from occasional spellings with *o*, the change has not affected the spelling. The rounding of *a* did not take place when it was followed by a velar consonant *k*, *g* or [ŋ], as in *wax*, *wag* and *twang*. The unrounded vowel in *swam* is due to the analogy of other preterites of the same class of strong verbs, such as *began* and *ran*.

Before nasals *a* varied with *o* in Middle English. By the end of the Middle English period forms with *a* had generally replaced those with *o* except before *ng*, as in *began*, *land*, beside *strong*, *song*. Preterites like *sang*, *sprang* are probably due to the analogy of other preterites of the same class of strong verbs, such as *began* and *ran*. Forms like *gang* and *hang* may be due to the influence of northerly dialects, where the rounding of *a* was less common than in the rest of the country.

Labial consonants tend to cause rounding of following vowels, and the influence of preceding labials often prevented the sixteenth-century change of [u] to [ʌ] or led to the restoration of the rounded vowel, especially when the vowel was followed by [ʃ], [tʃ] or *l*, as in *full*, *pull*, *bull*, *pulpit*, *bushel* and *butcher*. Occasionally, as in *cushion*, the rounded vowel is found before [ʃ], even when there is no preceding labial consonant. The un-rounded vowel is often found in later loan-words such as *bulb*, *pulse*, *fulminate*.

The [juː] which arose from late ME [iu] became [uː] about the end of the seventeenth century after *l*, *r*, [dʒ] (written *j*), and [tʃ] (written *ch*), as in *fruit*, *lute*, *June*, *chew*, beside *accuse*, *new*. There is some fluctuation between [juː] and [uː] after *l* and *s*, as in *absolute*, *resolution*, *suit*, *assume*.

A number of changes have affected the length of vowels during the Modern English period. We have seen that the consonant *r* tended to lengthen an immediately preceding vowel. Similar lengthening was caused by other consonants, notably by voiceless fricatives. One of the most obvious differences between Northern and Southern English speech is in the pronunciation of *a* before such fricatives. This variation is the result of a sound-change which took place in the South, but not in the North, except as the result of Southern influence. Before *f*, *s* and [θ] the [æ] which arose from ME *a* was in the seventeenth century lengthened to [æː] which became [ɑː] in the eighteenth century, as in *after*, *staff*, *fast*, *grass*, *path*. Even in the South there are some exceptions:

(*a*) Before antevocalic *-ss-*, *-ff-*, as in *classic*, *passage*, *chaffer*, beside *class*, *pass*, *chaff*.

(*b*) In lightly stressed words, such as *hath*, *hast*.

(*c*) In some French loan-words not in everyday use, such as *aspect*.

In the seventeenth century *o* was lengthened to [ɔː] before *f*, *s*, or [θ], but lengthening was not invariable, and today a long vowel is heard only occasionally in words like *off*, *coffee*, *cross*, *froth*.

During the eighteenth and nineteenth centuries both long and short vowels were lengthened under certain conditions, although the distinction between originally long and short vowels is kept. Sometimes the tendencies cut across each other. Vowels tend to be longer:

(*a*) When they are open, as in *hard* beside *bead*.

(*b*) Finally, as in *bee* beside *beat*.

(*c*) Before voiced consonants, as in *bead* beside *beat*.

(*d*) In monosyllables, as in *hard* beside *harder*.

(*e*) When they occur in words that have strong sentence-stress.

In American speech there is a tendency to lengthen all short vowels.

Shortening of long vowels has taken place during the Modern English period, sometimes under conditions that cannot be very exactly defined. One small group of words in which shortening took place can be distinguished: the [ɔ:] which arose from ME *a* before *l* was often shortened during the eighteenth century before *ls* or *lt*, although some speakers still pronounce these words with a long vowel at the present day. Examples are *alter*, *salt*, *false*, and *palsy*.

Some Modern English shortenings were caused by consonant groups in compound words which were no longer regarded as such. Examples are *breakfast* and *nickname*. In some compound words there is fluctuation in the length of the vowel because some speakers think of the words as compounds, and are therefore influenced by the long vowel of the simple word, while other speakers do not. Examples are *gooseberry* and *toothbrush*.

Shortening before single consonants in monosyllabic words took place occasionally in Old and Middle English, but it became much more common in the Modern English period. Certain consonants have favoured shortening of a preceding long vowel: ME [ɛ:] has often been shortened before dental or alveolar consonants, as in *dead*, *death*, *red*, and [u:] (from ME [o:]) has often been shortened before plosives, as in *blood*, *book*.

Shortening of vowels in Modern English has been spread over

several centuries, and in some words, such as *group*, the process is taking place today. As a rule it is difficult to fix even the approximate date of shortening, but there is sometimes evidence which enables us to relate the shortening of vowels to other sound-changes, and this evidence makes it clear that shortening took place at different dates in different words. For example, when shortening of ME [e:] took place before the fifteenth-century change of [e:] to [i:], we have [ɛ] in pronunciation at the present day; when shortening took place after the change of [e:] to [i:], we have [i]. Examples are *brethren*, *friend*, beside *nickname*, *riddle*, *grit*.

Similarly, if shortening of ME [o:] took place before the fifteenth-century change of [o:] to [u:], we have [ɒ] at the present day; if it took place after the change of [o:] to [u:] but before the sixteenth-century change of [u] to [ʌ], we have [ʌ]; if it took place after the change of [u] to [ʌ], we have [u]. Examples of the three developments are: *blossom*, *shod; blood*, *brother, flood, month; book, stood, good*. This seems the most natural explanation of the forms that occur, but it has been suggested that the vowel in words like *stood* may be a compromise between [ʌ] and [u:], in which case it may have been shortened early. There is a fourth class of words in which the vowel has never been shortened, as in *mood, food*. Before *k* shortening was probably late, and has not taken place in Scots, and in some Northern dialects. Examples are *hook, book, took*.

Before we pass on to the consonants, it will be well to give some account of the development of vowels in lightly stressed syllables. All sound-changes are difficult to date, and those in lightly stressed syllables are particularly so. There is a good deal of variation among different speakers in their treatment of such syllables, and the same speaker may treat them differently on different occasions, weakening and dropping lightly stressed vowels more in colloquial than in formal speech. The reduction of lightly stressed vowels is carried further than most speakers realize. Generally speaking, we can say that such vowels have become [i] or [ə], according as they were front or back, with the exception that before liquids all vowels have either tended to become [ə] or have disappeared. Two influences, which are always at work, complicate the picture: the influence of spelling and the analogy of related strongly stressed forms. Thus *ambition* has [æ] in the lightly stressed first syllable, perhaps by the influence of the spelling, whereas *affair* and *allow* have [ə]. The analogy of *spasm* may account for the [æ] in the lightly stressed first syllable of *spasmodic*. Since many lightly stressed vowels have thus fallen together, there has been much confusion in spelling. The *a* in *thousand* (OE *pūsend*) and the *o* in *ribbon* (OF *riban*) may be considered to be the result of such confusion.

In lightly stressed final syllables ending in a consonant *e* has generally disappeared, although there are some groups of exceptions. In the inflexional endings of nouns and in the third person singular of the present indicative of verbs, *e* has disappeared except after sibilants [s, z, ʃ, ʒ, tʃ, dʒ]. Examples are *cats, dogs, runs* beside *houses, dishes, catches*. In the preterite and past participle of weak verbs, *e* has disappeared in pronunciation except after *t* and *d*, although it generally remains in spelling. Thus we have *loved, raced* beside *ended, abated*. The *e* has been preserved in a few old past participles now used as adjectives, such as *dogged, beloved*, and in the archaic verbal endings *-est*, *-eth*, as *comest, cometh*.

One sound-change is concerned both with the vowels of lightly stressed syllables and with consonants. It is important because the sounds affected happened to occur in a number of common suffixes. When *i* was preceded by a consonant and followed by a lightly stressed vowel, it became [j] at the beginning of the seventeenth century, and then, when the preceding consonant was *t* or *s*, the [j] combined with it to give [ʃ], as in *pension, special, ambition, partial*. Similarly the group [zj] has given [ʒ] in such words as *pleasure* and *leisure*. The group [dj] often became [dʒ], and this pronunciation has remained in a few words, such as *grandeur, verdure, soldier*, but in most of the words that once contained the group [dj], the pronunciation [dj] or [di] has been restored by the influence of the spelling, as in *idiot, tedious* and *educate*. After other consonants we now have [j] or [i], with [i] especially common after [ɹ]. Examples are *opinion, guardian, material, historian*.

One of the most notoriously difficult groups of letters in Modern English is *ough*, and foreigners learning to pronounce English are inclined to be bitter about the many different

pronunciations represented by this spelling. Some of the variations are to be explained by a consonant change which took place
during the fifteenth and sixteenth centuries when the voiceless
velar fricative [x], spelt *gh*, had a twofold development: it
became [f] finally but disappeared when followed by *t*. Regular
examples are *cough, rough, laugh* beside *brought, sought, doughty,
taught*. The [f] in *laughter* is due to the analogy of *laugh*. The
forms *bough* and *plough* are due to the analogy of the plural (OE
bōgas, plōgas) in pronunciation, although the spelling goes back
to singular forms in which the velar fricative was unvoiced when
it occurred finally (OE *bōh, plōh*). The archaic form *enow* goes
back to the plural OE *genōge* whereas *enough* goes back to the
singular OE *genōh*.

Two consonant changes can be regarded as to some extent
complementary to each other: one is the change of [d] to [ð]
between a vowel and the ending *-er* and the other is the change
of [ð] to [d] after [r]. The first of these changes took place only
in native words and occurred at the beginning of the Modern
English period in such words as *father* (OE *fæder*), *mother* (OE
mōdor), *hither* (OE *hider*) and *gather* (OE *gæderian*). It did not
take place in French loan-words such as *powder* and *consider*, and
it did not affect *dd*, as in *adder* and *ladder*. Words like *leader* and
rider may be new formations after the operation of the change
or they may be due to the analogy of the verbs *lead* and *ride*.
The change of [rð] to [rd] has not been an invariable one. Most
words containing this group show double forms in Middle and
Modern English, and at the present day *rd* has been standard-
ized in some words and *rth* in others. Examples are *burden* (OE
byrþen), *murder* (OE *myrþrian*), *afford* (OE *geforþian*), beside
farthing (OE *fēorþing*), *further* (OE *furþor*). A similar change of
[ð] to [d] has taken place before *l*, as in *fiddle* (OE *fiþele*) and
Bedlam, from *Bethlehem*.

Many consonants have disappeared in Modern English.
Perhaps the most important change of this kind is the loss of *r*
medially before consonants and finally unless the next word
begins with a vowel and belongs to the same breath-group.
This change took place in the eighteenth century, but the *r* is
always kept in spelling as in *arm, heard, order*. The *r* is usually
silent before consonants, as in *I fear them*, but is pronounced

before vowels, as in *I fear it*. This pronunciation of final *r* when the next word begins with a vowel is known as 'linking *r*'. Some speakers have extended the use of *r* by analogy to words where there is no historical justification for it, and where there is no *r* in spelling, with the result that *r* may be heard after *India* in a phrase like *India and China*. This misuse of *r* is known as 'intrusive *r*'.

Initial *h* is generally pronounced as an aspirate in present-day English. The two groups of words where it is regularly omitted are French loan-words, like *hour* and *honour*, and lightly stressed words. In both these groups the initial *h* is sometimes restored in pronunciation by the influence of the spelling, as in *hotel, he, him*. In the pronoun *it* (OE *hit*) initial *h* has disappeared in both spelling and pronunciation because of the lack of stress.

Initial *k* and *g* disappeared in pronunciation in the late seventeenth century when immediately followed by *n*, as in *knave, knight, gnaw, gnash, gnat*. Initial *w* disappeared in pronunciation before *r* in the eighteenth century, as in *write, wrestle, wreath*. The consonant *w* often disappeared between *s* and a back rounded vowel and at the beginning of a lightly stressed syllable from the beginning of the Modern English period and occasionally even earlier, but in most words *w* has been restored either by the influence of the spelling or on the analogy of related words. The loss of *w* in pronunciation has proved lasting in *sword* and in place-names like *Norwich* and *Southwark*. Early spellings like *solen* and *sowlen* for *swollen* show loss of *w* which has later been restored, possibly on the analogy of *swell*.

CHAPTER V

Spelling

ENGLISH spelling is notoriously difficult, and foreigners learning English are bewildered by the lack of correlation between spelling and pronunciation. Those whose native language is English have been for so long accustomed to the vagaries of English spelling that they take them for granted, but it is not uncommon to find even well-educated Englishmen who will admit cheerfully, or even with a touch of pride, that they cannot spell. At the other extreme there are many people who seem to resent the few permissible variations in spelling that have been left to us, and who will argue about the respective merits of *standardize* and *standardise* or of *judgment* and *judgement* with a ferocity worthy of a better cause. In a perfectly consistent system of spelling there would be one symbol for each sound in the language, or at least one symbol for each phoneme. It is immediately obvious that present-day English is very far from this state. For example, the central vowel [ə] is represented in many different ways, some of which may be illustrated by the words *about, father, neighbour, pleasure, the, theatre*. On the other hand, the letter *a* is used to represent several entirely distinct sounds, such as those in *about, gate, cat, father, talk*. One reason why English spelling is misleading is that we overwork the alphabet. There are more phonemes than letters in present-day English, and we waste three letters of the alphabet (*c, q* and *x*) by using them to represent sounds which we can represent in other ways. It is inevitable, therefore, that some symbols have to be used to represent more than one sound.

An even more important reason for the unreliability of English spelling as a guide to contemporary pronunciation is that for the last three centuries or more English spelling has changed little whereas pronunciation is constantly changing. English spelling therefore often represents pronunciation as it used to be rather than as it is today. It provides evidence for which the student of the history of the language has reason to be grateful although the user of the language has reason to despair.

Another reason for the variety of English spelling is that more than one system of spelling conventions has been at work. Some of our spelling conventions go back to Old English and others were introduced by French scribes during the period of Norman and French ascendancy which followed the Norman Conquest. This is the explanation of the difference between the spelling of the sound [s] in *mouse* and *mice*: the *s* is the native spelling, whereas the *c* is a French spelling made possible by the fact that Old French [c] became [s] next to front vowels. The influence of Latin spelling conventions was less far-reaching than that of French but it has made its small contribution to the confusion. By French influence the spelling *th* was used to represent the two sounds [θ] and [ð], heard in *thin* and *then* respectively. Latin influence has added a third pronunciation: the *t* heard in *Thames* and *Anthony*. In *Thames* (OE *Temes*) Latin influence has affected the spelling of the vowel as well as that of the initial consonant: in Modern English we have the pronunciation derived from the Old English form but the spelling from the Latin form. It is natural that the influence of foreign spelling conventions should be most strongly marked in loan-words, especially since many of them have been borrowed in comparatively recent times through the medium of literature. The earliest loan-words into English, like *chalk* and *cheese*, were borrowed into the spoken language and have developed like native words, but more recent borrowings reflect the spelling conventions of the languages from which, or through which, they were borrowed. Thus we have *ph* as a spelling for [f] in many words of Greek origin such as *telephone* and *philosophy*, and *c* as a spelling for [s] before front vowels in words such as *cede* and *receive*, which were borrowed from French. Some Modern English words have two pronunciations because they have reached Modern English by more than one route. Thus, *cinema* and *Celtic* are pronounced with [k] if those who use the words follow the pattern of words borrowed directly from Greek or Latin, but with [s] if they treat them as though they were borrowed directly from French.

A fourth reason why English spelling does not always present a true picture of the pronunciation is that forms from various provincial dialects have passed into Standard English pronunciation although the dialectal pronunciation is not always recorded in spelling. Thus, we should expect *one* to be pronounced with the diphthong that is found in the related word *only*; the initial *w* that occurs in the pronunciation of *one* is borrowed from some local dialect. Similarly we find an imperfect correspondence between sound and spelling in some words as a result of the threefold development of OE *y* (p. 84). In Standard English *y* has become *i*, but in the South-East it became *e* in late Old English and in the South-West it remained, spelt *u* as the result of French influence, until the end of the Middle English period. The verb *kiss* (OE *cyssan*) shows the regular development, but *busy* (OE *bysig*) has the South-Western spelling with the Standard English pronunciation, while *bury* (OE *byrgan*) has the South-Western spelling with the pronunciation generally associated with the South-East, though not confined to that area.

Uncertainty about the pronunciation represented by a particular spelling is increased by the fact that many words are used much more often in writing than in speech. When a speaker wants to pronounce such a word, he generally resorts to analogy, and there is room for a good deal of variety in pronunciation according to the analogy which the speaker invokes. For example, in pronouncing *inveigle* he may decide that the *ei* should be pronounced as in *receive* or as in *eight*, and in pronouncing *gaseous* he may pronounce the *a* as in *gas* or as in *nature* and the *s* as in *gas* or *Asia* or *pleasure*.

Another contributory cause of the confusion of Modern English spelling is to be found in what are called inverted spellings, which is liable to occur whenever a sound-change has taken place. When a sound-change takes place, the change is sometimes, but not always, recorded in spelling. Hence, after a sound-change has taken place there often occur side by side two different forms of the same word, one with a spelling representing the old pronunciation and one with a more phonetic spelling representing the new pronunciation. When the resultant variation in spelling is extended to other words in which the sound-change in question has not taken place, an inverted spelling is said to occur. An example of such a spelling is the frequent use of *y* for ME short *i* or for the long *i* which has given the diphthong [ai] in Modern English. Such spellings were made possible by the sound-change which caused OE *y* to become *i* in the Northern and East Midland dialects of Middle English.

Spelling is one of the most valuable of our sources of evidence in the study of the history of a language, although it is clear that the evaluation of this evidence is by no means straightforward. The first task of a student of the history of the English language is to decide whether variations in spelling reflect variations in pronunciation or whether the variant spellings are simply different ways of representing the same sound.

Many attempts have been made to reform English spelling, and some of them have had a permanent effect on the language, but the influence of spelling reformers has for the most part merely touched the fringe of the problem, changing the spelling of individual words or of a small group of words. The efforts of reformers have sometimes had an effect opposite to the one intended: they have led to the introduction of a few variant spellings, which have gained widespread, but not universal, acceptance, with the result that inconsistency is now added to diversity. A reader of English must be prepared to meet with *civilisation* beside *civilization* and *connection* beside *connexion*, and a writer often has difficulty in maintaining consistency. There may be a conflict of views between a writer and his printer, and when there is most writers are content to let the printer use his own 'house style', but lovers of accuracy are sometimes confronted with problems, as when there is a conflict between the 'house style' and the spelling of a quotation.

The fundamental problem of spelling reform is to strengthen the connexion between speech and writing. An extreme solution of the problem is provided by Alexander Melville Bell's 'visible speech', a system of phonetic transcription in which the symbols represent the position of the organs of speech. Very few reformers, however, go further than aiming at a system of spelling in which a given sound is always represented by the same letter and a given letter always represents the same sound.

Reform of spelling is not the only way of bringing pronunciation and spelling into closer accord; another way of achieving the same result is by altering our pronunciation to make it agree more closely with the spelling. We have done this in a few words, but the immediate result of introducing spelling pronunciations, like that of introducing reformed spellings, is simply to add to the number of variant pronunciations. We thus have the historically correct pronunciation [fɔɹɛd] and [wɛskit] side by side with the spelling pronunciations [fɔəhɛd] and [weistkout] for *forehead* and *waistcoat*. Eventually one of the variants may disappear from the language but the two forms often exist side by side for several centuries.

One of the earliest English spelling reformers was the thirteenth-century versifier Orm who in his *Ormulum* made consistent use of various spelling devices, especially the doubling of consonants.

The spelling reformers who were active at the time of the Renaissance had a different aim from Orm and from the reformers of today. They were concerned not with the consistent representation of pronunciation but with etymology, real or supposed. Since the zeal of the reformers was greater than their etymological knowledge, some of the new spellings which they introduced were not justified. There is, for example, neither phonetic nor etymological justification for the *s* in *island* (OE *iegland*). It was introduced on the assumption that the word was related to OF *isle* and Latin *insula*, and if there is any thorough-going attempt to make English phonetic the *s* will have to be either dropped again or pronounced.

The advantages of spelling reform are obvious, although they are sometimes exaggerated by its advocates. Unfortunately the disadvantages of a thorough reform are even greater than the advantages. It is not always realized how many changes would be needed to make English spelling phonetic. A passage of present-day English transcribed into the phonetic symbols of the International Phonetic Association differs very considerably from the same passage in conventional English spelling. A child would probably find mastery of the phonetic symbols easier than that of English spelling conventions, but to achieve any saving of time the new spelling would have to replace the old; if the old and the new systems existed side by side, the difficulties of readers of English would be increased rather than lessened. In a country with a high proportion of illiteracy or with few printed books, such a thorough change would be practicable, but the task of rewriting and reprinting all existing English books worthy of preservation would be an overwhelming one. Another drawback of phonetic spelling is the lack of uniformity of the spoken language. Although present-day English spelling is often described as chaotic, it is less chaotic than Middle English spelling, which owed some of its lack of uniformity to the fact that it was more phonetic than English spelling of today: it reflected the varied state of contemporary pronunciation. Moreover, the pronunciation of English is constantly changing, and we have reason to be grateful that spelling is not constantly changing along with it. If we were committed to the principle that spelling must be phonetic, we should have to sacrifice the advantage of comparatively stable spelling that we have enjoyed for the last three centuries. English presents special problems to the spelling reformer because of the various circumstances, mentioned at the beginning of this chapter, which have made our spelling so unphonetic. If our spelling were reformed on the model of native words, the etymology of Latin and French loanwords would be obscured, and etymology is an indication of the relationship of words which is useful even to those who know no foreign language. Phonetic spelling would disguise the connexion between *nation* and *national* and between *photographic* and *photographer* and would introduce a misleading identity of form to *cession* and *session*, *symbol* and *cymbal*, *allowed* and *aloud*. Some short words in common use are pronounced differently according to the degree of stress. It is easy to recognize three different pronunciations of words like *shall* and *can*: one with the vowel [æ] used when the words are strongly stressed, a second with [ə] and a third with no vowel at all. Phonetic spelling of such words would introduce difficulties that are clearly not insuperable, since we are familiar with the three forms in speech, but it is well to remember that the introduction of phonetic spelling would not always lead to simplification.

These disadvantages apply only to thorough spelling reform; they do not apply to the piecemeal removal of some of the more obvious anomalies. The only objection to such minor changes is the innate conservatism of the users of a language, but experience shows that in linguistic matters this conservatism can be surprisingly strong.

OLD ENGLISH

The loss of early records prevents us from knowing much about spelling during the earliest periods of the history of the English language. The Germanic peoples in early times used a special alphabet known as the runic alphabet. The letters of this alphabet were made up mainly of straight lines and so were especially suitable for inscriptions carved on wood or stone. Two runic letters were adopted into the Old English alphabet, which was based on a Celtic variety of the Latin alphabet. The two runic letters passed out of general use during the Middle English period and were replaced by *w* and *th* respectively, but the letter *þ*, which was used to represent *th*, remained in use in the words *the* and *that* when it was no longer used in other words. It somewhat resembled a *y*, and, when its origin had been forgotten, it was sometimes mistaken for a *y*. This is the origin of the sham archaism *ye* for *the*.

Beside the two runic letters, the Old English alphabet included a new letter formed by putting a stroke through *d*, and this 'crossed *d*' was used, like the runic letter *þ*, to represent the sounds which we represent by *th*. We use *th* to represent two sounds, the voiced [ð] and the voiceless [θ], and the existence of two Old English letters to represent the sounds could have afforded a useful way of distinguishing between them, but the distinction seems never to have been made with any consistency. Some scribes preferred *þ* and others *ð*, while others would use now one and now the other apparently without any consistent principle. In addition to these two ways of representing the sounds, the earliest Old English texts sometimes use the spelling *th*, which passed out of use during the Old English period until it was re-introduced by the influence of French scribes after the Norman Conquest. It is interesting to see that even at this early period, the writers of English did not make the most efficient use of the material at their disposal for the representation of speech-sounds.

The use of *þ*, *ð* and *th* to represent the same sound illustrates one way in which Old English departed from the ideal of having one sound corresponding to one symbol, which is the character-istic of a phonetic language. The converse divergence, by which one symbol represents several different sounds, is also found. The most overworked Old English letter was ʒ, which is usually transcribed as *g* in modern editions of Old English texts. It was used to represent a voiced velar plosive, as in *gōd* 'good', a voiced velar fricative, as in *būgan* 'to bow', and a voiced palatal fricative, as in *geong* 'young'. The letter *c* had by the end of the Old English period come to have two distinct pronunciations: before consonants and back vowels it was a velar plosive as in MnE *come*, whereas before front vowels (except those which have become front as a result of front mutation) it had become an affricate consonant, like the *ch* in MnE *choose*. In late Old English *k* is sometimes used as a spelling for *c* when it has the former pronunciation but not when it has the latter. Another spelling device which came into use in the Old English period was the insertion of an *e* between *g*, *c* or *sc* and a following back vowel to show that the consonant had a palatal pronunciation. Thus we find *sceacan* beside *scacan* 'to shake' and *þencean* beside *þencan* 'to think'.

On the whole, however, Old English spelling gives a better picture of what we may reasonably believe to have been the contemporary pronunciation than does that of Modern English. For example, there were no silent consonants in Old English, and hence four consonants were pronounced in OE *cniht* 'boy' instead of two as in its Modern English equivalent *knight*. Again, Old English double consonants, except perhaps when they occurred at the end of a word, were pronounced double or long, whereas in Modern English they are normally pronounced as though they were single. Double consonants are pronounced as double or long in Modern English only in the few compound words, like *book-case*, or consecutive words pronounced without a pause between them, like *ill luck*, where the final consonant of the first element is the same as the initial consonant of the second element.

The greater consistency of Old English spelling as compared with that of Modern English is more apparent in the vowels than in the consonants, chiefly because the vowels have changed more than consonants in the course of the history of English. The letters representing vowels had the so-called 'Continental' values; that is, they were pronounced approximately as they were in most European languages other than English. The letters *a, e, i, o* and *u* when they represented long vowels were pronounced almost like the vowel sounds in *calm, say, feel, go* and *shoe*, except that the Old English vowels were probably pure vowels rather than diphthongs. The length of vowels is important in the study of the development of English because many sound-changes affect long vowels while leaving short vowels unaffected and *vice versa*. For example, from the point of view of the history of the English language, the difference between Old English long and short *a* is as important as the difference between *a* and *e*. Old English long *a* has today given [ou], as in *home* (OE *hām*) whereas short *a* has given [ei], as in *name* (OE *nama*). Vowel-length is generally not indicated in Old English manuscripts, though we find in Old English the beginnings of the device with which we are familiar today of doubling a vowel to show that it is long, as in *food* and *see*. In Old English manuscripts accents are sometimes written above vowels, and these may have been intended to indicate vowel-length but they may also have been used to indicate stress. It is usually an easy matter to decide from comparison with other languages or from the later development of the word in question whether an Old English word had a long or short vowel, and in grammars it is usual to place a horizontal stroke over long vowels and to leave short vowels unmarked.

MIDDLE ENGLISH

The change in spelling conventions was one of the most noticeable features of the transition from Old to Middle English. The influence of French scribes made itself felt in two ways. The more obvious way was in the introduction into English of spelling conventions which had previously been found only in French, but another result of the French influence, more important for the study of the history of English pronunciation, was that French scribes represented more or less phonetically the sounds that they heard, whereas Anglo-Saxon scribes were strongly influenced by West Saxon scribal tradition. For example, [f] was voiced to [v] when it occurred between voiced sounds in Old English, but the spelling *f* continued to be used to represent medial [v] as well as initial and final [f] until the Middle English period, when the voiced sound began to be spelt *u* or *v*. The modern practice of using *v* to represent the consonant and *u* to represent the vowel did not prevail in Middle English. The tendency then was to use *v* initially and *u* medially whether the sound to be represented was vowel or consonant.

During the Middle English period some Old English letters passed out of use. On the other hand the Old English spellings *ea* and *eo* remained in use after the sounds they represented had become monophthongs. Since OE *ēa* became [ɛ:] in Middle English, the spelling *ea* came to be used to represent [ɛ:] of any origin, and it has remained in use to the present day in words such as *eat* (OE *etan*) and *deal* (OE *dǣl*), where the *ea* is an inverted spelling, beside *leap* (OE *hlēapan*), where the spelling with *ea* is used nearly a thousand years after the disappearance of the pronunciation which it represented. The spelling *eo* has been less persistent. It remained in frequent use in Middle English after the monophthongization of the diphthong which it represented, but it is used only occasionally today, as in the French loan-words *enfeoff* and *people*.

Another Old English letter which remained in use long after the pronunciation which it represented had changed was *y*. In Old English this letter represented a front close rounded vowel, but in Middle English in the Northern and East Midland dialects it was unrounded to [i]. Hence during the Middle English period *y* is often used as a spelling to represent [i] whether long or short, as in *myhte* beside *mihte* 'might', *wys* beside *wis* 'wise'. In the later Middle English period some scribes tried to restrict the spelling *y* to express [i:], keeping the spelling *i* for the short vowel. Another tendency was to use the spelling *y* next to letters like *n*, *m* and *u*, where *i* might lead to confusion. Middle English scribes, like many people today, often failed to distinguish clearly between letters made up of short minims, and therefore *n* is liable to be confused with *u* and *m* with *in* or *ni*. The use of *y*, when it was available as an alternative spelling, lessened the likelihood of confusion.

Some of the spelling conventions introduced by Anglo-Norman scribes have had a permanent effect on English spelling. From about the middle of the thirteenth century *o* was used for *u* next to letters like *n*, *m* and *u*. This spelling was made possible by the falling together of *o* and *u* in Anglo-Norman, and it served a purpose similar to that served by the use of *y* for *i* in similar positions. Spellings with *o* for *u* have often survived to the present day, as in *come* (OE *cuman*), *son* (OE *sunu*). In the latter word the spelling convention has provided a useful means of distinguishing between two homophones, since *sun* (OE *sunne*) has not preserved the use of *o*, although spellings like *sonne* are common in Middle English. In Old English there had been no distinction in spelling between long and short *u*, but during the thirteenth century the use of *ou* for *ū* became common, and it thus became possible to distinguish between long *u*, spelt *ou* and short *u*, spelt *u* or *o*. A variant of the spelling *ou* was *ow*, and this variant was preferred at the end of a word, as in *cow* beside *house*.

Anglo-Norman influence did not always have the effect of causing English spelling to represent differences of sound more accurately. It introduced a new ambiguity in the use of *u*. Side by side with the native use of this spelling to represent [u], as in *full* and *sun*, we find *u* often used in Middle English, as a result of Anglo-Norman influence, to represent the front close rounded vowel [y] in those Southern and westerly dialects in which the sound remained in Middle English. Forms like *dude* 'did' (OE *dyde*) and *hude* 'hide' (OE *hȳdan*) are common in Middle English, although in Modern English they have for the most part been replaced by forms with *i* from other dialects.

In the spelling of consonants Middle English showed an advance on Old English in that various sounds which were in Old English represented by a single letter came to be more accurately distinguished from each other. This is especially true of the various sounds represented by OE ȝ(*g*). A slightly modified form of the Old English letter ȝ was used in early Middle English to represent the palatal fricative [j] especially when it occurred initially as in ȝer 'year' (OE *gēar*). In later Middle English, as in Modern English, this sound is spelt *y*. The symbol ȝ had several other functions in early Middle English. It was used to represent the velar fricative [ɣ] in words like *boʒe* 'bow' (OE *boga*), but when this sound was vocalized to [w] the need for a special symbol to represent it disappeared. It was sometimes used to represent the voiceless fricatives, whether velar [x] or palatal [ç], which had been spelt *h* in Old English, in such words as *souʒte* 'sought' (OE *sōhte*) and *niʒt* 'night' (OE *niht*). In later Middle English these sounds came to be spelt *gh* or, especially in Scottish dialects, *ch*. The letter ʒ was often confused with *z*, and when it passed out of use printers sometimes used *z* for ʒ, just as *y* was sometimes used for *þ*. There are survivals of this confusion in the present-day spelling of some Scottish words and names such as *Menzies*, *Dalziel* and *capercailzie*, the pronunciation of which causes trouble to the uninitiated. A new form of the letter *g* was introduced from the Continent to represent the velar plosive in words like *good* (OE *gōd*), and this is the shape of the letter with which we are familiar today. The sound represented in Old English by *cʒ* had by the Middle English period become an affricate [dʒ] and was written *gg* in early Middle English, later *dg*, as in *brugge* beside *bridge* (OE *brycg*). The same sound was spelt differently in French loan-words, where by the influence of French spelling it was represented by *j* or *i* initially and by *g*, later *dg*, medially, as in *iustice* 'justice' (OF *justice*), *juge* 'judge' (OF *juge*).

The sounds represented by OE *c* were not so various as those represented by *g*, but there was enough difference between two of the sounds represented by *c* in late Old English to make it desirable to distinguish between them in spelling. From about the middle of the twelfth century the spelling *ch* was used to represent the affricate consonant [tʃ], which was the usual pronunciation of *c* before front vowels in late Old English. This spelling has remained until the present day, as in *choose* (OE *cēosan*). When the sound was doubled the usual Middle English spelling was *cch*, which was later replaced by *tch*. Already in Old English the spelling *k* had sometimes been used when for any reason [k] kept its velar pronunciation before front vowels. We thus find *kyning* beside *cyning* 'king'. In Middle English the practice of using *k* to represent [k] before front vowels became more widespread, and *k* was also used instead of *c* before *n*, probably for the palaeographical reason that in many Middle

English hands *cn* was liable to be mistaken for *m*. Before back vowels and before the consonants *l* and *r*, the spelling *c* continued to be used to represent [k], as in Old English. This distinction between *c* and *k* continues in use at the present day, and we therefore have *knee*, *king* and *keen* beside *climb*, *creep* and *come*. Medially and at the end of a word we find in Middle English both *c* and *k*, as in *clerc* beside *clerk*. For velar *cc* we find *ck* or *kk*, as in *lockes*, *lokkes* 'locks of hair'. The group [kw], which had been spelt *cw* in Old English was in Middle English spelt *qu* because of French influence, as in *queen* (OE *cwēn*), and the sound developed from OE *sc*, which was probably [ʃ], was spelt *sh*. In French the spelling *c* was used to represent [s] next to front vowels, and this spelling was used in Middle English, not only in French loan-words but also in some words of native origin, such as *ice* (OE *īs*) and *cinder* (OE *sinder*).

MODERN ENGLISH

There have been few striking innovations in English spelling since the Middle English period. The most marked feature of English spelling since that time has been a tendency to restrict the freedom of choice: one of several possible spellings has become the invariable one, though freedom of choice still exists in a few words, such as *show* and *shew*, *gray* and *grey*, *waggon* and *wagon*. Sometimes alternative spellings of a word have become associated with different meanings, and have thus come to be regarded as different words; examples are *metal* and *mettle*, *flour* and *flower*. During the sixteenth and seventeenth centuries the great printing houses had a stabilizing influence on English spelling, and they brought about a number of improvements, such as the omission of final -*e* in many words, the exclusive use of *j* and *v* as consonants and of *i* and *u* as vowels, and the use of *ea* to represent the development of ME [ɛ:] and of *oa* for the development of ME [ɔ:], but there was much variation in spelling until about the middle of the seventeenth century.

During the Middle English period the spellings *ee* and *oo* were often used for *ē* and *ō* respectively, whether open or close. During the sixteenth century it became usual to keep the spellings *ee*, *oo*, only for the sounds developed from ME [e:] and [o:]

respectively, and this is the general practice at the present day. The spelling *ie* was also used for ME [e:], partly as a result of French influence; examples are *keen, see; cool, doom; field, priest*. Another way of indicating vowel-length was by the addition of a final *-e*. Final *-e* came to have this significance because of the lengthening of short vowels in open syllables in the thirteenth century. These new long vowels were nearly always followed by an *e* in the next syllable, and this *e* came to be regarded as a sign that the vowel of the preceding syllable was long. When final *-e* was lost in pronunciation it came to be used as a mere spelling device and was added to words such as *here* (OE *hēr*), where it had no etymological justification. This convention does not account for all the examples of the addition of final *-e* in spelling. There was much uncertainty in the use of final *-e* in both late Middle English and early Modern English, and often the addition or omission of final *-e* seems to depend on such accidental circumstances as the whim of the writer or printer, or the printer's convenience in filling up a line of prose at a time when spaces between words could not be so easily varied as they can by printers of today.

The use of *y* as a spelling for *i* to avoid confusion next to letters like *n* and *m* ceased to have much value when black-letter type gave way in the sixteenth century to the Roman type that we know today, since in Roman type there is less danger of confusion. Similarly, the Middle English tendency to use *y* for long *i* became unnecessary after the use of final *-e* to indicate length became general. The early seventeenth century saw the establishment of the present usage, which is to prefer *i* initially and medially but *y* finally. Thus we have *beautiful* beside *beauty*, *cried* beside *cry*. There are some exceptions to this general principle: *y* is always written before *i*, as in *dying*, in order to avoid the writing of double *i*, and it is generally used as the final letter of the first element of a compound word, because of the influence of the simple word, as in *shyness* and *ladyship*. Greek loan-words generally have *y* corresponding to Greek υ, as in *synonym* and *psychologist*.

The use of double consonants in Modern English does not always correspond with the Old English practice. During the Middle English period double consonants were simplified in pronunciation, although they have remained in spelling in many words until the present day as a result of the tendency of spelling always to lag behind pronunciation. Examples are *inn, kiss, quell,* and *sell.*

The most frequent function of double consonants in Modern English is to indicate that a preceding vowel is short. They were able to perform this function in Middle English because long vowels were shortened before double consonants, and the use of some such device was necessary because the lengthening of short vowels in open syllables of disyllabic words had had the result that a vowel, when followed by a single consonant and another vowel, was assumed to be long. Hence the doubling of a consonant to indicate that a preceding vowel is short is especially common when the consonant is followed by a vowel. We thus have *slipped* beside *slip, robbing* beside *rob,* and *stirred* beside *stir.* After lightly stressed vowels doubling of consonants is less common, but even in these positions we find *p, c,* and *l* doubled, with the added complications that the doubled form of *c* is spelt *ck* and the doubling of *l* is not found in American spelling. Thus we have *edited* beside *rebutted, reference* beside *referred* and *occurrence,* but *worshipped, mimicked* and *traveller* (beside American *traveler*). In a few words, such as *bias(s)ed,* uniformity has not been achieved, and in *(un)paralleled* the spelling with single *l* is the usual one even in England.

CHAPTER VI

Accidence

THE history of English accidence has been in the main one of progressive simplification, with occasional departures from this general tendency, such as the introduction of Scandinavian personal pronouns and of a few Latin and Greek nouns which have kept their original plural forms. Although the Old English inflexional system is complicated in comparison with that of today, there is evidence that it represents a simplification of a much more complex system of inflexions in the parent language, and it is simpler than the inflexional systems of Greek or Latin.

NOUNS

There were several different declensions of nouns in Old English, and four cases were distinguished: nominative, accusative, genitive and dative. In some declensions some of the cases fell together; this was especially true of the nominative and accusative. Already in Old English there was a tendency for nouns to pass by analogy from the smaller declensions into the larger, and this tendency became more marked in Middle English, with the result that today the great majority of English nouns belong to a single declension, and there are only occasional survivals of the other Old English declensions.

The Old English declension which served as the basis for the inflexion of most of our nouns today consisted of masculine nouns and may be represented by OE *stān* 'stone'.

	SING.	PLURAL
Nom. Acc.	*stān*	*stānas*
Gen.	*stānes*	*stāna*
Dat.	*stāne*	*stānum*

In Middle English the ending *-as* of the nominative and accusative plural became *-es* and was extended by analogy to the other

cases of the plural. The dative singular fell in with the nominative and accusative singular. Hence in the declension of Modern
English nouns the chief question that has to be settled is how the
noun forms its plural, although the forms of the genitive sometimes call for comment. The Middle English plural ending -*es* is
preserved in Modern English, pronounced [-əz] or [-iz], only
after sibilant consonants, as in *glasses, topazes, churches, hedges,
dishes.* After other consonants the *e* of the ending -*es* has disappeared in pronunciation although it has sometimes remained
in spelling. When the noun ends in a vowel or a voiced consonant, the plural ending is pronounced [z]; after a voiceless
consonant it is pronounced [s]. Examples are *bees, dogs* and
sides beside *cats* and *gates.* In native English nouns ending in -*f*,
the *f* is usually voiced and spelt *v* in the plural when it is preceded by *l* or a long vowel or diphthong, as in *wolves, knives.*
This is because the *e* of the ending was once pronounced and *f*
was voiced when it occurred between voiced sounds. After short
vowels and sometimes after long vowels, the voiceless consonant
has been restored by analogy with the singular, as in *cliffs,
deaths, beliefs.* In nouns ending in -*th* the final consonant is often
voiced, but analogical forms with [θ] are usual in some words.
Thus we have *mouths, oaths* beside *deaths, healths.* In nouns ending
in [s] the voiceless consonant is usually kept in the plural, as in
horses, but [z] is found in *houses.*

In most nouns the genitive singular and plural are identical
in pronunciation with the nominative plural, but towards the
end of the seventeenth century we find the beginnings of the
spelling convention, which is still in general use, of inserting an
apostrophe before the -*s* of the genitive singular. If we regard an
apostrophe as an indication that a letter or a sound has been
omitted, there is no historical justification for making a distinction between the genitive singular and the nominative plural,
since both these forms had the ending -*es* in Middle English. It
is clear, however, that the apostrophe has been found to serve a
useful purpose as an aid to the identification of cases, but it is
not essential, since the spoken language manages to dispense
with it without any real ambiguity. An even more arbitrary
convention than the use of '*s* was the addition of an apostrophe
after the *s* to indicate the genitive plural. This convention

became established towards the end of the eighteenth century. One difference between the genitive singular and all cases of the plural is that singular forms do not show voicing of *f*, and we therefore have *wife's* beside *wives* and *wives'*, *calf's* beside *calves* and *calves'*.

The declension to which most neuter nouns belonged in Old English differed from the declension of *stān* only in the nominative and accusative plural, which had the ending *-u* after short stems but no ending after long stems. Some of these plural forms without inflexional endings have survived until the present day, notably in *sheep* and *deer*. By analogy the use of uninflected plurals has been extended to other nouns, especially those indicating measure and number. Thus *couple*, *dozen*, and *score* are never inflected when they are preceded by a numeral, and expressions like *he weighs fifteen stone*, *twenty head of cattle*, and *five yoke of oxen* are commonly used. The noun *fish* has two forms of the plural, the use of which depends on whether we are thinking of a collective mass or not: we say *a boatload of fish* but *two small fishes*. Unchanged plurals with a collective sense are especially common with reference to hunting: a hunter shoots duck and waterfowl, but a farmer feeds his ducks and fowls.

A large number of nouns in Old English belonged to the weak declension, which included masculine, feminine and neuter nouns, all of which had the ending *-an* in the nominative and accusative plural as well as in the genitive and dative singular. This ending became *-en* in Middle English, and in Southern dialects the *-en* was extended to many nouns which originally belonged to other declensions, such as *honden* 'hands', *deden* 'deeds'. The genitive plural of all nouns of this declension ended in *-ena* in Old English and *-ene* in Middle English, and this ending too was often extended in Southern dialects to nouns of other declensions, as in *kingene*, gen. pl. of *king*. In Modern English the only noun which keeps the weak plural ending in its simple form is *ox*, pl. *oxen*, but three nouns have double plurals: *children*, *brethren* and *kine*. *Child* belonged in Old English to a declension of nouns which formed their nom. pl. in *-ru*, and *children* has its *r* from this declension. The other two nouns formed some of their oblique cases in Old English by changing the vowel of the stem, and they have taken on the weak plural ending as well; both can be regarded as archaic except for the religious use of *brethren*. There may be a development of the weak gen. sing. ending in *Lady Day* beside *Lord's Day*. OE *hlǣfdige* 'lady' was a weak feminine noun, and its gen. sing. ending became *-e* in Middle English, and this lightly stressed *-e* has now disappeared. The genitive form *lady's* is analogical.

Some nouns formed their nominative and accusative plurals in Old English by changing the vowel of the stem. The reason for the change of vowel was that in primitive Old English these nouns had an ending containing *i* in some of their oblique cases, and the *i* caused front mutation of the stem-vowel and then disappeared. Not many Old English nouns belonged to this declension, but about half of them have kept this method of forming the plural at the present day, with the result that we have the plural forms *feet*, *teeth*, *men*, *geese*, *mice*, and *lice*. In Old English these nouns had vowel mutation in their dative singular, and feminine nouns sometimes had it in their genitive singular, but these mutated forms have not survived in the singular in Modern English.

Nouns borrowed from foreign languages often keep their original plurals. Most of the examples are from Latin, but several other languages have also contributed irregular plurals. Examples are: Latin *vertebrae*, *papyri*, *genera*, *addenda*, *series*; Greek *phenomena*, *stigmata*; Italian *libretti*; French *plateaux*, *mesdames*; Hebrew *cherubim*; Arabic *fellaheen*. Sometimes double forms occur, one of them with a foreign plural and the other a new formation based on the analogy of native words, as in *banditti* beside *bandits*. The double forms are not always interchangeable; they may be specialized with different meanings. Thus we speak of the *indexes* of books but of *indices* in mathematics.

In native words, as well as in loan-words, variant plural forms sometimes come into existence, and here too there may be differentiation of meaning. *Brothers* are related to each other by blood, *brethren* by membership of some religious or secular community. *Clothes* has acquired a collective sense 'garments', whereas the analogical new formation *cloths* means 'pieces of cloth'. *Pence* is collective, while *pennies* is used of individual coins.

The method of forming the plural of compound nouns varies

with the age of the compound and the extent to which we are
conscious of the separate identity of its components. At one
extreme we have nouns which are in origin compounds, although no one but an etymologist is conscious of this fact. Such
words are *woman* (OE *wīfmann*) and *barn* (OE *bere-ern* 'barley
house'), and they naturally form their plurals like simple nouns.
Woman, like *man*, forms its plural by vowel mutation and the
variation in vowel of the second syllable has affected the pronunciation of the first syllable. Old compounds and those new
ones which represent a unified idea are treated as simple nouns.
If the final element of the compound is a noun, it has the same
plural form as it would have as a simple word. Examples are
womanhaters, washerwomen, horsemen, good-for-nothings. But in many
compounds, especially those consisting of a noun followed by an
adjective or a prepositional phrase, we single out the noun
element from the compound and give it the plural inflexion
when we wish to form the plural. An example is *passers-by.* In
popular speech the *s* is sometimes added to the whole compounds, as in *mother-in-laws* beside more usual *mothers-in-law*, and
the genitive ending -*s* is always so added, as in *my sister-in-law's
opinion.*

ADJECTIVES

Simplification of accidence has been carried further in adjectives than in any other part of speech. In Old English there
were two separate declensions of adjectives: the weak, used
after the definite article and in some other positions, and the
strong, and both declensions were highly inflected. In Middle
English the inflexional endings were greatly simplified, and by
the time of Chaucer most of them had been weakened to -*e*,
pronounced as a separate syllable, although the OE gen. pl.
ending -*ra* survives in Chaucer as -*er* in expressions like *oure aller*
'of us all' or *alderbest* 'best of all'. In the fifteenth century final
lightly stressed -*e* disappeared in pronunciation, and today most
adjectives are indeclinable in the positive. In Chaucer adjectives borrowed from French occasionally have the ending -*s*
in the plural, especially when they follow the noun, as in *places
delitables*, but the practice was short-lived.

The comparative of adjectives was formed in Old English by the addition of the suffix *-ra*, the superlative by the addition of *-ost*, or, less often, *-est*. These suffixes have today become *-er* and *-est*, and they are added to loan-words as well as to native words, but some adjectives, especially those of more than two syllables, are generally compared by the insertion of *more* and *most* before them instead of the addition of suffixes. Thus we have *cold, colder, coldest* and *brave, braver, bravest* but *beautiful, more beautiful, most beautiful*. The comparative *elder* and the superlative *eldest* have preserved the front mutation which was commonly found in the comparative and superlative of adjectives in Old English, since the suffixes at one time contained an *i*, which modified the quality of the stem-vowel. *Elder* and *eldest* now survive only in a rather specialized use applied to family relationsips; elsewhere they have been replaced by *older* and *oldest*, which are new formations levelled from the positive after the operation of front mutation.

Some adjectives form their comparative and superlative from a root different from that of the positive. These are words of frequent occurrence, and they have, in consequence, been able to preserve their irregularity until the present day. They had variant forms both in Old English and in Middle English, but the following list of forms in Old English and Chaucer will indicate the main lines of development of the forms.

OLD ENGLISH			CHAUCER		
gōd	betera	betst	good	bettre	best
yfel	wyrsa	wyrst	evil	werse	werst
mycel	māra	mǣst	moche	more	moost
lȳtel	lǣssa	lǣst	litel	lasse	leest

Some adjectives derived from adverbs have been influenced by analogy in the comparative and superlative. *Far* is from OE *feorr*, and the regular development of the comparative of this adjective appears in Chaucer as *ferre*. The Modern English forms *further* and *furthest* are the comparative and superlative of *forth*, which has been confused with *far*, and in *farther* and *farthest* the confusion has led to a change of stem-vowel. The most likely reason for the disappearance of the comparative *ferre* is that it was liable to confusion with the positive, which was often spelt *fer* in Middle English. *Near* has had a similarly complex history. The positive, comparative and superlative of this adjective were in Old English *nēah, nēarra* and (in non-WS) *nēhsta*. These three forms have given Modern English *nigh, near* and *next*. The old comparative *near* is now used as the positive, and a new comparative and superlative have been formed from it by the addition of *-er* and *-est*.

A number of superlatives ending in *-most* occur in Modern English, such as *foremost, inmost* and *utmost*. In origin this suffix is quite distinct from the superlative *most*, although the two have been confused. Beside the normal superlative suffix *-est* (earlier *-ist*), Old English had traces of an old superlative suffix *-ma*, as in *forma* 'first'. Many Old English words had both suffixes combined to form what was historically a double superlative ending, as *innemest* 'inmost', *lætemest* 'latest'. The suffix *-mest* was then identified with *mest* from OE *mǣst* 'most', and when this was replaced by the variant *most* from OE *māst*, the *o* was extended to the suffix, giving forms like *utmost* and *hindmost*. A further stage in the piling up of suffixes occurred when the suffix *-most* was added to a comparative ending in *-er* to give forms like *uppermost* and *uttermost*.

ADVERBS

Apart from the different forms for the comparative and superlative, adverbs are not inflected in Old English, but some of them preserve in a fossilized form the inflexional endings of other parts of speech. There were several different ways of forming adverbs in Old English. The most common was by the addition of the ending *-e* to an adjective, as in *wīde* 'widely' beside *wīd* 'wide'. If the adjective ended in *-e* there was usually no distinction in form between the adjective and the adverb, and when final *-e* disappeared in pronunciation in the fifteenth century many more adjectives and adverbs came to be alike in form. This is the origin of the construction, generally regarded as ungrammatical in present-day English, of the apparent use of an adjective in place of an adverb, as in the sentence *Come quick!*

A more distinctive way of forming adverbs in Modern English is by the use of the suffix *-ly*. Old English had a common adjectival suffix *-līc* and an adverbial suffix formed from it in the usual way by the addition of *-e*, as in *sōþlīce* 'truly' beside *sōþlīc* 'true'. Both of these suffixes have given *-ly* in Modern English, as in the adjective *kindly* and the adverb *truly*. Although we have some adjectives in *-ly*, the suffix is felt to be characteristic of adverbs, and it is still a living suffix by means of which we can form new adverbs from adjectives.

Other suffixes were used to form adverbs in Old English, and some of these have survived in particular adverbs. OE *-mǣlum* survives in *piecemeal*, and OE *-lunga* may survive in *headlong* and *sidelong*. The variant *-linga* has given a few archaic adverbs like *darkling* and has played a part in the creation of two verbs by a process of back formation: *to grovel* and *to sidle* have resulted from a misdivision of the adverbs *groveling* and *sideling*, the *-ing* having been mistaken for the ending of the present participle.

A number of adverbs had their origin in the oblique cases of nouns: the gen. sing. ending *-es* is found in OE *ealles* 'completely' and *dæges* 'by day', and the dat. pl. ending *-um* in *wundrum* 'wonderfully' and *stundum* 'sometimes'. The genitive ending survives in Modern English in the adverbs *needs* and *once*, and it has been added to some words in which it did not occur in Old English, such as *always* (OE *ealne weg, ealneg*), and *nowadays* (OE *nū on dæge*). The dative plural ending survives in the archaic *whilom*.

Adverbs are in the main compared like adjectives, although some adverbs, like *here* and *there* are incapable of comparison. A few monosyllabic adverbs, like *fast*, *high* and *near*, add *-er* in the comparative and *-est* in the superlative, but the usual method of comparing adverbs is by the use of the separate words *more*, *most* and *less*, *least*. Adjectives which are compared irregularly show similar irregularities when they are used as adverbs, with the occasional substitution of other words, such as *well* in place of the adjective *good*.

PRONOUNS

Demonstrative

In Old English there were two demonstrative pronouns which were both used also as adjectives. One of these pronouns has given Modern English *that* and the definite article *the*; the other has given *this*, *these* and *those*. A comparison of the Old English forms of these pronouns with their Modern English developments will serve to illustrate how great the simplification of English accidence has been.

The first demonstrative, which was already in Old English used as the definite article, had the following declension:

| | SINGULAR | | | PLURAL |
	Masculine	Neuter	Feminine	All genders
Nom.	sē	þæt	sēo	þā
Acc.	þone	þæt	þā	þā
Gen.	þæs	þæs	þǣre	þāra
Dat.	þǣm	þǣm	þǣre	þǣm
Instr.	þȳ, þon	þȳ, þon		

The other demonstrative had the declension:

| | SINGULAR | | | PLURAL |
	Masculine	Neuter	Feminine	All genders
Nom.	þes	þis	þēos	þās
Acc.	þisne	þis	þās	þās
Gen.	þisses	þisses	þisse	þissa
Dat.	þissum	þissum	þisse	þissum
Instr.	þȳs	þȳs		

It will be seen that, in spite of the wide variety of forms of the definite article in Old English, the form which has now established itself as the invariable one is not among them, and there is none of the Old English forms which can have served as its direct ancestor. Old English had a word *þe*, which was used as an indeclinable relative pronoun meaning 'who' or 'which', but Modern English *the* is derived from early Middle English *þe*, which goes back to the Old English nominatives *sē* and *sēo* with substitution of initial *þ* from the plural and the other forms of the singular. The replacement of the various inflected forms of the article by the indeclinable *þe* took place very early in Northern and Midland dialects of Middle English, but in Southern dialects inflected forms continued to be used side by side with *þe* until the fourteenth century. Although the definite article is now uninflected, a few fossilized traces of old inflexions survive, chiefly in proper names. The surname *Atterbury* preserves a trace of the dative singular feminine (OE *æt þǣre byrig*), while *Attenborough* preserves the development of the dative singular masculine *þǣm*, a form of the article that could have been used only when the Old English system of grammatical gender had been weakened. The initial consonant of the names *Nash* and *Noakes* is derived from the dative inflexion of a preceding definite article with misdivision. Similarly the archaic phrase *for the nonce* is derived from ME *for then ones*, where *then* is from the OE masculine or neuter dative singular *þǣm*. The first *the* in an expression like *the sooner the better* is a survival of the Old English instrumental *þȳ*.

The ME nominative and accusative singular neuter *þat*, *þet*, used as a definite article, survived longest when followed by *one* and *other*, and then by misdivision *þet one* and *þet oþer* became *þe tone* and *þe toþer*. This is the origin of *tother*, which has survived in occasional colloquial use until the present day. Apart from this fragmentary survival, *that* has ceased to be a definite article, but it has preserved two of the other uses of OE *sē*, *þæt*, *sēo*, as a demonstrative adjective and pronoun. The plural *þā* became *tho* in Middle English, except in Northern dialects, and was used as the plural of the definite article and also as the plural of the demonstrative *that*. The first of these functions was taken over by *the*; the second was taken over by *those*, which was derived from OE *þās*, the nominative and accusative plural of *þes*, *þis*, *þēos*. The other two demonstratives which have survived in Modern English, *this* and *these*, are derived from the same paradigm. *This* is derived from the Old English nominative singular neuter, and *these* is from a new plural form *thēse*, *thēose*, which arose in Middle English with the vowel partly from the nominative singular feminine *þēos* and partly from a variant form of the dative plural *þeossum*, in which the *eo* arose from *i* by a sound-change caused by the following *u*.

Personal

The inflexions of personal pronouns have been remarkably well preserved in English, partly, no doubt, because they occur so frequently that they have been able to resist the influence of analogy. There were many variant forms in Old English, but the following were the most common:

	FIRST PERSON			SECOND PERSON	
	Sing.	Plural		Sing.	Plural
Nom.	*ic*	*wē*		*þū*	*gē*
Acc.	*mē*	*ūs*		*þē*	*ēow*
Gen.	*mīn*	*ūre*		*þīn*	*ēower*
Dat.	*mē*	*ūs*		*þē*	*ēow*

	THIRD PERSON			
	Sing.			Plural
	M.	N.	F.	All Genders
Nom.	*hē*	*hit*	*hēo*	*hīe*
Acc.	*hine*	*hit*	*hīe*	*hīe*
Gen.	*his*	*his*	*hire*	*heora*
Dat.	*him*	*him*	*hire*	*him*

Besides singular and plural pronouns, there were separate forms for the first and second person dual, used when two persons were referred to. These did not survive beyond the early Middle English period, and they have no importance for the development of Modern English.

In Modern English the genitive of the personal pronoun is used only as a possessive adjective, and the forms will be discussed below along with those of the possessive pronouns.

The regular Middle English development of OE *ic* was *ich,* where the *ch* was simply a spelling for front *c*. Side by side with *ich,* all dialects of Middle English had *i*, later written *I*, which was in origin probably a lightly stressed form of *ich,* and as such had a short vowel. The form *I* came to be used in strongly stressed as well as in lightly stressed positions, and by the end of the Middle English period it had almost replaced *ich*. When *I* was used in stressed positions, the vowel was lengthened, and it is from this long vowel that Modern English *I* [ai] developed. This form is now used in lightly stressed as well as in strongly stressed positions.

The first person plural and the second person singular forms have developed regularly, except that Modern English *us* is derived from a form in which the long vowel has been shortened because of lack of stress. In the second person plural, *gē* has

regularly become *ye*, and *ēow* has become *you*. The initial consonant of *you* may be due to the analogy of the nominative *ye*. The
Modern English vowel [u:] is not regularly developed from the
Old English diphthong. It is probably from a lightly stressed
form [ju], with lengthening of the vowel when the pronoun
occurred in strongly stressed positions. This lengthening is
similar to that which took place in *I*, with the difference that the
lengthening of the vowel in *you* was too late to allow the long
vowel to take part in the Great Vowel Shift. The distinction
between the subjective *ye* and the objective *you* is preserved by
careful writers until the seventeenth century, although *ye* is
sometimes used as a lightly stressed form of the objective. Today
ye has been replaced by *you* in the subjective except in poetic and
religious use. A further extension of *you* has taken place at the
expense of the second person singular pronouns *thou* and *thee*.
The distinction between singular and plural forms is generally
maintained in Middle English, but in Chaucer and other
Middle English authors we sometimes find *you* as a respectful
way of addressing one person. At the time of Shakespeare *thou*
and *thee* were used as expressions of intimacy, as the cognate
words are used in many European languages. They were also
used to address inferiors, as in *Twelfth Night* (III. ii. 46), when
Sir Toby, persuading Sir Andrew to write a challenge to a duel,
says to him 'If thou thou'st him some thrice, it shall not be
amiss'. In Standard English of the present day *thou* and *thee* are
found only in poetic and religious use. Among members of the
Society of Friends *thee* is used as a subjective.

In the third personal pronoun the forms that have not survived in Standard English are the accusative singular feminine
and all the forms of the plural. Already in Middle English the
dative singular masculine had begun to replace the accusative,
and *hine* survived in literary use only until the early fourteenth
century. A descendant of the old accusative, pronounced [ən], is
very common in Southern dialects today and is applied to inanimate objects as well as to men.

In the neuter of the third personal pronoun *hit* has lost its
initial *h* both in pronunciation and in spelling because of the
lack of stress. Forms without *h* begin to appear in early Middle
English, but in Chaucer *hit* is more common than *it*, and *hit* is

found occasionally until the sixteenth century. In most of the personal pronouns the dative has replaced the accusative, but in the neuter singular analogy has acted in the opposite direction, thus introducing a useful distinction between the masculine *him* and the neuter *it*.

The origin of the pronoun *she*, which replaced OE *hēo*, is one of the unsolved problems of historical English grammar. The earliest recorded appearance of forms at all like *she* is in East Midland texts of the twelfth and thirteenth centuries, where *scæ*, *she*, and *sho* occur beside forms descended from OE *hēo*. Although none of the suggested explanations of the origin of *she* carries immediate conviction, there has been no lack of suggestions. One is that *she* arose from sentences in which OE *hēo* was preceded by a word ending in *s*, such as *wæs* 'was'. Another is that *she* is the result of a blend between the feminine demonstrative *sēo* and the personal pronoun *hēo*. There is evidence from place-names and modern dialects that *sh* may sometimes be derived from [hj], and it has been suggested that *she* may be derived from OE *hēo* through an intermediate stage containing this initial group. Although we cannot be certain what was the origin of *she*, it is easy to see why this form was preferred once it came to exist side by side with forms descended from OE *hēo*. In most dialects of Middle English OE *hēo* became *he*, and was therefore liable to be confused with the masculine nominative singular as well as with some forms of the plural. The objective *her* presents much less difficulty than the subjective. Like the masculine objective *him*, it has developed from the Old English dative form, which came to be used also as the accusative.

The *eo* of the genitive plural of the third personal pronoun arose from earlier *i*, which became *eo* by the influence of the *a* in the following syllable. Already in Old English the *eo* sometimes spread by analogy to the dative plural, giving *heom*, which became *hem* in Middle English. This form, with the loss of initial *h* which is common in lightly stressed words, survived in frequent use until the eighteenth century, generally written '*em*, and it is still occasionally heard in colloquial expressions like *That's the stuff to give 'em*. In general, however, the plural forms of this pronoun were replaced by the pronouns *they*, *them* and *their* borrowed from Scandinavian. These forms are found earliest in East Midland texts, and Orm, writing about the year 1200, has *þeȝȝ* in the nominative and *þeȝȝm* beside *hemm* in the dative. The nominative pronoun was borrowed a good deal earlier than the others, and many Middle English authors, including Chaucer, have the Scandinavian form *they* in the nominative but native forms in the other cases. The borrowing of pronouns from one language into another is rare, and the introduction of Scandinavian forms into English provides evidence of the closeness of the intermingling of the speakers of the two languages, and also, perhaps, of the need for new distinctive forms after the levelling of the older forms.

Reflexive

In Old English there were no distinctive forms of reflexive pronouns; personal pronouns were used with reflexive force. Thus we have *hē beþōhte hine* 'he bethought himself', *nō ic mē hnāgran talige* 'I do not think myself inferior'. This use of the personal pronoun as a reflexive became much less common in early Modern English. Examples occur in Shakespeare, as in *I confess me much guilty* (*A.Y.L.I.* I. ii. 172), and occasionally today, as in *I'll put the cushion behind me*.

The word *self* is frequently used in Old English as an adjective to strengthen a preceding personal pronoun, as in *ic self* 'I myself', *þū self* 'you yourself'. This construction, with *self* in the nominative in agreement with the pronoun, passed out of use in early Middle English. Already in Old English we find *self* preceded by the accusative or dative of a personal pronoun used as the subject of a sentence, and this construction proved more lasting. It has given us the forms of reflexive pronouns of the third person that we use today, such as *himself*. In the course of the Middle English period *self* came to be regarded as a noun, with the result that the possessive forms of pronouns were used with it. These forms are now used in the first and second persons, and in the plural, as a further sign that *self* is regarded as a noun, the plural form *selves* is used, as in *ourselves*. On the basis of these forms, there arose in the sixteenth century the forms *itself* and *oneself* with the variant *one's self*. In early Modern English these pronouns combined with *self* could be used instead of a personal pronoun as subjectives, as in *myself am Naples* (*The Tempest*, I. ii. 434), but today when they are used in this way they are generally accompanied by a personal pronoun, as in *I myself said so*. The same forms are used as reflexive pronouns, as in *He can dress himself*, *Don't trouble yourselves*. Many verbs which once required a reflexive pronoun are now used intransitively without any pronoun, as may be seen by comparing OE *hē reste hine* with its Modern English equivalent *he rested*.

Possessive

In Old English, the genitives of the personal pronouns were used also as possessive adjectives. We are familiar today with the latter use, but not with the former, and we no longer use constructions like the Old English *eall his* 'all of it' or *God ūre helpe* 'God help us'. The loss of the pronominal, as distinct from the adjectival, use of these forms goes back to early Middle English. When genitives were used as possessives in Old English they were inflected like adjectives and agreed with the nouns they qualified, but before the end of the Middle English period they had become indeclinable. The distinction between *my* and *mine* and between *thy* and *thine* came into existence in the Middle English period. At first the distinction was a purely phonetic one, like that between *a* and *an*: the final *n* of OE *mīn* and *þīn* was dropped before nouns beginning with a consonant but was kept in other positions. In course of time the forms without *n* have come to be used as possessive adjectives when immediately followed by a noun, whether the noun begins with a vowel or a consonant, while the forms with *n* are used as possessive pronouns. Thus we say *my book* but *This book is mine*. The differentiation in form between adjective and pronoun first began to appear in Northern dialects towards the end of the thirteenth century and spread to Midland dialects about a century later. In early Modern English there was a good deal of fluctuation between *my* and *mine* and between *thy* and *thine*, but in prose *my* and *thy* have been the normal adjectival forms since the latter part of the seventeenth century.

In the third person singular the masculine forms present least difficulty. In the masculine, *his* is used as both adjective and pronoun. In the feminine, OE *hire* survives unchanged in most Middle English texts, but we also find *here*, where the *e* may be due to the analogy of the nominative singular feminine with ME *e* from OE *ēo*. In Chaucer *hir(e)* is the only form, but by the sixteenth century *her* has become the usual adjectival form. The pronouns *hires* and *heres* begin to be used in Northern dialects towards the end of the thirteenth century and spread to Midland dialects about a century later. From these forms we get Modern English *hers*. In the neuter, *his* is preserved down to the seventeenth century. Side by side with *his*, from the fourteenth to the seventeenth century *it* is used as a possessive adjective, and Shakespeare uses both *his* and *it*. We also find *of it* and *thereof*. From *it* a new neuter possessive, *its*, was formed by the addition of the genitive ending *-s*. This form is first recorded at the end of the sixteenth century, but it is not found in the Authorized Version of the Bible (1611). It is the regular form today, although it is never used except adjectivally.

In the third person plural most Middle English texts have forms, such as *here* and *heore*, which were developed from OE *heora*, but even in the earliest Northern texts we find only forms with initial *þ* or *th*, borrowed from Scandinavian. In the East Midlands the *Ormulum* is the only early Middle English text which has any forms with *þ-*, and it has native forms with *h-* as well. Forms like *thair* and *their* spread from the North first to the East Midlands and then to the other dialects, and by the end of the fifteenth century *their* was the normal plural possessive adjective. When used as pronouns, the plural possessives, like the feminine singular, take final *-s*, giving *ours*, *yours*, *theirs*.

VERBS

The most important formal distinction of English verbs is that which divides most of them into two large groups known as strong and weak. Strong verbs form their past tense by changing the vowel of the stem without the addition of a suffix, as in *come*, *came* and *sing*, *sang*. Weak verbs usually form their past tense by the addition of *-d* or *-t*, both of which are sometimes spelt *-ed*; examples are *kissed*, *opened* and *loved*. The change of vowels in strong verbs is very old, and results from ablaut variation in Indo-European. All weak verbs originally had the same stem-vowel in the infinitive as in the past tense, and most of them still have, but for various reasons, which will be discussed in this chapter, some weak verbs, like *sell*, *sold* have vowel change as well as a suffix in the past tense, and some, like *bleed*, *bled*, have vowel change only. The number of weak verbs is very much larger than the number of strong, and new verbs which have been formed from nouns or borrowed from other languages since the Old English period are normally conjugated weak, although *take* (ON *taka*) is strong and *thrive* (ON *þrífa*) has both strong and weak forms. The strong verbs, on the other hand, are for the most part of frequent occurrence, and they form an important part of the picture presented by the English language at every period of its history.

The inflexions of verbs, like those of nouns and adjectives, have been greatly simplified in the course of the history of the English language. This simplification has been caused in part by the decay of inflexional endings, resulting from lack of stress, and in part by the operation of analogy.

The following were the usual endings in Old English:

Present Indicative Singular 1. -*e*, 2. -(*e*)*st*, 3. -(*e*)*þ*; Plural -*aþ*;
Present and Preterite Subjunctive Singular -*e*; Plural -*en*;
Imperative Singular -, -*e*; Plural -*aþ*;
Infinitive -*an*; Present Participle -*ende*;
Preterite Indicative Strong Singular 1. -, 2. -*e*, 3. -; Plural -*on*; Weak Singular -*de*, -*dest*, -*de*; Plural -*don*;
Past Participle Strong -*en*, Weak -*ed*, -*od*.

From this comparatively simple pattern there were many deviations which varied from one dialect to another. Two of these, which affected the forms of the present indicative, deserve special mention in view of their influence on the later development of the language. The first variation was in the West Saxon dialect, where the second and third persons singular lost the lightly stressed vowel of the inflexional ending. This loss of a vowel often led to the juxtaposition of two consonants which were difficult to pronounce together, and, when such a group arose, assimilation and simplification often took place. In non-West-Saxon dialects there was usually no loss of the lightly stressed vowel. Hence as the third person singular present indicative of *cēosan* 'to choose' and *grētan* 'to greet', West Saxon had *cīest* and *grēt*, while non-West-Saxon had *cēoseþ* and *grēteþ*. Monosyllabic forms descended from the Old English forms are found in Southern dialects of Middle English. The other variation was in Northumbrian, where the third person singular of the present indicative ended in *-es* beside *-eþ* and the plural ended in *-as* beside *-aþ*.

In Middle English the inflexional endings of verbs are preserved best in the South. Some texts show a great variety of forms, especially in the Midlands, but the following is the general picture of the endings of the present indicative.

	SINGULAR			PLURAL
South	1. *-e*	2. *-est*	3. *-eth*	*-eth*
Midlands	1. *-e*	2. *-est*, *-es*	3. *-eth*, *-es*	*-en*, *-e*, *-es*
North	1. *-e*	2. *-es*	3. *-es*	*-es*, *-is*

The Modern English forms of the first and second persons singular are regularly developed from the Old English forms. In the third person singular the two endings *-eth* and *-es* have existed side by side from Middle English until the present day. The forms in *-es* spread from the North to the East Midlands and the North-West Midlands in Middle English, and by the fifteenth century spread to London English. The spread of the forms in *-es* may have been helped by the analogy of the common verbal form *is*. In the fifteenth and sixteenth centuries forms in *-es* were more common in private letters than in literary texts, and they were probably thought of as colloquial. The First and Second Prayer Books of Edward VI and the Authorized Version of the Bible have *-eth*, and, on the rare occasions when forms in *-eth* are used today, they are usually archaisms in religious contexts based upon these models.

In the plural the Midland ending *-en* was borrowed from the subjunctive, and served a useful purpose in providing a plural form distinct from the third person singular when the Old English endings *-eþ* and *-aþ* had fallen together. During the Middle English period the final *-n* was sometimes lost, and the Midland form spread to other dialects and became the ancestor

of the Modern English form. Forms with final -*n* are found as
late as the sixteenth century and occasionally even later. They
were useful when metre required an extra syllable, as in the
Shakespearean example 'and waxen in their mirth' (*M.N.D.*
II.i.56); the ending -*eth* served the same purpose in the third
person singular.

Some Old English verbs, both strong and weak, had -*cg*- in
the infinitive beside -*g*- in the second and third persons singular
present indicative, and others had -*bb*- beside -*f*-. Such verbs are
licgan 'to lie down' beside *ligeþ* 'he lies down', *lecgan* 'to lay'
beside *legeþ* 'he lays', *secgan* 'to say' beside *sægþ* 'he says', *hebban*
'to lift' beside *hefeþ* 'he lifts', *habban* 'to have' beside *hæfþ* 'he
has'. The normal Modern English development of OE *cg* would
have been [dʒ], spelt *dg*, as in *bridge* (OE *brycg*), and OE *bb*
would normally have been simplified to *b*. The verbs *lie, lay, say,
heave* and *have* are from the stem of the third person singular
present indicative; if the Old English infinitives had come down
into Modern English they would have given **lidge, *ledge,
*sedge, *heb* and **hab*.

In early Middle English the present participle had the ending
-*inde* in the South, -*ende* in the Midlands and -*and* in the North.
During the Middle English period a new type of present participle, ending in -*ing(e)*, came into use. It is first recorded in
Southern dialects, and by the time of Chaucer it had become
the normal type; this is the ancestor of the Modern English
form. The present participle in -*ing* probably had its origin in
Old English verbal nouns ending in -*ung* or -*ing*. The transition
from verbal noun to present participle probably arose from the
loss of the lightly stressed preposition *on* through the intermediate stage *a*, pronounced [ə]. Thus, *What are you a-doing?*
'What are you engaged in the act of doing?' became *What are
you doing?*

In Old English, past participles usually had the prefix *ge*-,
provided that the verb had no other prefix. In early Middle
English this prefix became *y*-. It survived longest in Southern
dialects, but in later Middle English it generally disappeared,
though occasional survivals, such as the Miltonic *yclept* 'called',
are to be found in later English.

Strong Verbs

Strong verbs in Old English had four principal parts, and, on the basis of the vowel variation shown by these parts, the strong verbs are divided into seven classes. The principal parts were: (1) the infinitive, (2) the third person singular of the preterite, (3) the preterite plural and (4) the past participle. The variations in the stem-vowels may be illustrated by giving the principal parts of one verb of each class:

I	*rīdan*	'to ride'	*rād*	*ridon*	*(ge)riden*
II	*bēodan*	'to command'	*bēad*	*budon*	*(ge)boden*
III	*helpan*	'to help'	*healp*	*hulpon*	*(ge)holpen*
IV	*beran*	'to bear'	*bær*	*bǣron*	*(ge)boren*
V	*tredan*	'to tread'	*træd*	*trǣdon*	*(ge)treden*
VI	*faran*	'to go'	*fōr*	*fōron*	*(ge)faren*
VII	*hlēapan*	'to leap'	*hlēop*	*hlēopon*	*(ge)hlēapen*

Verbs of Class VII had a variety of vowels in the infinitive, and some of them had *ē* instead of *ēo* in the preterite. In verbs of this class the stem-vowel of the past participle was normally the same as that of the infinitive, and verbs which had *ē* in the preterite singular had the same vowel in the preterite plural.

The four principal parts give the stems that were used in the building up all the forms of an Old English strong verb. The stem of the infinitive was used also in the present indicative and subjunctive, the imperative and the present participle. Since the vowel of the inflexional endings of the second and third persons singular of the present indicative was *i* in primitive Old English, the stem-vowel of these forms generally shows the effects of front mutation, but the vowel without mutation was sometimes levelled out into these forms, especially in non-West-Saxon, on the analogy of such forms as the infinitive.

The second of the principal parts formed the basis of only two forms: the first and third persons singular of the preterite indicative, which were alike. The stem of the preterite plural was found also in the second person of the preterite singular and in the whole of the preterite subjunctive. In Middle English the stem-vowel of the second person was levelled under that of the other singular forms, and the ending -*e* was replaced by the more characteristic ending of the second person, -*est*, on the analogy of weak verbs or of the present indicative. Older forms of the second person singular without the ending -*est* survive occasionally in Chaucer and even later. Such forms are *founde*, regularly developed from OE *funde*, and *drank*, re-formed on the analogy of the first or third persons singular (OE 1, 3 sg. *dranc*, 2 sg. *drunce*.)

The ending -*en* of the past participle survived in Middle English as -*en* or -*e*, and it has generally been preserved as -*en* in Modern English except in verbs of Class III. In that class the -*en* has generally disappeared except in a few isolated forms used as adjectives, such as *drunken*, *bounden* and *molten*.

In Middle English the stem-vowels of each of the principal parts of each class of strong verbs underwent the normal sound-changes, with the result, for example, that the preterite singular of the first two classes came to have [ɔ:] and [ɛ:] respectively. A further influence that has done a good deal to modify the development of strong verbs has been that of analogy working in various ways. One of the results of analogy has been to reduce the number of principal parts of strong verbs from four to three by removing the distinction between the preterite singular and plural. The only survival of this distinction is in the preterite of the verb 'to be', where we have *was* (OE *wæs*) beside *were* (OE *wēron*). In Classes VI and VII of strong verbs and in a few other verbs, such as *cuman* 'to come' and *niman* 'to take', the preterite singular and plural already had the same stem-vowel in Old English. In Middle English analogy took place in more than one direction, and the direction depended in part on the dialect. In Northern dialects the vowel of the preterite singular tended to replace that of the preterite plural, and Middle English plural forms showing the results of this analogy are sometimes called Northern preterites. In the South and Midlands the distinction between the preterite singular and plural was preserved longer than in the North, but in the South-West and the South-West Midlands the vowel of the preterite singular was often replaced by that of the preterite plural or the past participle, especially when these two forms had the same stem-vowel. Preterite singulars showing the results of this analogy are sometimes

called Western preterites. In Modern English the various preterite forms no longer serve to distinguish between singular and
plural, but some verbs have generalized the vowel of the singular
and some that of the plural or past participle. In a few verbs,
especially in those of Class III, there is still fluctuation between
the two types. *Drank, sank, sang, began, swam* are descended from
the preterite singular; *sung, swum, bound* and *ground* are from the
preterite plural or the past participle. When the past participle
had a different vowel from the preterite plural, analogy sometimes caused the vowel of the past participle to be used in the
preterite, as in *froze, bore* and *got*. On the other hand, in early
Modern English the preterite was often used for the past participle, and in a few verbs it has become the normal form. For
example, the past participle *shone* is from the OE preterite
singular *scān*, and *held* is from the preterite *hēold*, the historically regular form of the past participle being the archaic
holden.

Another result of analogy has been the tendency of some
verbs to pass from one class into another. *Speak* passed from
Class V to Class IV when it re-formed its past participle (OE
gesprecen) on the analogy of forms like *boren*. Sometimes analogy
has led to the creation of a new set of principal parts which do
not fit into any of the old classes. *Slay* originally belonged to
Class VI and had in Old English the principal parts *slēan, slōh,
slōgon, geslægen*. Only the past participle *slain* is regularly derived from Old English, and this form represents one of the two
possible developments; the other development is found in ME
slawe (from the OE variant *geslagen*) and this form has not
survived into present-day English. The infinitive *slay* is a new
formation on the analogy of the past participle, and the preterite
slew is on the analogy of preterites of Class VII, such as *grew*
(OE *grēow*) and *blew* (OE *blēow*). The effect of analogy has
sometimes been that a strong verb has become weak, or, less
often, a weak verb has become strong. Strong verbs that have
become weak include *glide* and *writhe* from Class I, *creep* and
seethe from Class II, *carve* and *yield* from Class III, *fret* and *be-
queath* from Class V, *fare* and *laugh* from Class VI, and *weep* and
walk from Class VII. Weak verbs that have become strong include *stick* and *wear*. Some weak verbs have acquired strong

past participles in -(*e*)*n* without acquiring strong preterite forms; examples of such past participles are *chidden*, *hidden*, *sewn* and *shown*.

Weak Verbs

There were three classes of weak verbs in Old English. The first class formed its preterite in -(*e*)*de* or, after a voiceless consonant, in -*te*, and its past participle in -*ed*. The second class formed its preterite in -*ode* and its past participle in -*od*. The third class formed its preterite in -*de* and its past participle in -*d*. All verbs of the second class and a few verbs of the first class had the ending -*ian* in the infinitive; the other weak verbs had -*an*. Regular examples of the three classes are:

	INFINITIVE		PRETERITE	PAST PARTICIPLE
I	*dēman*	'to judge'	*dēmde*	*gedēmed*
	settan	'to set'	*sette*	*geseted*
II	*lufian*	'to love'	*lufode*	*gelufod*
III	*habban*	'to have'	*hæfde*	*gehæfd*

Most of the Old English verbs belonging to Class I had long stems, and these fell in with Class III in Middle English. They had -*e*(*n*) in the infinitive, and in the preterite they had -*de* after voiced consonants and -*te* after voiceless consonants. Verbs of Class II kept the *i* of the infinitive ending in Southern dialects of Middle English, as in *louie* 'to love', *þonki* 'to thank', beside Midland and Northern *loue*(*n*), *þonke*(*n*). The few verbs of Class I which had short stems fell in with Class II and had preterites in -*ede* in Middle English. In later Middle English the vowel *e* which preceded the *d* in the preterite and past participle disappeared in pronunciation except when the stem ended in *t* or *d*. After the loss of this *e* the *d* of the preterite ending generally became *t* by partial assimilation when the stem of the verb ended in a voiceless consonant. In early Modern English this change was reflected in the spelling of many words, such as *stript*, *whipt*, *drest*, but in most words the spelling with -*ed* has since been restored. We thus get the normal rule today that the preterite and the past participle are alike in having an ending which is spelt -*ed* and which has three pronunciations:

(*a*) after *t* or *d* it is pronounced [əd] or [id], as in *hated*, *appointed*, *ended*, *dreaded*;

(*b*) after voiced consonants other than *d* and after vowels it is pronounced [d], as in *loved*, *raised*, *dined*, *breathed*, *prayed*, *employed*;

(*c*) after voiceless consonants other than *t* it is pronounced [t], as in *liked*, *ceased*, *fixed*, *kissed*.

Some exceptions to this general development remain to be mentioned.

(*a*) Long vowels were shortened before double consonants in Old English and before certain consonant groups in Middle English. As a result, verbs ending in -*d* or -*t* often had a long vowel in the infinitive and a short vowel in the preterite and past participle, where the addition of an inflexional ending led to the creation of a double consonant or a consonant group. In early Modern English the double consonant of the preterite and past participle was simplified in both pronunciation and spelling, and the reason for the shortening was thus obscured. For example, ME *blēden* 'to bleed', preterite *bledde*, past participle *ybled*(*d*) has given MnE *bleed*, *bled*, and similarly we have *lead*, *led*; *hide*, *hid* (with a strong past participle *hidden*); *feed*, *fed*; *meet*, *met*; *keep*, *kept*. In the preterite and past participle *read* [ɹɛd] the spelling has been influenced by the infinitive. In *clad* from *clothe* (OE *clāþian*) there has been assimilation of *þd* to *dd* and shortening of the preceding vowel.

(*b*) Verbs ending in -*d* or -*t* with short stem-vowels now normally have preterites and past participles identical in form with the infinitive. In Middle English the preterite could sometimes be distinguished from the infinitive by its double consonant, but these double consonants have now been simplified. Examples are *cast*, *let*, *cost*, *thrust*, *spread*, *shed*. Some verbs, such as *knit* and *lift*, belonged to this group in early Modern English, but now have analogical preterites and past participles *knitted* and *lifted*, the old past participle *knit* being preserved in the phrase *well knit*.

(*c*) The ME ending -*te*, which was the usual preterite ending after voiceless consonants, was sometimes extended by analogy to other verbs, especially those with stems ending in *v*, *l*, *m*, *n*, *nd* or *ld*. When such verbs had a long stem-vowel, it was generally shortened in the preterite, and the present-day pronunciation often shows that the shortening took place in Middle English. Examples are *leave, left*; *bereave, bereft*; *dwell, dwelt*; *feel, felt*; *mean, meant*; *send, sent*; *build, built*, beside *believe, believed* and *fill, filled*. Some verbs have double forms in spelling, and sometimes the difference in spelling reflects a difference in pronunciation. Examples are *burnt, burned*; *spilt, spilled*; *learnt, learned*. Sometimes the form in *-ed* has a long vowel from the infinitive, while the form in *-t* shows shortening of the stem-vowel. Examples are *dreamed* [dɹiːmd] beside *dreamt* [dɹɛmt] and *leaned* [liːnd] beside *leant* [lɛnt].

(*d*) There were twenty Old English verbs belonging to Weak Class I which had front mutation in the infinitive but not in the preterite or past participle, and several of these have come down to Modern English, preserving their irregularities. *Sell* and *tell* are from OE *sellan* 'to give' and *tellan* 'to count'; the preterites *sold* and *told* are from the Anglian preterites *salde* and *talde*, which corresponded to WS *sealde* and *tealde*. *Dwell* (OE *dwellan*, pret. *dwealde*) has an analogical preterite *dwelt*, and *quell* (OE *cwellan*, pret. *cwealde*) has its preterite *quelled* on a slightly different analogy. *Buy* is from the third person singular present indicative of OE *bycgan*, and *bought* is regularly developed from the OE preterite *bohte*. *Teach* is from OE *tǣcan*, and *taught* may be from either of the Old English forms of the preterite *tǣhte* or *tāhte*, with shortening of the vowel. On the analogy of such verbs, especially the obsolete *latch* 'to seize' (OE *lǣcean*, pret. *lǣhte*), the Norman French loan-word *catch* has acquired a preterite *caught*. OE *worhte*, preterite of *wyrcan* 'to work', has given *wrought*, which is still used as a participial adjective, but the infinitive has been replaced by *work* from the cognate noun (OE *weorc*), and from this a new analogical preterite *worked* has been formed. *Think* and its preterite *thought* are from OE *þencan* 'to think' (pret. *þōhte*). *Methinks* and *methought* are from OE *þyncan* 'to seem' (pret. *þūhte*) influenced by the forms of *think*. *Beseech* and *besought* are from OE *besēcan, besōhte*, but *seek* probably had its *k* from the OE third person singular present indicative *sēcþ*, where the following *þ* prevented the *c* from becoming an affricate. *Bring* and *brought* are regularly developed from OE *bringan* and *brōhte*, but this verb was irregular in Old English in that the infinitive belonged to a related strong verb. Other verbs of this group have either become obsolete, like OE *þeccan* 'to cover' and *reccean* 'to narrate', or have acquired analogical preterites, like *reached*, beside the obsolete *raught*, preterite of *reach* (OE *rǣcean*, pret. *rǣhte, rāhte*) or *stretched*, preterite of *stretch* (OE *streccean*, pret. *streahte*).

(*e*) Only four verbs belonged to Weak Class III in Old English: *hycgan* 'to think', *secgan* 'to say', *libban* 'to live', and *habban* 'to have'. The first of these has not survived into Modern English. The present forms of the other three verbs are derived, not from the Old English infinitives, but from such forms as the third person singular present indicative *sægþ, liofaþ*, and *hæfþ*, in which there were single consonants. The *v* of *have* disappeared in Middle English when it was immediately followed by another consonant, with the result that we now have *hast, hath, has* and *had*.

Minor Groups

One small but important group of verbs shares some of the characteristics of both strong and weak verbs. The verbs of this group are known as preterite-present verbs because their present tenses are derived from old preterites. In origin they are strong verbs of which the preterite forms gained a present meaning and for which new weak preterites were made in Common Germanic. It is easy to see how the preterite of one verb may, by a change in one's point of view, come to be regarded as the present tense of another verb of slightly different meaning. For example, the preterite of a verb meaning 'to see' or 'to learn by seeing' came to be regarded as the present tense of a verb meaning 'to know'. Hence OE *witan* 'to know' is a preterite-present verb cognate with Latin *vidēre* 'to see', and this verb has survived in Modern English in *to wit* 'namely' and in the participial adjective *unwitting*, as well as in the archaism *God wot*.

Only a small number of the Old English preterite-present verbs have been preserved in Modern English. They are the verbs *can, dare, shall* and *may*, with their preterites *could, durst, should* and *might*, and the old preterites *must* and *ought*, which are now used also as presents. Even in Old English, preterite-present verbs were often defective; that is to say, many of the forms that we should expect to find did not occur. In Modern

English the process of loss has been carried further. The surviving forms are in very frequent use, but they are used chiefly
as auxiliaries to other verbs.

Can is regularly developed from the OE present indicative
singular *cann*, but *could* is not regularly developed from the OE
preterite, which was *cūþe*. The usual ME forms of the preterite
were *coude* (or *koude*) and *couthe* (or *kouthe*). The forms with *d* were
due to the analogy of other weak preterites ending in *-de*, and
the Modern English form *could* shows a further analogy in the *l*,
which is due to the influence of *should* and *would*, where the *l* is
etymologically justified. The vowel of *could* has been shortened
because of lack of stress. The adjective *cunning* is derived from
this verb, the infinitive of which in Old English was *cunnan*, and
uncouth is from the OE participial adjective *cūþ* 'known'.

Dare has almost ceased to be a preterite-present verb. The
two traces of its origin that it still keeps are the third person
singular present indicative *dare* (OE *dearr*), beside analogical
dares, and the preterite *durst* (OE *dorste*), which is now old-
fashioned and is gradually giving way to the analogical form
dared, a form which has been in existence since the sixteenth
century. The *u* of *durst* is due to the analogy of such forms as the
OE present indicative plural *durron*, which have not survived in
Modern English.

Shall is from OE *sceal*. In strongly stressed positions the Old
English form became [ʃɔːl] in early Modern English, just as
OE *eall* has given Modern English [ɔːl]. The pronunciation
[ʃɔːl] became obsolete during the eighteenth century, and the
modern pronunciation [ʃæl] is from a Middle English lightly
stressed form. We now have new lightly stressed forms [ʃəl] and
[ʃl̩], in which the vowel has been still further reduced. In the
negative form *shan't* the *l* disappeared in the seventeenth century.
The lengthening of the vowel is probably due to the loss of the
following *o* rather than to the loss of the *l*, since a similar lengthening has taken place in *can't*. In the preterite Old English had
sceolde, and in Middle English this form gave rise to a strongly
stressed form *shōlde* beside a lightly stressed form *shŏlde*. The
strongly stressed form became [ʃuːld] in early Modern English,
and the Modern English, [ʃud] is derived from this.

May is regularly developed from the OE first and third

persons singular present indicative *mæg*. The OE second person singular was *meaht*, later *miht*, but this form became obsolete in late Middle English, and was replaced by *may(e)st*, a new formation from the first and third persons singular. In the preterite Old English had *meahte* beside *mihte*. The second form gave Modern English *might*; the first gave *mought*, which remained in use until the end of the seventeenth century, although it is now obsolete, except in dialects.

One Old English preterite-present verb was *mōt* 'I may', and it had the preterite *mōste*. The present forms of this verb became obsolete during the sixteenth century, and were replaced by the preterite *must*, derived from OE *mōste* by the fifteenth-century raising of [o:] to [u:], with subsequent shortening of the vowel resulting from lack of stress. There is a survival of the old preterite use of *must* in indirect speech, as may be seen by comparing *He said that he must go* (where *must* is a preterite) with *I must go* (where *must* is used in the present tense). Another Old English verb, *āgan* 'to possess', had the preterite *āhte*. The infinitive has given MnE *owe*, which now has the analogical preterite *owed*. The OE preterite *āhte* has given *ought*, which is used with both present and preterite meaning. It cannot be used as an infinitive, and that is the reason why the expression *you didn't ought* is ungrammatical.

There remain a few verbs which do not fit into any of the categories already considered. These are verbs which are used so frequently that they have been able to preserve many of the irregularities which are characteristic of the older stages of the language, whereas verbs of less frequent occurrence are more subject to the influence of analogy. The most important of these irregular verbs is the verb *to be*. One reason for the irregularity of this verb is that several different roots have contributed to the formation of the various parts of the verb. The usual West Saxon form of the first person singular present indicative was *eom*, but the Anglian dialects had *eam* or *am*, and it is from these that MnE *am* is derived. The MnE second person singular *art* and third person singular *is* are regularly developed from OE *eart* and *is*. The plural of the present indicative was *sint* or *sindon* in the West Saxon dialect of Old English, but Anglian, beside these forms, had *aron* and *earon*, and it is from these forms that we get MnE *are*. In strongly stressed positions the *a* was length-ened in Middle English because it occurred in an open syllable of a disyllabic word, and the regular Modern English develop-ment of this form would be [ɛə]. This pronunciation is now obsolete and has been replaced by [ɑ:], which is from the Middle English lightly stressed form with a short vowel. A new lightly stressed [ə] has now come into use. Another root which contributed to the formation of the verb meaning 'to be' was that found in the OE infinitive *bēon* and related forms, of which the most common were: present indicative first person singular *bēo*, second person singular *bist*, third person singular *biþ*, plural *bēoþ*; present subjunctive singular *bēo*, plural *bēon*. The form *be* was used as an indicative until the seventeenth century, but it is no longer used in this way in Standard English. In present-day English *be* is the only form surviving of the infinitive, the sub-junctive singular and plural, and the imperative, and from it have been formed the present participle *being* and the past part-iciple *been*. In the preterite indicative Old English had first person singular *wæs*, second person singular *wære*, third person singular *wæs*, plural *wæron*. These forms have regularly given MnE *was* and *were*. This is the only Modern English preterite which has preserved the old distinction between the singular and the plural, but *was* was often used for *were* colloquially in early Modern English. In the sixteenth century the form *were* of the second person singular preterite indicative was replaced by the new formations *wast* and *wert*; with *t* from the present *art*. *Were* is still used in the singular as a subjunctive and in the plural as both indicative and subjunctive. In strongly stressed positions OE *wære* and *wæron* became [wɛə] in Modern English, and this pronunciation is still occasionally heard; the usual pronuncia-tion [wə:] is developed from the lightly stressed form of the verb.

The remaining irregular verbs are *do*, *go* and *will*. *Do* and its preterite *did* are regularly developed from OE *dōn* and *dyde*. The pronunciation of *don't* is due to the influence of the spelling. In *dost*, *doth*, *does* and *done* shortening of the vowel, no doubt caused by lack of stress, took place after the fifteenth-century raising of [o:] to [u:] but before the sixteenth-century change of [u] to [ʌ]. The ending *-th* in the third person singular present indicative remained in *doth* and *hath* longer than in other verbs; these two forms were common in the eighteenth century.

The Old English verb which has given *go* was *gān*, and it had its preterite *ēode* from a different verb. In Middle English, *ēode* became *ȝede, ȝode,* later *yede, yode,* and these forms were still used by Spenser, although even in the sixteenth century they were felt to be archaisms. The Modern English preterite *went* came to have its present sense in Middle English. In origin it is the preterite of OE *wendan* 'to turn'.

Will and *wilt* are regularly developed from the Old English forms *wille* and *wilt*. The preterite in Old English was *wŏlde,* and in Middle English this gave rise to a strongly stressed *wōlde* and a lightly stressed *wŏlde*. Modern English *would* is derived from the strongly stressed form, in which [o:] became [u:] in the fifteenth century, and the [u:] was shortened after the sixteenth-century change of [u] to [ʌ]. The development of the word is thus parallel to that of *should*. In the present tense, beside forms with *i*, Middle English had *wol(l)e,* with *o* from the preterite and *wul(l)e,* with *u* resulting from the rounding influence of the preceding *w*. The variant with *o* survives in Modern English in the contracted form *won't*.

CHAPTER VII

Syntax

WHEN we examine the syntax of Old English prose, we find that in many ways it resembles the spoken English rather than the written English of the present day. As compared with Modern English, Old English prose is undisciplined. The figure known as *anacoluthon*, which consists of the change of a construction in the middle of a sentence, is common: we find sentences beginning in the third person and continuing in the first person, or beginning with reported speech and changing to direct speech. Another characteristic of Old English syntax is a fondness for clauses linked together by the conjunction *and*, whereas today we prefer conjunctions which show what is the relationship between clauses. The first type of construction, which places clauses side by side, leaving the reader to work out the connexion between them, is known as *parataxis*, while the second type, which subordinates one clause to another, is known as *hypotaxis*. The syntax of Old English is natural in that it reflects the succession of mental images as they occur, whereas Modern English syntax imposes a discipline which makes clear the relation of one idea to the next.

Another change in English syntax has been a tendency to move from the concrete to the abstract, a tendency well illustrated in the history of English prepositions, which originally for the most part indicated relationship of place, but which have come to express a wide variety of abstract relations.

Side by side with this tendency there has been a tendency to attach greater importance to logic in matters of syntax, and the results of this may be seen if we compare the syntax of Chaucer or Shakespeare with that of the present day. A good illustration is provided by our changed attitude to the double negative, the double comparative and the double superlative. In Old and Middle English the idea of negation was often expressed several times in a single sentence. Thus, Chaucer says of the Knight

> He nevere yet no vileynye ne sayde
> In al his lyf unto no maner wight

By a refinement of logic, we have come to believe that two negatives make an affirmative, and the vigour of expression achieved by the piling up of negatives is now reserved for vulgar speech, as in the sentence, *I'll never do nothing no more for none of you, no, never no more*. Similarly, Middle English and Elizabethan writers could make a comparative or a superlative more emphatic by combining two ways of expressing comparison: the addition of suffixes and the use of the separate words *more* and *most*. Thus, Shakespeare could combine *unkindest* and *most unkind* in *This was the most unkindest cut of all*. Modern English, with its preference for logic rather than emphasis, rejects such constructions.

One of the most important changes in English syntax since Old English times has been the growing importance of word-order. Old English had its own rules governing the order of words in a sentence, but so long as the language was highly inflected, word-order was not important for the expression of meaning. Today it is very important. The normal way of indicating that a noun is the subject of a sentence is to place it before the verb, whereas, if the noun is the object, it follows the verb. Hence we find the subjective replacing the historically correct objective in passive constructions of verbs with two objects, one direct and the other indirect. The oldest form of this construction was of the type *A book was given (to) him*. When it was thought necessary to emphasize the importance of the indirect object, it was placed first: *Him was given a book*. This was felt to be contrary to the usual pattern of English sentences and so the objective pronoun was replaced by the subjective, and we thus get the usual Modern English idiom: *He was given a book*.

One way in which word-order has been made to compensate for the loss of inflexional endings is in the use of an indirect object without a preposition. When a preposition is used, the indirect object follows the direct object and the preposition makes it clear which is which, as in *He gave a book to the man*. If no preposition is used, the indirect object is placed between the verb and the direct object, as in *He gave the man a book*.

Many books on English usage contain examples of sentences where a ludicrous effect has resulted from a failure to pay attention to word-order. All that is necessary to avoid such awkward sentences is to place adjectival and adverbial phrases as near as possible to the word which they qualify. The adverb *only* should modify the clause or phrase which immediately follows, it, but, in the words of Mr G. H. Vallins, '*only* always tends to slip in as near as possible to the main verb',[1] and we thus have a conflict between the word-order of the precisian and that of colloquial usage. The precisian would say *He died only a week ago*, whereas in ordinary usage most people would say *He only died a week ago*.

English syntax has been influenced a good deal by that of foreign languages, chiefly Latin and French. Foreign influence on syntax is less easy to trace than foreign influence on vocabulary, because it is always possible that a construction has developed independently in the two languages in question, but Latin influence certainly reinforced, if it did not introduce, such syntactic features as the absolute construction and the accusative with the infinitive. The first of these constructions is found in Old English, where a participle and a noun or pronoun joined with it are put in the dative when used absolutely. It is used freely by Milton, and survives in present-day English in such expressions as *weather permitting*. The accusative with the infinitive was commonly used in Old English after certain verbs, such as *hātan* 'to command' and *hīeran* 'to hear', but in later English the number of verbs after which it could be used was greatly extended, and it is now quite a common construction, as in *I know him to be a good man*.

The influence of Latin upon English syntax has been increased by the prominent place accorded to Latin in the English educational system. Until recent years the grammarians who formulated the rules of 'good' English had been trained in the study of Latin syntax and, consciously or unconsciously, they sought to make English sentences conform to the pattern of

[1] *Good English*, The Language Library, p. 39.

Latin sentences. Similar influences were at work on many English authors who, until about the end of the seventeenth century, generally held the view that Latin was a more respectable language than English. Thus we find that Dryden in the first edition of his *Essay of Dramatic Poesy* had many sentences ending with prepositions, but in later editions he revised these sentences, altering, for example, *the age I live in* to *the age in which I live*. The first version represents natural English syntax and is an idiom of long standing in the language; the revised form is the result of applying the rules of Latin syntax to English, and, perhaps, of remembering the etymological meaning of the word 'preposition'. It may be noted that many people are indirectly influenced by the rules of Latin syntax without realizing the ultimate source of that influence.

The influence of French syntax is perhaps to be seen in the word-order of Middle and Modern English, which is more fixed than that of Old English. The Old English method of forming the comparative and superlative of adjectives was by the addition of suffixes which have today given *-er* and *-est*. This method of comparison is now used only for short words which are felt to be well-established in the language. Long adjectives and those which are obviously loan-words are compared by coupling with them the words *more* and *most*, a construction which is probably imitated from the French use of *plus* and *le plus*. Thus, we say *fair, fairer, fairest*, but *beautiful, more beautiful, most beautiful*, and *naive, more naive, most naive*. A minor instance of the influence of French syntax is in the position of adjectives. The normal position of an adjective in English is immediately before its noun, but some phrases of French origin have the adjective following the noun, as in *court martial, letters patent, malice prepense* and the English adaptation of the last phrase, *malice aforethought*.

Although English has lost many of its inflexional endings, those that remain sometimes cause trouble. It is one of the fundamental rules of the syntax of English, as of many other languages, that a finite verb should agree with its subject in number, but in all periods of English we find examples of false concord, as the lack of agreement is called. Sometimes the false concord is the result of uncertainty about what is the subject of the verb. A moment's thought is generally enough to remove this uncertainty, but most of us speak, and sometimes even write, at a speed that does not allow time for much thought. When a verb agrees with a noun that is not its subject, the verb is said to have been 'attracted' to the noun. Another kind of attraction is illustrated by the expression *these kind of people*, which has not yet gained universal acceptance, although phrases of similar type have been used in English for some centuries. In *King Lear*, for example, we find 'these kind of knaves' (II. ii. 104).

In Early English false concord is often the result of excessive distance between the subject and the predicate, resulting from the insertion of a long adjectival or adverbial clause. False concord is frequently found when the verb precedes its noun and the sentence is introduced by *there*. In most of the examples of this type of false concord the verb is either *is* or *was*, and it may be well to note that in Middle English and early Modern English these verbal forms were often used in the plural as well as in the singular.

In Modern English collective nouns are a fruitful source of apparently false concord, and endless discussions take place to decide whether such nouns as *committee* or *crowd* should take a singular or a plural verb. It is mere pedantry to say that such nouns must always take a singular verb, and the possibility of using either a plural or a singular verb permits a useful distinction to be made. Collective nouns may be used with a singular verb if we think of the thing represented as a whole but with a plural verb if we are thinking of its members separately. Thus, we should say that a football team *was* victorious, but that the team *were* wearing striped shirts. The construction with a plural verb is found only with such collective nouns as denote living and moving beings; it cannot be used with nouns like *library* or *collection*, which denote inanimate objects, or those like *forest*, which denote fixed objects. Some nouns were originally plural but have now come to be regarded as singular. We therefore say *Phonetics is an interesting subject* and *The news is good*. One editor is said to have insisted that *news* is plural and should therefore take a plural verb. He sent a message to a reporter *Are there any news?* and received the reasonable reply *Not a new*.

Of the Old English cases of nouns, the genitive is the only one that has preserved a distinctive form in Modern English, and the functions that it performs have therefore a special interest. It performed a wider variety of functions in Old English than it does at the present day. It was most commonly used to indicate some sort of relationship between two nouns. The genitive could be possessive, subjective, objective, partitive or descriptive, and a number of verbs and adjectives took the genitive.

In Old English there were several different genitive endings, varying according to the declension. The ending *-es* or *-'s* is the only one that has survived into Modern English, and this has been supplemented by a new construction consisting of the preposition *of* followed by the uninflected form of the noun. The original meaning of *of* was 'from', but when the *of*-phrase is used today, the original meaning of the preposition is not as a rule remembered. Since the Old English period the *of*-phrase has been constantly encroaching on the genitive in *-s*, and in present-day use the latter is almost confined to persons and personified objects and to a few set phrases, such as *at my wit's end*. There is a difference in word-order between the two constructions: the genitive in *-s* usually precedes the noun which governs it, whereas the *of*-phrase follows the governing noun.

Sometimes we find the *of*-phrase used together with the genitive in *-s*, as in *This is a book of my brother's*. There is a similar construction with possessive pronouns, as in *He is a friend of mine, It is no business of theirs*.

Another way of expressing the genitive may be illustrated by the inscription which caused a lot of trouble to the members of the Pickwick Club: *Bil(l) Stumps His Mark*. The *his*-genitive, as it may be called, is found occasionally as early as the Old English period. It was very common in early Modern English, and it is occasionally found even today. It undoubtedly owed some of its currency to the resemblance in pronunciation between the lightly stressed form of *his* and the genitive inflexion *-es*, and many speakers of early Modern English probably regarded the *s*-genitive as a contraction of the *his*-genitive. Other possessive pronouns were used in a similar way without any confusion with the inflexional ending.

The possessive use of the genitive is the one most familiar to-day. The term is used to indicate not only possession in the strict sense, as in *the miser's wealth*, but also close association, as in *the day's work*. When personal pronouns are used possessively, we now generally use the genitive of the personal pronoun as a possessive adjective, as in *my house, his son*, but the construction with *of* is always used when the pronoun is modified by a relative clause, as in *the words of him who came*. More often, in such a construction, we substitute a different pronoun, such as *one* for the singular or *those* for the plural of the personal pronoun. In Early English, before the genitive of the personal pronoun had become a mere possessive adjective, it could be used as the antecedent of a relative clause, as in *into his hands that hates me* (*Henry the Eighth* III. i. 118).

Another kind of genitive is the partitive, used to describe the whole of which only a part is in question, as in *three of the men*. In Modern English an *of*-phrase is used, but in Old English inflected partitive genitives were common, as in *māðma menigeo* 'a large amount of treasure' (*Beowulf* 2143). With the decay of inflexional endings which took place in Middle English, the genitive plural often lost its distinctive form and appeared to stand in apposition to the governing noun. Sometimes in Middle English the two constructions were confused, as in *Oon of the grettest auctour that men rede* (Chaucer's *Nun's Priest's Tale* l. 164). This is a mixture of an *of*-phrase used with the function of a partitive genitive *one of the greatest authors* and the construction with apposition *one the greatest author*.

One special form of the genitive which has grown up during the Modern English period is known as the group genitive. This consists of the addition of the genitive inflexion to the last word of a group of words that can be regarded as expressing a single idea even though it belongs logically to an earlier noun in the group. Thus, we say *somebody else's hat, the King of England's son*, and *the Wife of Bath's Tale*, but in the early manuscripts of the *Canterbury Tales* we find either *the Tale of the Wyf of Bathe* or *the Wyves Tale of Bathe*. The group genitive has come into existence because in Modern English the inflected genitive is generally placed immediately before the governing noun, whereas in Old English the position of the genitive was more variable. The group genitive can be used only when the group of words in question is felt to be a unit with the force of a single word, but this unity of meaning alone would not have led to the departure from strict logic, as may be seen from the fact that the plural inflexion is not added to the last word of a group in the same way. We say *the Queen of England's power* but *the Queens of England*. The recognition of a group genitive in the second half of the sentence makes sense out of apparent nonsense in the old catch sentence: *The son of Pharaoh's daughter was the daughter of Pharaoh's son*.

The decay of inflexional endings has had the result that it is impossible to tell from the form whether a noun is in the subjective or the objective case. Pronouns, however, have often preserved the distinction between one case and another, and in doing so they present problems to speakers of English. One of the most frequently discussed problems is whether to say *It is I* or *It is me*. The latter expression gained ground so quickly that it is now the usual idiom, especially in colloquial speech. In Old English the sentence occurred in the form *Ic hit eom* 'I it am', and this construction survived in early Middle English. In later Middle English the word-order was changed, and in Chaucer we find *It am I*. In English the subject of a sentence generally precedes the verb, and one result of the changed word-order was that *it* was regarded as the subject of the sentence. The verb was then changed from the first person to the third in order to agree with the supposed subject. The sentence thus took the form *It is I*, which it kept for several centuries and which is still regarded by many speakers as the correct form. As early as the sixteenth century we find instances of the replacement of *I* by *me*, which probably arose because the pronoun here follows the verb, and the objective case generally follows the verb. The same tendency has been at work with other pronouns, although many speakers who habitually say *It's me* hesitate before saying *It's him* or *It's us*. The construction *It's me* may be defended by saying that *me*, originally accusative and dative, has in course of time taken on another function: it is now the disjunctive form of the pronoun which may be used in emphatic positions, just as the French *moi* not only may but must be used instead of *je* in the sentence *C'est moi*. Jespersen sums up what is happening to English pronouns: 'On the whole, the natural tendency in English has been towards a state in which the nominative of pronouns is used only where it is clearly the subject, and where this is shown by close proximity to (generally position immediately before) a verb, while the objective is used everywhere else'.[1]

The opposition offered by prescriptive grammarians to the idiom *It's me* has had the result that many speakers have gained the impression that *I* is in some way more respectable than *me*, and they consequently sometimes use *I* after prepositions or as the object of a verb when *me* is grammatically correct. This misuse of *I* is generally confined to sentences in which the pronoun is preceded by *you* or a noun, since these have the same forms for the subjective and the objective, and by separating the preposition or the verb from the pronoun they prevent the speaker from realizing that the objective case is required. The use of *I* for *me* is not a recent development; there are several examples in Elizabethan English, as in *All debts are cleared between you and I*, (*Merchant of Venice* III. ii. 319 f.).

Just as the objective case is generally used after a verb, so there is a tendency to use the subjective before a verb. This is one of the reasons why the pronoun *who* is tending to replace *whom*, and NED states that *whom* is 'no longer current in natural colloquial speech'. This tendency is not a recent development; there are many examples of the use of *who* for *whom* in Shakespeare and other Elizabethan dramatists. As a result of the frequent use of *who* for *whom*, the idea has grown up with many speakers that *whom* is a more correct form than *who*, and some speakers consequently use *whom* in sentences where *who* would be correct. An example is the sentence *I sent for the man whom I knew had done it*. The pronoun *whom* is the subject of *had done* and so should be the subjective *who*. The use of *whom* in such a sentence may be due in part to a confusion with the accusative and infinitive construction, as found in a sentence like *I sent for the man whom I knew to have done it*.

There are many different ways of introducing a relative clause. It is possible to use *who* or *whom* for persons and *which* for animals or things; it is possible to use *that* to refer to any antecedent, alive or inanimate; and it is possible to have no relative pronoun expressed. Thus, one can say *This is the man whom I saw*, *This is the man that I saw*, or *This is the man I saw*. In a famous

[1] *Essentials of English Grammar*, p. 136.

essay 'The Humble Petition of *Who* and *Which*' (part of *Spectator* No. 78) Steele deplored the practice of using the demonstrative pronoun *that* as a relative, and made the pronouns *Who* and *Which* complain: 'We are descended of ancient Families, and kept up our Dignity and Honour many Years, till the Jacksprat *That* supplanted us'. Steele here misrepresents the historical facts, since *that* as a relative pronoun is much older than either *who* or *which*; the fondness which Steele and his contemporaries showed for *who* and *which* was probably due to the influence of Latin syntax. The oldest method of introducing a relative clause in English was by putting the principal and the relative clauses together without any joining word; it is thus misleading to speak of the omission of the relative pronoun in the sentence *This is the man I saw*. The next stage was to use the demonstrative pronoun *sē*, *þæt*, *sēo* as relatives, either alone or together with the indeclinable relative particle *þe*. As early as the ninth century, the neuter demonstrative *þæt* came to be used for all genders in both the singular and the plural, and in early Middle English the masculine *sē* and the feminine *sēo* passed out of use as relatives. The relative particle *þe* also died out in early Middle English, perhaps because it was liable to be confused with the definite article, which had by then acquired the same form. The two texts of Layamon's *Brut* illustrate the trend: there are many passages where the earlier version has *þe* as a relative while the corresponding passage in the later version has *þat*. The use of interrogative pronouns as relatives had its origin in the indefinite pronouns *swā hwā swā* and *swā hwilc swā*, both meaning 'whoever', which were used as relatives. There are instances of the use of *which* and *who* as relatives as early as the twelfth and thirteenth centuries respectively, but it was not until some centuries later that *who* came to be generally accepted as a relative.

One advantage of the use of interrogative pronouns as relatives is that they are inflected. In the nominative we can refer to a human antecedent by either *that* or *who*, but if we wish to use the possessive we must say *whose*, as in *I met a man whose name I did not know*. In order to express the possessive case of the relative, it was once possible to use *that* followed by the appropriate form of the possessive pronoun, as in the sentence quoted by NED (sv.

That sense 9) from Malory: *There came a man that sire Tristram afore hand had slayne his broder* (*Arthur* VIII. xxxv. 327). This rather clumsy construction has now passed out of use, except in dialects.

Some grammarians make a distinction between *that* and *who* or *which* according to the nature of the relative clause. Relative clauses are of two kinds: defining and non-defining. A defining clause helps to limit or define the antecedent, which without the relative clause would either have a different sense or would make no sense at all; a non-defining clause parenthetically gives additional information about a clause that is already sufficiently defined. An example of the first type of clause is 'This is the house *that Jack built*'; an example of the second is 'My brother, *who lives in the country*, enjoys good health'. Those who make a distinction between *that* and *who* or *which* often use *that* for defining clauses and *who* or *which* for non-defining clauses. The advantages of *who* and *which* in distinguishing between persons and things, in having a possessive *whose*, and in being suitable for use after prepositions, have led to the frequent use of these pronouns even in defining clauses, and the usual way of distinguishing between a defining and a non-defining clause is by inserting a pause in speech or a comma in writing before the latter type of clause but not before the former.

Since the relative pronoun *that* is indeclinable, its agreement with its antecedent is somewhat obscured, but the agreement can often be inferred from the form of the verb in the relative clause, as in the sentence *These are the books that have influenced me.* Sometimes the form of a verb shows that a speaker has chosen the wrong antecedent, as in the sentence *It is one of the best books that has ever been written on the subject.* The antecedent should be *books* but the singular verb *has* shows that the speaker imagines it to be *one*. A similar kind of attraction is found as early as the Old English period, as in ðās lēasan spell lǣrað gehwylcne monn ðāra ðe wilnað helle ðīostro tō flīonne . . . 'these false stories teach everyone of those who wishes to flee from the darkness of Hell . . .'

Some of the most important differences between the syntax of Old English and that of Modern English are in the use of impersonal verbs. One change has been a reduction in the number of impersonal verbs. These are verbs which are used only in the third person singular and which state in the most general way that an action is taking place or that a state of things is in existence. The impersonal verbs which have survived are chiefly those describing the weather, such as *it is raining* or *it thunders*, and expressions formed with the verb *to be*, such as *it is time for me to go*. Impersonal verbs may be used either alone or accompanied by a noun or pronoun indicating the person or thing affected. In Old English, impersonal verbs which took an oblique case often had no subject expressed, as in *mē þyncþ* 'it seems to me', but in Middle English the use of the pronoun *it* became general with all impersonal verbs. The old construction without *it* survived in *methinks* and *meseems*, both of which mean 'it seems to me', and in *if you please*. Historically *you* is not the subject of *please* but its object (cf. Latin *si vobis placet*, French *s'il vous plaît*), and *please* has no final *s* because it was originally subjunctive. Now that the pronoun *you* has to serve as both subjective and objective, it is regarded as the subject of *please*. Evidence of this may be found in parallel expressions with other pronouns where the subjective and the objective are not identical in form. Thus we say *if I please* and *if they please*.

Perhaps the most common instance of an impersonal verb without an expressed subject in Modern English is the expression *as follows*, used to introduce a list of things. Since impersonal verbs are not now very common, many people do not recognize that *follows* is here used impersonally and consequently alter it to *follow*.

The reasons why many impersonal verbs have become personal during the course of the history of the English language are partly psychological and partly linguistic. The psychological cause was a growing realization that what happens to us is to a large extent the result of our own actions. The frequent impersonal constructions in Old English are in keeping with a belief in the subordinate nature of purely human actions which caused the hero of the Old English poem *Beowulf* to describe in a strikingly detached way his slaying of a sea-monster; *heaþorǣs fornam mihtig meredēor þurh mīne hand* 'the onrush of battle destroyed the mighty sea-beast by means of my hand' (*Beowulf* 557 f.). The linguistic cause of the change from impersonal to personal constructions was the decay of the inflexional ending of the dative case of nouns. As a result of this decay, the subjective and objective cases of nouns and some pronouns became identical in form. What had previously been the object of an impersonal verb could then easily be regarded as the subject of a personal one. Once the change from impersonal to personal use was established, it spread to pronouns which have preserved the distinction between the subjective and the objective. Hence *it likes me* has become *I like*.

The inflexional system of the Indo-European verb was extremely complicated. Some idea of its extent may be gained from a language like Greek, which has preserved a very elaborate system of verbal inflexions, whereas in Old English the verbal system had been very considerably simplified. The history of the English verb is concerned very largely with the development of new devices, especially auxiliary verbs, to express shades of meaning which in many other Indo-European languages are expressed by the use of inflexional endings. In highly inflected languages there are different verbal forms for the first, second and third persons and for the singular and plural numbers. In English most of these distinctions have disappeared without any loss of efficiency, since the person and number are indicated with sufficient clarity by the subject, whether noun or pronoun. There are, however, other things that we need to know about a verb, and many of these cannot be inferred from its context. One of these things is its tense. The simplest division of tenses is into past, present and future, but the number of necessary tenses is more than three. We may wish to describe a past, present or future state resulting from a completed action, and so we get the tenses known respectively as pluperfect, perfect and future perfect. Again, in a complex sentence we may wish to describe the time of the event mentioned in the subordinate clause in relation to the tense of the principal verb. We thus get tenses such as the secondary future and the secondary future perfect, which describe respectively an action and the completion of an action which was in prospect at some point in the past. The ordinary future and future perfect are illustrated by the sentences *He says that he will go* and *He says that he will have gone before noon*. The secondary future and future perfect are illustrated by *He said that he would go* and *He said that he would have gone before noon*.

We are interested not only in the tense of a verb but also in what are called verbal aspects. The aspect of a verb indicates what sort of action it describes. One important distinction is whether the action is thought of as instantaneous, as in *he killed the man*, or continuing, as in *he was saying*. Other aspects call attention not to an act as a whole but to only one point, either the beginning, as in *she burst out laughing*, or the conclusion, as in *she stopped crying*. Another aspect is the iterative, which indicates a succession of similar acts, as in *he keeps getting annoyed*. In some verbs the aspect is implicit in the meaning of the verb, as in *to frequent* or *to work*, but in many verbs the aspect is expressed by means of adverbs or auxiliary verbs.

Already in Old English we find the beginnings of several of the devices by which our verbal system has been enriched. The most common method of enrichment has been by the use of auxiliary verbs, but other devices have sometimes been used. For example, in Old English the pluperfect was expressed by the simple preterite accompanied by the adverb *ǣr* 'formerly'. One of the most important developments in the history of the English verb has been a great extension in the use of expanded forms of the verb. These are forms made up of some part of the verb *to be* followed by the present participle, and they are sometimes called progressive because their chief function is to indicate that an action is, was, or will be in progress. Already in Old English we occasionally find expanded forms such as *hīe feohtende wǣron* 'they were fighting', but they became much more common during the Middle English period. It is not until the time of Chaucer that we find an expanded perfect of the type *we have been waiting*. One reason for the increased frequency of expanded tenses during the Middle English period was that the present participle came to be identical in form with the verbal noun, and the expanded verbal forms were reinforced by the construction *on* (later *a*) followed by the verbal noun, as in *he rode a-hunting*.

A later development was the extension of expanded verbal forms to the passive. The verbal noun in Early English often had passive significance, as in *the house is (a)-building*, but from the closing years of the eighteenth century we find the expanded passive of the type *the house is being built*. In the course of the nineteenth century this passive construction met with a good deal of opposition from grammarians and we still avoid using it with any parts of the verb *to be* other than the simple present or past tense.

The wide variety of forms of the English verb may be illustrated in two ways. One way is to begin with a grammatical concept and show in how many different ways the concept may be expressed. The other way is to choose one verb and show how varied are its uses. The different ways of expressing the future tense will serve to illustrate the first method of approach; the uses of the verb *to do* will illustrate the second.

In Old English there was no separate tense to describe future happenings; the present tense had to serve for both present and future. We can still use the present tense in this way, although we now have many other ways of expressing the future. When the present tense is used for the future, the sentence generally contains some indication of time which prevents ambiguity, as in *I start for London tomorrow*. The expanded form of the present, as well as the simple form, is sometimes used for the future, as in *He is going home next week*.

The usual way of expressing future time is by means of the auxiliary verbs *shall* and *will*. The distinction between these verbs in present-day English is full of complications, and observance of the very elaborate rules has unfortunately sometimes been regarded as a shibboleth, as when NED says 'to use *will* in these cases is now a mark of Scottish, Irish, provincial, or extra-British idiom'. Already in Old English we find *willan* and *sculan* used as auxiliaries in contexts where they can be regarded as simply indicating the future, but in Old English there is usually some idea of volition in *willan* and of obligation in *sculan*. In present-day English the broad distinction between *shall* and *will* is that we use *shall* in the first person and *will* in the second and third persons to express the simple future, and we reverse the process in order to express the emphatic future. In colloquial use the auxiliary *will* is tending to replace *shall*. Confusion between the two verbs in colloquial use has been helped by the frequent reduction of both verbs to *'ll*, as in *I'll go*.[1]

---

[1] For a full discussion of the use of *shall* and *will* see H. W. and F. G. Fowler, *The King's English* pp. 133-154, and Charles C. Fries 'The Periphrastic Future with *Shall* and *Will* in Modern English' in PMLA 40 (1925) 963-1024.

Another way of expressing the future, which is especially common in colloquial use, is by the use of *going to*, as in *I'm going to send for it tomorrow*. A more literary idiom is *to be about to*. Another way is by the use of the infinitive after some part of the verb *to be*, as in *He is to go to Leeds tomorrow*. These methods of expressing the future often carry with them some other shade of meaning beside simply futurity. For example, *He is to go* carries with it a hint of compulsion or inevitability. In the 'block language' of newspaper headlines a special development of this construction is found: the use of a noun followed by an infinitive without the verb *to be*, as in *Film Star to Wed*.

The large number of different syntactic functions that can be performed by a single verb is illustrated by the history of the verb *to do*. In Middle English *do* followed by the infinitive generally meant 'to cause', and thus it made up for the loss of many Old English causative verbs.

Another use of *do* followed by an infinitive is as a periphrastic form of the present or past tense. This use may have arisen out of the causative use. The periphrastic construction with *do* was rare in Old English, but became common during the fourteenth century, and was at its height during the sixteenth and seventeenth centuries. In Shakespeare there often seems to be no distinction in meaning between the simple past tense and *did* followed by the infinitive.

During the Modern English period the auxiliary *do* has come to be used in a number of specialized functions. One of these is to add emphasis to a statement, as in *I do like apples*. A similar use of *do* is to strengthen an imperative, and in this construction *do* can be used with the verb *to be*, as in *Do be quiet!*

Another use of *do* is in negative statements. The construction with *do* is normal with all full verbs, but not with auxiliaries. Thus we say *I do not know* but *I will not agree to it*.

Another use of *do* is in questions, where it helps to reconcile two conflicting tendencies. The general tendency in English sentences is to put the subject before the verb, but in questions the verb generally precedes its subject. A convenient way of reconciling these two contradictory requirements when one is asking a question is to begin the question with an auxiliary verb and to place the subject between the auxiliary and the main verb. When the sentence does not contain an auxiliary verb, one is provided by the use of *do*. Hence we say *Have you heard it?* and *Do you hear it?*

Another important use of *do*, found as early as the Old English period, is as a substitute for a verb that has been mentioned previously. Sometimes *so* is added when the verb *do* is used in this way. Examples are *I hoped to come but I was not able to do so* and *He promised to come but he didn't*.

In poetry archaic constructions are often used, and we therefore find constructions like *he cometh not* and *Stands the Church clock at ten to three?* corresponding to which prose would have constructions with *do*.

Auxiliary verbs can often be used to meet the needs of courtesy or diffidence. The simple imperative has long been avoided in English except in rather special environments such as the schoolroom or the drillyard. Even the addition of *please* often seems inadequate to tone down the brusqueness of a command. We generally substitute a request for the imperative, and there is a wide variety of different expressions available, such as *will you, would you mind, I wonder if you would, perhaps you will*, or, in extreme cases, *I suppose that there wouldn't by any chance be such a thing as a cup of coffee*, pronounced with appealing intonation.

One function that has been in very large measure taken over by auxiliary verbs in Modern English is that of expressing the subjunctive mood. The term 'subjunctive', in its etymological sense, would describe the form of a verb used in a subordinate clause, but this description has never been wholly appropriate as far as English is concerned. Even in Old English the indicative was often used beside the subjunctive in subordinate clauses, and, on the other hand, the subjunctive was often used in principal clauses to express a wish, as in *Ābrēoðe his onginn!* 'May his enterprise come to naught!' The underlying principle which determined the use of the subjunctive in subordinate clauses in Old English was that the subjunctive was required in all dependent statements which do not express a fact. In Modern English the subjunctive is used only in certain types of clause and in some stereotyped expressions.

In Old English the subjunctive was expressed by distinctive inflexional endings, and one reason for the loss of distinctively subjunctive forms has been the decay of many of these endings. Some subjunctive forms survive occasionally today in formal or literary use, as in *lest he misunderstand me*. The only survivals of subjunctive forms in common colloquial use today are *be* and *were*, and even these are often replaced by indicatives. It does not follow that, apart from these forms, the subjunctive is extinct in English. It is true that we use the indicative today in many sentences where the subjunctive would have been used in Old English, but there are many others in which we express the subjunctive mood by the use of auxiliaries, such as *may, might, would,* and *should.* When *should* is used as an auxiliary to express the subjunctive, it loses its preterite meaning and may refer to present or future time, as in *if he should come*.

The subjunctive is still used in simple sentences and in principal clauses to express a wish, but the form without auxiliary is used only in a few fixed phrases, such as *God bless you!* The more usual way of expressing a wish is by the use of the auxiliary *may,* as in *May he prosper!* In clauses introduced by *as if* and *as though* we still use the subjunctive form *were,* and after *lest* we use the subjunctive, either in its simplest form, *lest he fall,* or made up of an auxiliary and the infinitive, *lest he should fall.* One use of the subjunctive that is still very common is in the formal language of notices and regulations after verbs of commanding or requesting: *It is requested that a stamped addressed envelope be* (or *should be*) *enclosed with all applications.*

The infinitive is a verbal noun, and in Old English it had some of the inflexions of a noun. The nominative and accusative ended in *-an*; the dative, which was always preceded by the preposition *tō,* ended in *-enne.* With the decay of inflexional endings in Middle English and early Modern English, the two forms of the infinitive became identical, and the infinitive with *to* has taken over many of the functions of the old nominative infinitive, with the result that the infinitive with *to* is now much more common than the bare infinitive. This development was no doubt aided by the need felt by speakers for some distinctive mark of the infinitive, to replace the mark which had been provided in Old English by the inflexional ending. The preposition *to,* when used with the infinitive, still sometimes has its old function of indicating purpose, as in *I have come to see you,* but more often it is felt to be merely the sign of the infinitive. The simple infinitive without *to* is still used, chiefly after auxiliary verbs, as in *He will come*, beside *He is going to come*. We are so accustomed to thinking of *to* as a part of the infinitive that a prejudice has grown up against separating the preposition from the verb. The 'split infinitive' is one of the best-known English grammatical solecisms, and one whose importance is often exaggerated. The construction consists in the separation of the word *to* from an infinitive by the insertion of some word or words, as in *to really know*. In present-day usage the inserted words are always adverbs or adverbial phrases, but in the oldest examples, which are recorded from the fourteenth century, it is the object of the infinitive that is so used. Thus, in *Sir Gawain and the Green Knight*, v. 1540 we have *to trwluf expoun* 'to expound true love'. The term 'split infinitive' is not altogether a happy one because, as Jespersen has pointed out,[1] *to* is not an essential part of the infinitive. There is no historical reason why *to* should immediately precede the infinitive of which it is a sign, though it is naturally desirable that the two words should not be very far apart. One advantage of a split infinitive is that the construction makes it perfectly clear which word is qualified by the adverb, whereas a refusal to split an infinitive sometimes leads to ambiguity. One may say that splitting an infinitive is not the deadly sin that it is sometimes represented to be, but that it is not often necessary.

One construction which has become common in recent years is the use of *to* by ellipsis to stand for an infinitive clause whicn has already been expressed either by the speaker or by someone else. In reply to the question *Are you going to the theatre tomorrow?* one could reply *I intend to*. In Elizabethan English the preposition *to* in such a context would generally be followed by the pronoun *it*, as in *But shall we dance, if they desire us to't?* (*Love's Labour's Lost* V. ii. 145).

One use of the infinitive with *to* that has grown in popularity is to replace a subordinate clause. The older type of subordinate clause was introduced by *that* and contained a subject and a finite verb. This type of clause can still be used, but the infinitive

[1] *Growth and Structure of the English Language*, p. 191.

is a more concise form of expression which may be used when the subject of the infinitive is either the subject or the object of the principal verb, as in *I am anxious to go* and *I persuaded him to go.* In the fourteenth century this construction began to be extended to sentences in which there was no noun or pronoun in the principal clause which could serve as a subject for the infinitive. In such sentences the preposition *for* was used as an indication of the change in subject, as in *I am eager for him to go.* A different use of *for* with the infinitive is found as early as the thirteenth century; the use of *for* as well as *to* before the infinitive in order to indicate purpose, as in *forr uss to clennsenn* in *The Ormulum* v. 1384. Later the idea of purpose was weakened, and *for to* was used, like *to*, as a mere sign of the infinitive. It was very common in the sixteenth century and was much used by unskilful poets in search of an extra syllable. Today it is regarded as a vulgarism.

Although in Old English the infinitive was a noun, in course of time it has come to have some of the properties of a verb: a passive as well as an active voice and a perfect as well as a present tense. The Old English infinitive could be used in either an active or a passive sense, and the active infinitive with passive meaning is found today in sentences such as *I am to blame* and *This house is to let.* In the Middle English period the infinitive with passive function gradually acquired passive form, and was expressed by the verb *to be* followed by a past participle. This construction too is frequently found today, as in *This house is to be sold.*

The development of a perfect form of the infinitive followed soon after the development of a perfect tense. It took the form of the infinitive *have* followed by a past participle. In the earliest examples the *have* is not preceded by *to*, but at the present day *to* is regularly used. The normal use of the perfect infinitive is to describe events that are past in relation to the time of the principal verb. Thus, we say *I was glad to have escaped* but *I was glad to see you there.* A fairly common construction, but one which cannot be regarded as good English usage, is the use of the perfect infinitive to express time contemporaneous with that of the principal verb, as in the sentence *I should have liked to have gone.* Since there is no future tense of the infinitive in English, the present infinitive is used to indicate time either contemporaneous or in the future with reference to that of the principal verb.

CHAPTER VIII

Semantics

FOR most of those who speak and write English the study of meaning, or semantics as it is sometimes called, is undoubtedly the most important branch of the subject, yet it is a branch which until recent years has been badly neglected. This neglect of semantics has had its effect on some Modern English translations of Old English poetry. For example, the Old English poem *Beowulf* contains the line:

> flota fāmi-heals fugle gelīcost. (l. 218)

William Morris's translation of this line is:

> the foamy-neck'd floater most like to a fowl.

This translation illustrates the unfortunate results which follow when one branch of study is developed while another branch is neglected. A knowledge of etymology and phonology shows that *fowl* is derived from OE *fugol*, but to use *fowl* as a translation of *fugol* is to ignore the development that has taken place in the meaning of the word. OE *fugol* meant 'bird', but the word *fowl* is now generally restricted to domestic birds which can be used for food, and to use *fowl* as a translation of *fugol* is to ignore the semantic development of the word.

Although the neglect of semantics is to be regretted, it is easy to see how it came about. It is much less easy to discern general principles at work in semantics than in phonology. The best way to study semantics is to examine the meaning of particular words in their contexts, and it is no accident that the increased interest in semantics in recent years has been accompanied by an increased interest in practical criticism, the detailed study of a short passage of prose or verse. All careful readers, whenever they lived, have been students of semantics, even though many of them may never have heard the word.

The aim of the present chapter is to see how far general

principles can be discerned in the development of meaning of English words and what are the chief kinds of semantic change. If such general principles can be seen at work, the history of one word may throw light on the history of others.

When we give a name to an object we select one of its many characteristics which we choose to regard as the significant one. Semantic change takes place because the various people who use that name do not agree about which characteristic is the significant one, and the same speaker may have different characteristics of a given object in mind on different occasions. For example, when he refers to a book, he may be thinking of the physical shape of a particular volume or the contents or the ideas expressed in the book.

In learning the meanings of words we very rarely seek for a precise definition, and there are many words in everyday use the approximate meanings of which most people understand although they would have difficulty in framing a satisfactory definition. Most of us acquire our knowledge of the meanings of words from the contexts in which the words occur, and misunderstanding is probably a good deal more common than we realize. Most of us can probably remember instances of such misunderstanding, especially among children. One such instance is that of an Englishman, living in the Sudan with his family, who used to take his small son for a daily walk to see the statue of General Gordon sitting on the back of a camel which is one of the sights of Khartoum. When the Englishman had to leave Khartoum, he suggested to his son that they should go and say goodbye to Gordon. The boy enthusiastically agreed, and as they were leaving the statue for the last time he was struck by a thought that had not occurred to him before: 'Daddy, who is that funny man on Gordon's back?' The story affords a good illustration of the working of one type of semantic change, since father and son were habitually using the same word with different meanings, and it was only by accident that the transfer of meaning was disclosed.

The usual safeguard against misunderstanding of meaning is that we meet most words in many different contexts, and the number of possible meanings of a word is thus narrowed down to one which will fit all the contexts in which we have met the word. The dangers of relying on a single context are too obvious to need stressing, and may be illustrated by the schoolboy's definition of an adage as 'a kind of cage in which cats were once cruelly kept'.[1] Context is of the greatest importance for the understanding of meaning, as may be seen by glancing at a large dictionary. For example, NED records more than two hundred main senses of the word *set* as noun or verb, most of them in current use, and many of these main senses are sub-divided. In view of the complexity of the English language and the haphazard way in which most of us acquire a knowledge of the meaning of words, the surprising thing is that we manage as well as we do.

The meaning of a word may be changed as a result of its repeated use in a particular kind of context. In addition to its central meaning it acquires additional shades of meaning which may lead to confusion if the word is used carelessly or un-scrupulously. A barrister may ask a witness if he 'admits' that a statement is true. If there is nothing discreditable about the statement and if the witness has made no attempt at conceal-ment, the use of the word 'admit' is inappropriate; it subtly puts the witness in the wrong.

The most obvious help given by context to the understanding of the meaning of a word is in its identification. The English language contains a fairly large number of homophones, words that are pronounced alike but that are of quite different mean-ing and origin, like *bear* as a noun and a verb and *bare* as an adjective, and some writers on language, notably Robert Bridges, have seen in these homophones a real threat to the efficiency of the language as a means of expression. Yet homo-phones present little real ambiguity because the context generally makes it immediately clear which word is intended. Anyone who fails to understand the meaning of the sentence 'The Englishwoman is proud of the reputation for cooking she bears' is just being perverse. But the help offered by context goes further than this. It can make it clear that specialization of meaning has taken place, as in the sentence *He began life as a bank clerk*, where *life* clearly means 'working life'. Very often

[1] See *Macbeth* I. vii. 45.

an implied contrast will make clear which sense of a word is intended, as, for example, man as opposed to woman or man as opposed to God. Further, the context can reveal whether a word is used with emotive value. There is a clear difference between the meaning attached to the word *rose* in a text-book of botany and its meaning in a poem like Edmund Waller's 'Go, lovely rose!'

The emotive values of words form an important branch of the study of semantics. Emotive values may be defined as those which are concerned with the expression of feeling as distinct from purely intellectual meaning. Because words with emotive values may be used deliberately or unconsciously to distort the truth, it is particularly important to be conscious of their true nature. Two convenient and self-explanatory terms that have been used to describe words of this kind are *purr-words* and *snarl-words*. To describe any important idea it is usually an easy matter to find both purr-words and snarl-words, but it is not always easy to find words that are completely free from emotive value. For example, *valiant* and *frugal* are purr-words while *foolhardy* and *niggardly* are snarl-words.

The emotive values of words cause difficulty to foreigners learning a language, because dictionaries do not as a rule give any warning of their nature. When a foreigner says 'Poor small boy!' instead of 'Poor little boy', he is speaking unidiomatically because the word *small* is not emotive enough. The converse mistake is more common, as in an advertisement of a tourist agency which quoted different rates for 'collective travelling' and 'lonely travellers'. The word *lonely* is unsuitable because it has emotive associations that are not present in the word *alone*.

The emotive content of words has always to be taken into account in the discussion of development of meaning because it does not remain constant. The emotive content of a word, like its intellectual content, may change because a speaker and his hearers use the word differently. It may change as the result of some particular event which can be dated. For example, *appeasement* became a snarl-word in 1938 as a result of the Munich Agreement.

The emotive content of words is one of the reasons why there are so few exact synonyms in any language. A book like Roget's

Thesaurus lists large numbers of words which can be loosely described as synonymous with each other, but a glance at such a list makes it clear that most of the words are not exact synonyms in the sense that they can replace each other in any given context without causing any change in intellectual or emotive meaning; they are partial synonyms which can replace each other in some contexts but not in others. There are, of course, other reasons beside the emotive content why exact synonyms are rare, chief of which is the vagueness of the sense of many words, especially those which refer to abstract ideas. Another reason is that some words, especially loan-words, are thought of as more respectable and 'literary' than others, and are thus preferred by some people and shunned by others for the same reason. NED defines *commence* as precisely equivalent to the native *begin*, but the test of substituting one word for the other in various contexts shows that the two words are not precisely equivalent. Anyone who said 'It's commencing to rain' would be understood, but most hearers would feel that the remark was not idiomatic English. Touchstone shows himself to have a good command of synonyms and near-synonyms when he says to William, 'Therefore, you clown, abandon,—which is in the vulgar leave,—the society,—which in the boorish is company,— of this female,—which in the common is woman; which together is, abandon the society of this female, or, clown, thou perishest; or, to thy better understanding, diest; or, to wit, I kill thee, make thee away, translate thy life into death, thy liberty into bondage' (*As You Like It* V. i. 45–53). The status of words can change as much as the meaning, as may be seen by comparing *female* and *woman*. Few people today would share Touchstone's opinion that *female* is the more courteous word, although *woman* is sometimes avoided as vulgar, as by the woman who attended the out-patients' department of a hospital suffering from the effects of a bite which puzzled the doctor until the patient admitted that it had been caused by 'another lidy'.

Legal documents contain large numbers of synonyms and near-synonyms. The original reason for their inclusion was a laudable desire to make sure that nothing was accidentally excluded, but their use can become a mannerism, and the various categories described in a legal document often seem to overlap if they do not coincide with each other. It is an interesting exercise in the study of near-synonyms to decide the exact meanings of the words quoted rather ruefully by a struggling clergyman from the sentence pronounced on an offending vicar: 'That he by law be deprived of all the profits, glebes, fruits, tithes, rents, salaries, dues, rates and emoluments'.

The existence of synonyms may be regarded as one aspect of multiple meaning: synonymy describes the state of things where we have several names corresponding to a single sense. Another aspect of multiple meaning is the converse of synonymy and is called polysemy: the existence of several senses corresponding to a single name. Semantic change leads to the growth of polysemy because, when a change of meaning takes place, the word in question often keeps its original sense side by side with the new sense. The growth of polysemy may be assisted by ellipsis. For example, the noun *glass* may be used to form compound words to describe various objects made of glass, such as *eye-glass* or *drinking-glass*, and then by ellipsis the first element of the compound may be omitted and *glass* used to describe any object made of glass. The full compound may be used when there is any danger of ambiguity.

We often find semantic changes proceeding along similar lines in different words. These may be regarded as parallel developments resulting from the fundamental likeness of human beings or from similarity of circumstances, or they may be due to semantic borrowing. Thus *calling* and *vocation* are both used in the sense of 'occupation' and they are both derived from words meaning 'to call, summon'.

One result of semantic change is that a knowledge of etymology is often necessary to enable us to understand the sense in which a word is used by an older English author. The Book of Common Prayer (1662) contains such petitions as 'Prevent us, O Lord, in all our doings with thy most gracious favour', where *prevent* (Latin *praeventus*, pp. of *praevenire*) is used in the etymological sense of 'go before'. In *A Midsummer Night's Dream* (II. i. 92) Titania speaks of rivers which 'have overborne their continents'. This use of *continents* is not current today, but it is a natural development of the etymology: 'things which contain or hold in', hence 'banks'.

Words differ in the extent to which they are liable to undergo semantic change. There are many classes of words, such as prepositions, conjunctions, articles, pronouns, and auxiliary verbs, whose chief function at the present day is to describe the relations which exist between other words. From the synchronic point of view these 'empty' words have little independent meaning, but are in the same category as syntactic processes such as word-order and the use of inflexional endings. From the historical point of view, however, we can speak about their semantic development, since many of them are derived from full words, and even words whose sole function is to describe the relations between other words may develop in meaning to describe different kinds of relationship. Most English prepositions have a bewildering variety of meanings, most of which can be traced back to relationship in space. For example, the preposition *for* originally meant 'in front of'. A person or thing standing in front of anyone may be either a support or an obstacle, and so we have two distinct groups of derived meanings. The larger group, derived from the idea of support, includes such meanings as 'in support of', 'instead of', and 'because of'; from the ideas of obstruction or opposition we get the meaning 'in spite of, notwithstanding', as in Burns's line 'A man's a man for a' that'.

Most kinds of semantic change are examples of linguistic innovation, but there is one type of change of meaning which results from linguistic conservatism. This takes place when a word retains its original form but its meaning changes because the object which it describes has changed. The change is of two kinds: the object itself may change or our knowledge of the object may grow. The first kind of change may be illustrated by *pen* and *paper*. The word *pen* originally meant 'feather' (Latin *penna* 'wing, feather') and it was first used when the normal type of pen was a quill pen. *Paper* is ultimately from Greek *papyrus*, but the word has continued in use when paper is made from a large number of other materials. Changes of meaning resulting from changes in our knowledge of the object described are frequently to be found in the history of science. Thus, *electric* originally meant 'pertaining to amber' (Greek ἤλεκτρον 'amber') because it was when amber was rubbed that the effects of electricity were first observed. Similarly *oxygen* is from French *oxygène* 'acidifying principle', from a derivative of Greek ὀξύς sharp', because oxygen was at one time thought to be essential to the formation of acids. Again *atom* meant originally 'a body too small to be divided', and was borrowed, through Latin and French, from Greek ἄτομος, 'indivisible'. The word has survived into an age when the etymological meaning of the word is unfortunately no longer applicable.

This aspect of semantics is closely bound up with social history. *Window* is a word whose etymology arouses both our respect and our sympathy for the Scandinavians who coined the word (ON *vindauga* 'wind-eye') and brought it to England: respect for the poetic ingenuity which saw the resemblance between a window and the human eye, and sympathy for the housing conditions of those for whom a window was simply a hole for the wind to blow through.

A glance at any large dictionary will show that many of the most common words in a language have several very different meanings all current at the same time. It is often possible to explain this wide diversity by showing that the different senses are all developments of one central idea. This process is known as *radiation*, because the simplest meaning may be regarded as standing at the centre while the derived meanings proceed from it in every direction like rays. Thus *head* has many different senses illustrated in such phrases as *the head of a school, sixpence per head, the head of a page, to come to a head, to lose one's head, six head of cattle*. These senses have little in common, but they all derive from special applications of the central idea of *head* as a part of the body. The principle of radiation is simple, but it can be complicated in various ways. There are not many words whose central idea is so easy to discern as it is in the example quoted, and it is an oversimplification to regard all words as having had one primary meaning from which their other meanings may be derived. The central meaning from which secondary meanings have radiated may become obsolete, and each of the secondary meanings may become a centre of further radiations.

This last possibility leads to a process to which has been given the name *concatenation* 'linking together' (from Latin *catēna* 'chain'), an adaptation of the French term *enchaînement*. The successive changes in meaning are like the links of a chain. Each stage in the development can be seen to belong to one of the recognized types of semantic change, but the final meaning may differ very considerably from the original one. The development of meaning of *cardinal* will serve as an example. The word is from French *cardinal*, which is from Latin *cardinālis*, an adjective from *cardo* 'a hinge'. As often in loan-words, the earliest stages of the semantic development of the word took place before its introduction into English. The stages are:

(*a*) pertaining to a hinge.

(*b*) hingeing, of fundamental importance, as in 'cardinal virtues' and 'cardinal points of the compass'.

(*c*) (as a noun) a church dignitary connected with one of the *cardinal* or 'parish' churches of Rome.

(*d*) one of the seventy ecclesiastics who constitute the Pope's council, and who wear scarlet hats and robes.

(*e*) a scarlet cloak worn by ladies.

(*f*) (as noun or adjective) scarlet.

(*g*) bird with scarlet plumage.

The last three senses are highly specialized and are not the most common ones current today, but the usual Modern English sense (*d*) is sufficiently far removed from the original sense to illustrate the process of concatenation, and the example shows also that it is not only the original meaning which may pass out of use; some of the latest links in the chain may be forgotten while earlier links survive.

Examples of concatenation are innumerable. *Treacle* is ultimately derived from Greek θηριακός 'pertaining to a wild animal'. The stages of development are: a remedy for the bite of a wild animal, a remedy in general, a remedy in the form of a syrup, syrup in general, sugary syrup. *Candidate* is from Latin *candidātus* 'a person dressed in white'. Since the Romans wore their whitest robes when standing for election to any office, we have the meaning 'white-robed applicant for office' as a link between the original and the present-day meanings. *Person* is borrowed through French from Latin *persōna* 'an actor's mask'. It then came to describe either the actor or the part that he played, and then it joined the words, like *wight* and *body*, used to describe a human being of either sex.

Many kinds of semantic change result from the figurative use of language, and probably the most common of the figures of speech is metaphor. It is so common that any kind of figurative language is liable to be called metaphorical, often mistakenly. The essential characteristic of a metaphor is that it is based on similarity, and it differs from a simile in that it is condensed. A simile is usually a literally true statement, since it simply points out a resemblance, whereas a metaphor as a rule is not literally true; but we are so accustomed to metaphors that we usually have no difficulty in detecting what is the literal truth which is expressed in disguised form in the metaphor.

The context is important for the understanding of a metaphor as it is for the understanding of other words. If a speaker refers to a rock it is well to know whether he has in mind the building of a house or the sailing of a boat. Many words have been used so often as metaphors that the metaphorical sense is more familiar than the literal sense, and these are called 'faded metaphors'; the term itself is a metaphor. These faded metaphors account for the mixed metaphors or the so-called 'Irish bulls' to which some very eloquent speakers are prone. They generally show that a speaker is using a metaphor unthinkingly, like the man who prayed, 'If there be any spark of goodness in us, water that spark'. To defend this would be going too far, but a mixture of metaphors is often the result of exuberance of imagination which causes the speaker to move rapidly from one image to another before completing a sentence. Examples abound in Shakespeare, as for example, when Lady Macbeth reproaches her husband:

> Was the hope drunk,
> Wherein you dress'd yourself? hath it slept since,
> And wakes it now, to look so green and pale
> At what it did so freely?[1]

So long as metaphors are vividly felt as such, they are the concern of the student of literature or of rhetoric; it is the faded metaphors which have most interest for the student of language. Sometimes a literal meaning of a word is preserved side by side with a metaphorical one, as in *dull* and *bright*, and it is usually

[1] *Macbeth* I. vii. 35–38.

easy to see when such words are used metaphorically. There are other words whose literal meaning has been almost or quite forgotten, and it is only those who have some knowledge of etymology who realize that they are metaphors at all. Such words are *to thrill* (which originally meant 'to pierce' and is related to the second syllable of *nostril*), *to fret* (OE *fretan* 'to devour'), and *depend* (Latin *dependere* 'hang from'). Without investigation of the history of a word, it is not always easy to say which is the literal and which the metaphorical sense. The names of parts of the human body are often used metaphorically, as in the *head* of a school, the *foot* of a page, the *eye* of a needle, and the *heart* of the matter, but in the word *chest* the process is reversed; the literal meaning of the word is 'box', and the use of the word to describe part of the body is metaphorical.

One result of the fading of metaphors is that we do not always realize the vividness of poetic imagination that has been shown in the building up of our vocabulary. This tendency has been helped by the phonetic changes which have disguised the connexion between words originally the same. *Daisy* originally meant 'eye of day'; *tulip* is ultimately from the Persian word which has also given *turban*, and that was the older meaning; *easel* meant 'ass', and the word has acquired its present sense because, like an ass, an easel has to bear a burden; *tribulation* meant 'threshing', and the history of the meaning of the word reflects the belief that suffering may have a purifying effect. This is one of many words which show that the study of semantics can help to throw light on the history of ideas.

There is one psychological process which has linguistic results similar to those of metaphor. This is *synaesthesia*, which NED defines, in one of its senses, as 'production, from a sense-impression of one kind, of an associated mental image of a sense-impression of another kind'. Thus, when we speak of 'good taste', or of 'a clash of colours' we are using synaesthetic imagery, which may have had its origin in genuine synaesthesia, but which is probably for most of us simply one kind of metaphor. Some synaesthetic images are so well established that their synaesthetic origin is lost sight of, as, for example, when we speak of a soft voice or a sweet sound. It may be that the meaning of *soft* and *sweet* had become generalized before the adjectives were coupled with these particular sounds. *Eager* is another word in the development of which synaesthesia has played a part. It is from OF *aigre* 'sharp, sour', and the earliest recorded English sense is 'pungent, acrid, keen to the taste or other senses' (cf. *vinegar* from OF *vinaigre*). When we say that we *feel* sorry for someone we are using a metaphor based on physical sense-impression, since the earliest sense of the word recorded by NED is 'to handle (an object) in order to experience a tactual sensation'.

Simile and metaphor are figures of speech based upon the similarity between two objects. There are two figures of speech, metonymy and synecdoche, which are based not on similarity but on contiguity. The contiguity which forms the basis of these figures need not be physical contact; it is often based upon the association of ideas. Metonymy is the figure by which an object or idea is described by the name of some closely related object or idea. The relation may be of many different kinds. It may be that of a container to the thing contained, as when we speak of drinking *claret cup*. It may be that of instrument and result, as when we say *tongue* for *language*. It may be that of material and product, as in *copper* for *penny*. Very often metonymy leads to the use of an abstract term for a concrete object or the converse. *Bombast* originally meant cotton-wool, which was used for padding, but the figurative sense 'inflated or turgid language' has completely ousted the concrete sense. *Fustian* has had a similar development, but both concrete and abstract senses of that word are still current. *Battle* is an example of the use of an abstract term in a concrete sense: the earliest English sense is 'hostile encounter', but the word was for a long time used in the sense 'a body of troops in battle array'. *Thews* is from OE *þēaw* 'custom', which was later specialized with the sense 'good quality'. From the sixteenth century *thews* was used in the plural to indicate physical strength, and later, perhaps by association with *sinews*, it came to mean muscles or tendons. *Premise* is a technical term in logic meaning a previous statement from which another is inferred, and in legal documents the plural *premises* was used to refer back to anything that had already been mentioned. In a title deed a detailed description of a piece of property was set out at the beginning, and in later parts of the document *the premises* was used to avoid repetition. Hence the word has now acquired the concrete sense of buildings and grounds.

Synecdoche is the figure by which the name of a part is applied to the whole, or, conversely, the name of the whole is applied to a part of it. A familiar example is the use of *hands* to describe the people working in a factory. Since *hand* in its literal sense is a word in common use, it is clear to everyone that in the example quoted the word is used figuratively, but synecdoche is closely related to two extremely common processes which often take place without users of a language being aware of what is happening. These are extension and specialization. These two kinds of semantic change take place when speaker and hearer fail to agree about the size of the group to which a particular object belongs. Just as a man belongs to a family and also to a larger group, such as a nation, which includes the family, so any object may be regarded as belonging either to a large group or to a smaller subdivision of that group. If the speaker has in mind a smaller group than that envisaged by the hearer, extension of meaning is likely to take place; if the speaker has in mind a large group while the hearer is thinking of a smaller one, there will be specialization.

Extension has taken place in a large number of English words. *Quarantine* is so called because it originally lasted for forty days, whereas now the word is used whatever the duration of the precaution. *Panier* was originally a bread-basket, but the word is now used to describe a receptacle for other objects. The original meaning of *journey* was a day's walk or ride, and a *journal* was a periodical which appeared daily, but we can now speak without incongruity of a week's journey, and many journals are published quarterly. *Dilapidated* is derived from Latin *lapis* 'stone' and was originally applied only to stone build-ings. *Arrive* was at first appropriate only to an arrival by water, since it is from French *arriver*, which is from a derivative of Latin *rīpa* 'shore, bank'. *Rival* meant originally 'one who uses the same brook as another' (cf. Latin *rivus* 'stream'), and the development of meaning suggests that disputes about water rights were common. *Salary* is from French *salaire*, which is from Latin *salārium*, a sum of money given to Roman soldiers to enable them to buy salt; the use of the word in its present sense was no doubt originally a protest at its inadequacy.

In many words extension has gone about as far as it can go, and to words of this kind the term 'generalization' can most properly be applied. There are many English words, which once had a quite precise sense, which have acquired a meaning so vague that they can stand for almost anything. They have come to mean 'things in general', and they derive from the context in which they are used any more precise meaning which they possess. Such words include *thing* (OE *þing* originally 'discussion', ON *þing* 'legislative assembly'), *state* (OF *estat* related to Latin *stāre* 'to stand'), *condition* (OF *condicion*, related to Latin *condĭcere* 'to agree upon'), *matter* (OF *matere*, from Latin *māteria* 'stuff, materials used for building'), *article* (OF *article* from Latin *articulus* 'joint'), *circumstance* (OF *circumstance*, related to Latin *circumstāre* 'to stand round'). Another extreme form of extension is the tendency, particularly noticeable in slang, for adjectives of the most varied origins to become either vague terms of approval or vague terms of disapproval. Standard English examples are *good, nice, fine, excellent, admirable* beside *bad, worthless, mean, evil, vile,* and many others. These are not exact synonyms, but the English language has a sufficient number of these vague terms to make it worth while to resist the attempts which are constantly being made to add to their number.

One kind of extension that has contributed a good deal to the growth of the English vocabulary is the formation of words from proper names. The transition from proper names to common nouns is a gradual one and it is not always easy to say at what point the change takes place. Christian names, surnames and place-names have been drawn upon. *Jack* is used in a variety of senses, such as a small ball sent down as a mark at bowls and a tool used to lift a motor-car. *Guy* was a distinguished name in medieval England, as in the romance of Guy of Warwick, but is used as a common noun with the sense 'grotesque figure' because of the custom of burning Guy Fawkes in effigy. The word has taken on a more favourable sense in America, where 'regular guy' is a more complimentary description than it is in England. Surnames have become verbs to describe activities associated with particular men. *To boycott* is derived from the name of Charles Boycott (1832–1897), at one time agent for Lord Erne's estates in County Mayo, and the verb came into use in 1880 to describe the treatment of Boycott organized by the Irish Land League. *To burke* is derived from the name of William Burke (1792–1829) who joined with Hare to suffocate a number of people in order to dispose of their bodies to the anatomist Robert Knox. Words derived from proper names have sometimes undergone an interesting semantic development. *Dunce* is from the name of Duns Scotus, an eminent medieval scholar. At the time of the Renaissance the work of the medieval Schoolmen fell into disrepute, and so *dunce* came to be used contemptuously. Words from place-names are usually names of products and have often undergone a change of form, as *copper* from Cyprus, *sherry* from Jerez in Spain, *currant* from Corinth, and *damask* and *damson* from Damascus. Other words derived from proper names that have undergone a change of form as well as a change of meaning include *tawdry* (from *Saint Audry*, a reference to the fair held in June at Saint Etheldrida's shrine in the Isle of Ely), *maudlin* (from Mary *Magdalene*), and *bedlam* (from *Bethlehem*, the name of a thirteenth century London priory which became an asylum for the insane).

Specialization of meaning has taken place in a large number of words, and many words have undergone both extension and specialization at different stages of their history. *Generous* meant originally 'of noble birth'. It was then extended to apply to anyone who had the qualities that one might expect to find in a man of noble birth. The sense has now been restricted to a selection of those qualities, especially to open-handedness. The importance attached to this quality is illustrated by the specialization of other words, such as *bounty* (OF *bontet* 'goodness') and *charity* (OF *charite*, from Latin *cāritas* 'love'). A number of terms of abuse which could at one time be applied to either men or women are now applied only to women. Examples are *termagant* (from *Teruagant*, the name of a supposed Saracen god), *shrew* (OE *scrēawa* 'shrew-mouse', supposed to have a venomous bite), and *hoyden*, which is not recorded before the end of the sixteenth century and is not found with its present feminine sense until nearly a century later. *Starve* (OE *steorfan*), like its German cognate *sterben*, originally meant 'to die'. The meaning has been specialized in Standard English to mean 'to die of hunger', whereas in many dialects it has been specialized to mean 'to die of cold' and later the participial adjective *starved* has been weakened to a synonym for 'cold'.

Some words were originally used of either good or bad things but have been specialized to refer to either one or the other. When *retaliate* was first introduced into English in the seventeenth century, it could be applied to benefits as well as to illtreatment. *Censure* originally meant 'opinion', not necessarily 'unfavourable opinion', as in the advice of Polonius: 'Take each man's censure' (*Hamlet* I. iii. 69).

When the meaning of a word has been specialized, it is not uncommon to find the older sense preserved in a proverbial phrase, a compound, or a cognate word. *Meat* (OE *mete*) originally meant 'food', and the older sense is preserved in *sweetmeat* and in the proverb *One man's meat is another man's poison*. *Tide* (OE *tīd*) meant 'time', as in the proverb *Time and tide wait for no man*. The specialization of one of a pair of cognate words is very common, but it is sometimes concealed by the divergence in form of the two cognate words. *Spice* is cognate with *species* and was once used with that sense. *Poison* is cognate with *potion* and *treason* with *tradition*. In each of these pairs the French word is the more highly specialized while the word borrowed directly from Latin keeps the wider sense. *Cattle* (ONF *catel*) once meant 'property', and this sense was common in English until the sixteenth century. In an agricultural society living animals are one of the chief forms of property, and from the beginning of the fourteenth century we find that the word has the specialized meaning 'live stock'. It was applied to any living creatures, such as pigs, hens, and bees, that could be kept for profit. Fitzherbert (1523) says: 'Shepe in myne opynyon is the mooste profytablest cattell that any man can haue'. The word has now been still further specialized to mean bovine animals, and the older sense 'property' has been preserved in *chattel*, which is the Central French doublet of *cattle*.

Sometimes specialization results from a change in the meaning of a suffix. The etymological meaning of *tobacconist* is 'one who has something to do with tobacco'. It once meant a man who smoked tobacco, but it now has the more restricted sense of one who sells it. Another occupational term which has been specialized is *grocer*. The word is from OF *grossier* 'a wholesale dealer' (cf. OF *gros* 'great'), and has thus undergone both extension (to include a retail dealer) and specialization (to refer to one particular class of commodities).

When a word has been specialized in meaning, the narrower sense does not always drive out the other sense; we often find the two senses existing side by side for centuries. When Edgar in *King Lear* (III. iv. 149) speaks of 'mice and rats and such small deer', he is using *deer* (OE *dēor*) in the sense 'animal' which is its usual meaning in Old English, but the specialized sense which the word has today is recorded as early as the ninth century. *Cousin* had both a wide and a specialized meaning from the time when it was borrowed into English at the end of the thirteenth century until the eighteenth century, when the wider sense 'kinsman or kinswoman' became obsolete, except for special uses, as in royal proclamations.

Specialization often involves the figure of speech known as ellipsis by which some words are omitted or left to be understood. For example, a *nonconformist* or a *dissenter* may be mentioned without any specification of what it is to which he fails to conform or from which he dissents. One of the most startling instances of specialization accompanied by ellipsis is *total abstainer*, and there is similar ellipsis in *prohibition* and *temperance reformer*.

Euphemism is the figure of speech by which one seeks to disguise the real nature of an unpleasant idea by giving it an inoffensive name, and many words have changed their meanings as a result of being used as euphemisms. Closely related to euphemism are the taboos which have led to the use of *dash* and *darn* for *damn* and which lead many people to avoid mentioning God. The taboo comes into being because of the importance and emotional power of the idea to be expressed. The motives for respecting such taboos are sometimes complex, as when Thomas Hardy at the conclusion of *Tess of the D'Urbervilles* writes 'the President of the Immortals, in Æschylean phrase, had ended his sport with Tess'. At some stages in the history of the world, for example in nineteenth-century America, there has been excessive indulgence in euphemism, with the entertaining result that it was thought indelicate to refer to the legs of a table, but euphemism is found to a greater or less extent at all periods of the history of the English language. The chief objection to its excessive use is that it casts a mantle of impropriety over the most innocent words and phrases because one's hearers suspect euphemism on all occasions even when none is intended. It has been said that one gains a much more sinister effect if, instead of calling a spade a spade, one calls it 'an instrument of a certain nature'.

The themes which have been most productive of euphemisms are death, sex, illness and excretion. Euphemisms for death are common in Shakespeare: Macbeth avoids mentioning the murder of Duncan by speaking of his 'surcease' (I. vii. 4) and his 'taking-off' (I. vii. 20), and the tribunes in *Julius Caesar* are said to have been 'put to silence' (I. ii. 290). The most common kind of euphemism involves specialization; an extremely vague word or phrase is used in the belief that the hearer will understand what special aspect the speaker has in mind. Thus, a very common way of referring to the possibility of death is to say 'if anything should happen to him', and a man who looks after funeral arrangements is known as an *undertaker*. This word cannot now be applied to anyone who undertakes other tasks than the care of the dead, and it has become so closely associated with death that the search for fresh euphemisms has begun. In the attempt to avoid what has now ceased to be a euphemism we sometimes see a revival of the original word that the euphemism was intended to avoid. Many undertakers now call themselves funeral directors.

The same process may be seen at work with words dealing with sex. The word *whore* is a very old euphemism and is cognate with Latin *cārus* 'dear, beloved'. We know that the euphemistic use is old because it is found in Gothic as well as in Old English and may well go back to Common Germanic. The word had certainly lost its euphemistic force by the eighteenth century, when Dr Johnson replied to Boswell's defence of Lady Diana Beauclerk: 'My dear Sir, never accustom your mind to mingle virtue and vice. The woman's a whore, and there's an end on't'.[1]

[1] Boswell's *Life of Johnson* ed. Birkbeck Hill, II. 247.

In the fifteenth century the word *harlot* came to be used with the same meaning. This word, derived from OF *harlot* 'vagabond', had been in use in English since the thirteenth century applied to men, sometimes as a term of insult but also used in the sense of 'good fellow'. Chaucer says of the Summoner:

> He was a gentil harlot and a kynde,
> A bettre felawe sholde men noght fynde.

Neither *whore* nor *harlot* passed completely out of use, but reluctance to use the words was strong enough to make further words necessary. The words were therefore reinforced by *strumpet, prostitute,* and by various paraphrases.

In describing illness euphemism is common. An example is *disease,* the original meaning of which was 'discomfort,' and the word is used by Chaucer in this sense. When the illness is mental, euphemism is particularly common. *Insane* simply means 'unhealthy' and is an example of specialization. Sometimes it is fear of the commonplace rather than desire for concealment that leads to the use of such phrases. In recent years the common cold has shown signs of becoming 'a virus infection'.

A common form of euphemism is the replacement of a word by the negation of its opposite. Examples are *untruthful, intemperate, unwise, impolite.* Another device is to use a Latin phrase, such as *felo de se* or *post mortem.* Initials are sometimes used, as in *m.d.* for *mentally deficient* and *t.b.* for *tuberculosis.* Slang is sometimes used euphemistically, as in an expression like *to kick the bucket,* and the evanescent nature of slang satisfies one of the needs of euphemism, which is that it is merely a temporary expedient, although it has lasting effects on the language.

Two opposite processes which have affected the meanings of many English words are elevation and degeneration. The two processes can sometimes be seen at work in the same word. *Fellow* (late OE *fēolaga,* from ON *félagi*) was originally a word involving neither praise nor blame; it meant 'one who lays down money' and so 'business partner'. Since a joint enterprise might be either for good or evil ends, the meaning of *fellow* developed in two opposite directions. As early as the fourteenth century it was used in a bad sense to mean 'accomplice'. The derogatory sense was reinforced by our national habits of reserve, which cause us to regard it as an insult if a comparative stranger addresses us familiarly and assumes that his familiarity will be welcomed. The word became a way of addressing a servant or a man of humble station and it then became a term of contempt. This development is illustrated in *Pickwick Papers* (chap. 15), where Mr Tupman is so deeply moved as to say to Mr Pickwick 'Sir, you're a fellow'. The elevation of meaning of the word has gone on side by side with the degeneration, and from the fifteenth century *fellow* was the name given to a member of a college. Hence it was used to describe a member of a learned society, with the result that today a Fellow of the British Academy or of the Royal Society has attained virtually the highest academic distinction attainable. A similar divergence in meaning of two words once nearly synonymous is to be seen in *knave* (OE *cnafa*) and *knight* (OE *cniht*), which both meant 'boy' in Old English.

Elevation, like degeneration, is a form of specialization. *Fame* (Latin *fāma*) originally meant 'report, talk', but the word has now been specialized in a good sense. As often, the older unspecialized sense is preserved in a particular phrase *a house of ill fame*. *Admire* now always implies to wonder with approval, but until the eighteenth century the word was used in a wider sense, close to that of Latin *mīrārī*. On the other hand, extension of meaning has often led to elevation. A word which once had quite a precise meaning is liable to become a vague expression of approval if it describes a quality which many people regard as admirable. The best-known example of this process is *nice*. This is from OF *nice*, which is from Latin *nescius* 'ignorant'. It is used in English from the thirteenth century, and all the early senses are derogatory. In the sixteenth century it was specialized in the sense 'fastidious, difficult to please', no doubt by people who thought this quality unattractive. But many people regard fastidiousness as evidence of good judgement, and therefore when the meaning of the word was once more extended, in the latter part of the eighteenth century, it became a term of praise, although the narrower sense 'precise, subtle' still remains, as in *a nice distinction*, and is worth preserving. The word has thus undergone a complete reversal of its original meaning.

Another word which has undergone elevation because of a

change in our attitude to the qualities it describes is *luxury* (OF *luxurie*, from Latin *luxuria*). In Latin and in its early occurrences in English this was a word implying strong blame; it was the name of one of the Seven Deadly Sins. The nearest modern equivalent is *lust*, a word which has undergone the opposite development to *luxury*, since in Old English it meant simply 'pleasure'. From the seventeenth century the meaning of *luxury* was extended to mean indulgence in anything choice or costly, without the implication that such indulgence was blameworthy. The usual meaning of the word today is something which is desirable but not indispensable, and it is often contrasted with *necessity*.

Several words which were originally used in derision to describe political or religious opponents have been accepted by those to whom they were applied and used either as colourless descriptive names or as terms of praise. Examples are *Lollard* ('babbler'), *Whig* and *Tory*. The earliest recorded meaning of *Whig* is 'yokel, country bumpkin'. The word is shortened from *Whiggamore*, the name given to adherents of a body of Covenanters who marched on Edinburgh in 1648. It was then applied to those who opposed the succession to the crown of James, Duke of York, afterwards King James II. From 1689 it was used as the name of a powerful political party, but since the middle of the nineteenth century it has been replaced, except as a historical term, by *Liberal*. The word *Tory* came into use at about the same time as *Whig*. From the middle of the seventeenth century it was applied to the dispossessed Irish who became outlaws and plundered the English settlers. It was applied as a nickname to the supporters of James II, and by the middle of the eighteenth century it had achieved such respectability that Dr Johnson could define it (1755) as 'One who adheres to the ancient constitution of the state, and the apostolical hierarchy of the church of England'.

Another instance of this kind of change is to be found in the name *the Old Contemptibles* applied to the British expeditionary force sent to France in 1914. The adjective *contemptible* was scornfully applied to the force by the Kaiser, and its startling inappropriateness appealed to a love of irony in the national character, with the result that it was adopted as a term of praise.

Such expressions often have a short life, however, and in a general knowledge examination one schoolboy hazarded the guess that *the Old Contemptibles* were the Preston North End football team.

Degeneration of meaning, or pejorative sense-development as it is sometimes called, is one of the commonest kinds of semantic change. The English have been accused of having a well-developed talent for discovering moral obliquity in others, and it may be that the frequent occurrence of degeneration in English words is a result of such a propensity. There are many words which originally described a man's low economic status which have in course of time come to denote bad manners or moral blame. Such words are *churl* (OE *ceorl*), *boor* (cf. OE *gebūr* 'dweller'), and *villain* (OF *vilein* 'feudal serf'); the meaning of the last word may have been influenced by *vile*. The adjective *base* now implies moral unworthiness, but originally it meant 'of humble birth'. When Hamlet says that he once regarded it as 'a baseness to write fair', (V. ii. 34) he means that he thought that the ability to write well was characteristic of a low social class, not that it was blameworthy. *Lewd* (OE *lǣwede*) originally meant 'not in holy orders'. It came to mean 'unlettered, untaught', and was then for many centuries a vague term of reproach. The modern sense 'lascivious, unchaste' is a specialization of this unfavourable sense. *Caitiff* is an Anglo-Norman doublet of *captive*, and its sense-development has a partial parallel in that of its French cognate *chétif*.

It is not only low social position and misfortune that have been regarded as blameworthy; the development of meaning of several English words reflects the widespread belief that people who have any special skill or knowledge are up to no good. *Cunning* is the present participle of the verb *can*, which meant 'know, am able'; its degeneration of meaning has a more recent parallel in the use of *knowing* as an adjective. *Sly* is from ON *slǣgr*, which meant 'skilful'. *Crafty* shows a similar debasement.

Terms of praise can undergo degeneration as a result of their being used insincerely or patronizingly. *Worthy*, both as adjective or noun, has degenerated in this way. The earliest meaning of *quaint* was 'skilled, clever'. As early as the thirteenth century it had acquired a bad sense, 'cunning, given to scheming', which it has since lost, but it was frequently used in the sense 'handsome, elegant'. It then came to mean 'unusual', and its use today is generally patronizing. *Silly* is from OE *sǣlig* 'blessed'; the stages in its development have been 'innocent', then 'harmless', then 'weakly foolish'. The ironical use of a word can also lead to degeneration, as in the use of *egregious*, which etymologically means 'out of the herd, outstanding', but is no longer a term of praise.

Degeneration of meaning is sometimes only temporary. Thus *promoter* originally meant 'one who furthers any project, whether good or bad', but in the fifteenth century it acquired the specialized sense of a professional accuser of offenders against the law. It is easy to see how the word then became a term of abuse. After the word had lost its older specialized sense it acquired a new one in connexion with the formation of joint stock companies in the nineteenth century. Since some of the enterprises promoted were unsound, the word again acquired a pejorative sense which it has never completely lost. Similarly *plausible* and *specious* still keep their specialized derogatory meanings. *Plausible* originally meant 'deserving of applause', 'praiseworthy', whereas now it means 'having an appearance of reasonableness or worth', with the implication that the appearance is misleading. Similarly, *specious*, like Latin *speciosus*, meant 'beautiful'. It has undergone two changes, one a transference from physical beauty to truth and the other, parallel with the development of *plausible*, a suggestion that it describes a deceptive appearance of truth not truth itself. Another example is *companion*. The original meaning was 'one who shares bread', hence 'comrade'. By the influence of the same tendencies which caused degeneration in the meaning of *fellow*, *companion* became a term of abuse and is so used by Shakespeare. It has now lost all its derogatory associations, and its derivatives *companionship* and *companionable* have gone further and generally imply approbation.

Development in the meaning of loan-words has sometimes begun to take place before the introduction of the word into English. The favourable and unfavourable meanings of *politician* are both found from the time of the first recorded English use of the word at the end of the sixteenth century, but the unfavourable sense is a specialized use of the word, which means

primarily 'one versed in the theory or science of government'.
The unfavourable sense was more widespread at the time of
Shakespeare than it is today, but even today *politician* is a mild
snarl-word. The corresponding purr-word is *statesman*.

Some words have acquired new associations which make their
use by older authors in certain contexts seem incongruous to
a modern reader. Romeo 'bears him like a portly gentleman'
(*Romeo and Juliet* I. v. 69). All that this means is that he carries
himself well, that he is handsome and of good bearing, but
today the word suggests corpulence. *Pompous* is another word
that can no longer be used as a term of praise. The original
meaning was 'magnificent, splendid', but it now suggests self-
importance and pretentiousness. *Puny* is a phonetic spelling of
puisne 'born later, junior'. The latter word has kept its colourless
technical sense, and is used only in legal contexts, usually as a
description of a judge, but *puny* has undergone degeneration.

Two processes which have something in common with
degeneration and elevation are weakening and strengthening.
Certain words, like *vexed* or *irritated*, are habitually used in
trivial contexts, while others, like *angry* or *enraged*, are suitable
for occasions when feeling is more intense, and the degree of
feeling associated with particular words has changed in the
course of the history of the English language.

Weakening of meaning results from the habitual use of particular words on unsuitably trivial occasions, whereas strengthening results from habitual understatement. In spite of our
supposed national fondness for understatement, weakening is
more common than strengthening. In the Old English poem
The Battle of Maldon one of the warriors on the losing side an-
nounces his intention to go on fighting by saying that men will
not be able to reproach him with having run away from the
battle after the death of his lord. To flee from battle and to fail
to avenge one's dead lord were two of the most serious offences
of which an Anglo-Saxon warrior could be guilty, yet the word
used for 'reproach' is *ætwītan*, which has given Modern English
twit. It is clear that the word has been very much weakened
since Anglo-Saxon times, since we now use *twit* only of trivial
offences. Another common Old English word that has been
weakened is *gilpan*, which has given *yelp*. In Old English it

meant 'to boast', but this sense is not recorded later than the fifteenth century. Since the beginning of the sixteenth century the word has had its modern sense referring to the cry of an animal, more shrill than a bark. The development of meaning is based upon metaphor and reflects a distaste for boasting. The weakening of the sense of *giddy* had begun before the first recorded occurrence of the word in late Old English. The etymology of the word suggests that it originally meant 'possessed by a god', but already in Old English this sense had been weakened to 'mad, foolish'. The word has undergone further weakening and now means 'frivolous, flighty'. Sometimes the essential meaning of a word remains unchanged, but there has been a change in the sort of context in which the word can be used. Thus OE *scūfan* was a dignified word that could be used in poetry, but its modern descendant *shove* has undignified associations.

The weakening of certain adverbs and adverbial phrases suggests that procrastination is a deeply rooted human characteristic. *Soon* (OE *sōna*) once meant 'at once, instantly', and so did *presently*, *by and by*, and the archaic *anon*. *Immediately* is now going the same way; the word is sometimes used in publishers' announcements to indicate that a book will be published within a few weeks. Similarly, expressions like *in fact, as a matter of fact, to tell the truth*, and *no doubt*, originally used to strengthen assertions, have been weakened, and generally have the opposite effect of throwing some doubt on the truth of a statement. It is easy to see how this change of meaning took place: it is chiefly doubtful statements that are in need of strengthening. Similarly adverbs used as intensives soon cease to have any meaning. It is doubtful whether *Thanks awfully* is really any stronger than *Thank you*. Sometimes intensive adverbs show a tendency to pile up, as in *Thank you very much indeed*. Another adverb that has been weakened is *literally*, and some incongruities result from the existence side by side of the legitimate use of the word, when there is an implied contrast with *metaphorically*, and the almost meaningless use which is a survival of an earlier attempt at emphasis. The result is a sentence like *He literally devoured the morning paper*, which summons up a picture which the author probably did not intend.

Another word that has been weakened is *amuse*, which is a derivative of the verb *muse*. The earliest recorded English sense is the intransitive one 'to gaze in astonishment', but the usual early sense is 'to cause to muse', 'to bewilder'. During the fifteenth century the word acquired a pejorative sense, which was common until the end of the eighteenth century although it has now been lost, 'to cheat, deceive'. The usual associations of the word today are with trivial or cheerful subjects. *Astonish*, although still fairly strong, is not so strong as it once was; the early occurrences of the word generally suggest a physical blow or the paralysing effect of such a blow. *Unkind* originally meant 'unnatural', whereas now it simply describes slightly disagreeable behaviour. *Naughty* is a derivative of *naught* and originally meant 'worthless'; it is now used either facetiously or with reference to the minor transgressions of a child. *Apparent* originally meant 'manifest, obvious', and it has kept this sense in the phrase *heir apparent* contrasted with *heir presumptive*. In other contexts *apparent* has undergone the fate of *specious* and *plausible* and is often used with an expressed or implied contrast with *real*. *Comfort*, both as noun and verb, and *comfortable* are from Old French and are derived from, or related to, Latin *confortāre* 'to strengthen', from *fortis* 'strong'. The earliest English meaning of the noun was 'strengthening' as an aid to the resisting of temptation; it is used today of things that are pleasant but not as a rule likely to strengthen one's character.

It is sometimes possible to see the effects of both weakening and strengthening on the meaning of the same word. *Drench* was originally the causative of the verb *drink* and is still so used with reference to giving medicine to animals. By what seems to have been a grim joke, the word was strengthened so as to mean 'to drown' or 'to be drowned'. A common proverbial expression in Middle English was *dronke ase a dreynt mous* 'drunk as a drowned mouse'. The modern sense is weaker than this, though stronger than the original sense.

Strengthening of meaning is illustrated in the history of *defy*, which originally meant 'to distrust', whereas now it means 'to declare one's distrust openly'.

One of the results of semantic change has been the divergence in meaning of related words or of variant forms of the same word. This divergence is encouraged when sound-changes have caused a divergence in pronunciation of the two words in question. Thus, the connexion between *miser* and *misery* has been disguised by the difference in vowel-length which results from the difference in the number of syllables in the two words. As a result the two words have had a different semantic development: *misery* has kept the wider meaning of wretchedness which was once associated with both words whereas *miser* has undergone specialization of meaning and is now applied to a person who suffers from a particular form of wretchedness. *Miser* had the wider sense in Spenser: Archimago seeks to arouse sympathy by describing himself as a 'humble miser' (*Faerie Queene* II. 1. 8). Similarly, various sound-changes have led to considerable divergence in form between certain verbs and their past participles, and the divergence of form has led to divergence of meaning. The verb *seethe* and the adjective *sodden* are descended respectively from the infinitive and past participle of OE *sēoþan* 'to boil'. The adjective *forlorn* is descended from the past participle of OE *forlēosan* 'to lose'.

The divergent semantic development of variant forms of the same word may be illustrated by a pair like *propriety* and *property*. The second word is an Anglo-Norman or Middle English modification of OF *proprieté*, from which *propriety* is derived more directly. The oldest recorded sense of *propriety* in English is 'ownership', or 'proprietorship'; it is not until the end of the eighteenth century that we find the word in its usual modern sense of 'correctness of behaviour or morals'. *Property* has kept its original meaning of 'ownership' but its usual sense today is 'material possessions'. Thus the two forms of the word have been conveniently specialized in different fields, one referring to things mental or moral, the other to things material. There has been a similar division of labour between *piety* and *pity*. Both words were borrowed from Old French, where *pitié* was the popular and *pieté* a more learned form, and both go back ultimately to Latin *pietās*. In classical Latin this meant 'piety', although the meaning of the word was extended in Late Latin to include 'pity, compassion', and this was the meaning of the two forms when they first appeared in Old French and, later, in Middle English. In Middle English both *pity* and *piety* are found with both the senses 'compassion' and 'piety', but by the end of the sixteenth century the two words had been differentiated with the senses that they have at the present day.

Another pair of words which go back to a common source are *whole* and *hale*. They are the developments in different dialects of OE *hāl*, which already in Old English had the two meanings 'entire' and 'in good health'. The Northern form *hale* was re-introduced into literary English at the beginning of the nineteenth century, largely by the influence of Sir Walter Scott, and Scott uses the form in both senses. In present-day English *whole* has taken over one of the meanings and *hale* the other. The older meaning 'in good health', which the adjective *whole* has lost, is preserved in the related verb *to heal* (OE *hǣlan*), which originally meant 'to make whole', and in the abstract noun *health* (OE *hǣlþ*).

Sometimes we have a whole group of words derived from a common source which have diverged in form. The most common cause of such divergence is the repeated borrowing of a word from some other language. Between one borrowing and the next the word may have changed its form in the language to which it is native, or the differences in form may result from different attempts to represent an unfamiliar sound. Whatever the reasons for the variation, it is unusual for the different forms to remain exact synonyms; the variation in form is seized upon as a convenient way of distinguishing between various senses of the word in question. Thus, *gentle*, *Gentile*, *genteel* and *jaunty* are all derived from French *gentil* 'high-born, noble', which is from Latin *gentīlis* 'belonging to the same race'. The four words illustrate different kinds of specialization. The oldest of them in English is *gentle*, which was used from the thirteenth century in the sense 'well-born'. At first it was used as a synonym of *noble*, but was afterwards distinguished from it and taken to indicate a lower degree of rank. The word was then applied to the behaviour that may be expected from a man of high rank and so came to mean 'courteous, polite'. It then acquired its usual modern sense 'mild, kind'. The sense of *Gentile* is derived from an earlier stage in the history of the word than that represented in Old French. The usual sense of the word, 'non-Jewish', is derived from the Vulgate and represents a specialization of the sense of Latin *gentīlis*. *Genteel* represents a re-adoption, at the end of the sixteenth century, of French *gentil*. It was at first borrowed in the form *gentile*, and the spelling *genteel* was adopted at the end of the seventeenth century to show that the suffix had the vowel-sound of French *ī*, whereas *Gentile* had the English diphthong. During the seventeenth and eighteenth centuries *genteel* was used in senses similar to those of *gentle*, but in the nineteenth century it underwent pejorative development and was applied in ridicule to those who attached too much importance to the external signs of social standing. The word has never com-pletely lost its derogatory associations, and NED says of it that 'in educated language it has always a sarcastic or at least playful colouring'. *Jaunty* has undergone a different kind of pejorative specialization. It is first recorded in the seventeenth century and represents an English attempt to record the contemporary French pronunciation. Like *genteel*, it first meant 'well-bred; gentlemanly', but it soon came to mean 'easy, sprightly in manner'. It was then applied to someone pretending to have those qualities, and when the word is used today there is usually an implication of self-satisfaction. There are many other pairs of loan-words in which there has been a divergence of meaning; among them are *human* and *humane*, *urban* and *urbane*, *curtsey* and *courtesy*, *mask* and *masque*, *saloon* and *salon*, *antic* and *antique*.

Divergence of meaning has sometimes taken place when the difference between two forms is merely one of spelling. *Flour* and *flower* are variant spellings of the same word. Dr Johnson in his *Dictionary* did not separate the two words and used the spelling *flower* for both, but some of his contemporaries recognized the modern distinction. *Flower* has the more recent spelling but it represents the older or botanical sense. One of its derived senses, recorded in English as early as the beginning of the thirteenth century and still current today, was 'the choicest among a num-ber of persons or things'. From this sense, by specialization, it came to mean the finest quality of meal from wheat or other grain, and then, by extension, any fine soft powder obtained by grinding seeds or grain. The spelling *flour* has now been re-stricted to this particular sense, and probably most speakers of English are unaware of any connexion between the two words. Similarly most people probably regard *metal* and *mettle* as different words, but *mettle* is simply a variant spelling of *metal*, once used indiscriminately for all the senses of the word but now confined to the figurative sense. The distinction in meaning is recognized in dictionaries from the beginning of the eighteenth century.

Sometimes divergence of meaning results from the misunderstanding of a prefix or suffix or from the use of different prefixes or suffixes. The word *demerit* has had two exactly opposite meanings: good qualities and bad qualities. The first of these senses is the older and the word is used in this sense by Shakespeare; the second sense is the one current today. The same opposition of meaning is found in French, from which language the word is borrowed, and it arose from a misunderstanding of the meaning of the prefix *dē-* in Latin *dēmerēri* 'to merit, deserve'. The prefix was intensive and meant 'completely, thoroughly'; it has the same meaning in *denude*. But another function of the Latin prefix *dē-* was to undo or reverse the action of a verb, and this is the usual function of the prefix in English. Hence *demerit*, both as noun and verb, came to mean the opposite of *merit*, and the two words were often contrasted in the same phrase.

Divergence of meaning resulting from the employment of different suffixes has been utilized in a very precise way by chemists, who attach different meanings to the suffixes *-ous* and *-ic*, as in *ferrous* and *ferric*. Among more everyday words *willing* and *wilful* have diverged in meaning: the former word has become weaker and the latter stronger. The original meaning of *willing* was 'wishful' but that meaning has now given way to a more passive meaning, 'ready to comply with the wishes of others'. Both of these senses were attached to *wilful* from the fourteenth to the sixteenth century, but they are now obsolete and the word is used to describe a person who has too much will, who is obstinately self-willed or perverse.

Sometimes the same suffix may have more than one meaning and its different senses may lead to differences in the meaning of the word of which it forms a part. In *Macbeth* (I. iv. 10) the thane of Cawdor is said to throw his life away 'as 'twere a careless trifle'. Here the suffix *-less* has a passive meaning and *careless* means 'not worth taking care of'. Today the suffix has an active meaning, 'not taking care'.

One branch of semantics is the study of what may be termed the life and death of words: the principles which determine when new words shall come into existence and when existing words shall become obsolete. Many such words present no problem. New words are borrowed from other languages or formed from native or foreign elements to meet new needs, and so we have new words like *aeroplane, television* and *skyscraper*. Less often, completely new words, bearing no relation to existing words, are coined, especially to describe commercial products, such as *kodak* and the innumerable improbable monosyllables used to describe new types of detergent. Even when words are coined in this way, it is sometimes possible to perceive a partial etymology, as with *vaseline* (cf. German *Wasser* 'water' and Greek ἔλαιον 'oil'). Some everyday words have been coined in comparatively recent times. For example, the word *gas* was coined by the Dutch chemist J. B. Van Helmont (1577–1644) on the basis of Greek word that has given English *chaos*, and his coinage has been adopted into most Western languages. An even more recent coinage is *blizzard*, a word of American origin first recorded in the nineteenth century and probably suggested by such words as *blow, blast*, and the suffix *-ard*, which has as its usual English meaning 'one who does to excess, or who does what is discreditable'. The word *doll*, a pet-form of *Dorothy*, is not used in its present sense until the eighteenth century; in Shakespeare its place is taken by *baby* or *puppet*. Other words for children's toys are even more recent: *gollywog* is not recorded before 1895, and *teddy bear* (named after Theodore Roosevelt) not before 1907. On the other hand some words pass out of use along with the things that they represent, and are either entirely forgotten or used only with reference to the past, and so we have lost words like *hauberk* 'coat of mail' (originally 'neck-protection') and *byrnie* 'corselet'.

Sometimes a word comes into existence to express an idea for which we already have an adequate number of words, but it appeals to the imagination of the user and of his hearers because it expresses an old idea more vividly than do existing words. This is the way in which slang words come into existence, but, since such words do not as a rule serve any real need, as soon as their novelty has worn off they tend to pass out of use. If they do satisfy a need, they generally pass into the standard language and are no longer regarded as slang. We thus have words like *bet*, *fun*, *shabby*, *trip* 'short journey', *blackguard*, *coax*, *simper* and *prig*, which were once slang but which are now well established in Standard English. Such words may undergo quite considerable semantic development. For example, *prig*, when the word was first borrowed from sixteenth-century thieves' slang, meant 'thief'. One word which has defied all the rules by remaining in English as a slang word for several centuries is *booze*, first recorded in English in a comic poem of the fourteenth century, reappearing in sixteenth-century thieves' slang, and widely current as slang today.

Sometimes a word passes out of use while its derivatives remain. *Rathe* 'early' is a word that has puzzled many readers of *Lycidas*, where Milton mentions 'the rathe primrose' (l. 142). The adjective is now obsolete, but its comparative, *rather*, is in very frequent use as an adverb. Again, the obsolescence of a word may cause a phrase in which it occurs to be misunderstood. The phrase *forlorn hope* is from the Dutch *verloren hoop* 'lost troop', a name given to a picked body of men chosen to undertake some dangerous enterprise. *Hoop* is cognate with *heap*, but does not occur in English except in this phrase. Hence the phrase *forlorn hope* is often misused in the sense 'a faint hope', the word *hope* being confused with a quite different native word. The same sort of thing can happen when it is only one sense of a word that has become obsolete. *Depart* originally meant 'to separate', but this meaning was forgotten at the time of the revision of the Prayer Book in 1661 when 'till death us depart' was altered to 'till death us do part'.

Sometimes we can only guess at the reasons why particular words have become obsolete. One reason may be that the word that disappears is felt to have unpleasant associations and so is replaced by a euphemism. The euphemism in its turn comes to have unpleasant associations and is then replaced by another euphemism. Such considerations may have accounted for the disappearance of some Old English words meaning 'to die', such as *ācwelan*, *sweltan* and *forþfaran* (a euphemism originally meaning 'to pass forth') and the restriction of meaning of OE *steorfan*, which has given *starve*. The word *die* is not recorded in Old English, though Middle English forms suggest that it occurred; the cognate word *deyja* is of frequent occurrence in Old Icelandic. Sometimes the reason why a word passes out of use seems to be that it is felt to be too weak to express the idea that it is used to describe and it is therefore replaced by a stronger word. Thus OE *weorpan* 'to throw' was replaced by *cast* (ON *kasta*), and this in its turn was replaced by *throw*, a word which has existed in the language since Old English times (OE *þrāwan*), although in Old English it meant 'to twist'.

One reason why words pass out of use may be that sound-changes have caused two words to become homophones. It is clear that the creation of homophones does not always lead to the disappearance of one word of the pair, for we have many such pairs of words in English which have remained in use for centuries after becoming homophones. We have seen that the context generally prevents ambiguity, and homophones tend to disappear only when the words concerned are likely to occur in the same sort of context; for example, when they are the same part of speech. Thus, there is little danger of confusion between *seal* the noun and *seal* the verb, but there is a real danger of confusion between the two verbs *let*, one of them (OE *lǣtan*) meaning 'to allow' and the other (OE *lettan*) meaning 'to prevent', with the result that the latter verb has nearly passed out of use, although it is used as a noun in connexion with games and in the expression *without let or hindrance*. It may be that similar causes have led to the obsolescence of *quean*, which became a homophone of *queen*. In some dialects the word *son* is virtually obsolete, and even in Standard English it is less common in the spoken than the written language. The danger of confusion with *sun* may be the reason.

CHAPTER IX

Present-Day Trends

IN THE first chapter it was suggested that the scientific inventions of the last few decades have done a good deal to restore the spoken language to the important position which in most living languages speech enjoys as compared with writing. The gramophone, the telephone, the wireless and the tape recording machine have to some extent done for the spoken language what printing did for the written. It is often said that the popularity of broadcasting is leading to an extension of the use of Standard English and a decline in the use of dialect. It is true that broadcasting has caused many people to become familiar with the sounds and intonations of Standard English who, but for the wireless, would have heard and spoken nothing but local dialects, but it does not follow that local dialects are declining. It is possible that broadcasting is causing an increase in the bilingualism which is already widespread in England, if we can apply the term to the use of two different varieties of the same language by one speaker. There are many countrymen who habitually listen to the cultured accents of a B.B.C. announcer reading the news bulletin and who understand what they hear but who would be horrified at the thought of speaking in the same way themselves. It may be noticed further that the influence of the B.B.C. works in more than one direction. Programmes like *Country Magazine* have greatly increased the knowledge of local dialects and the interest taken in them, and many of the talks are given by speakers with recognizable local dialects. Many of the best-known speakers of dialect are entertainers, and the association of dialect with music-hall comedians, though unfortunate, has some validity in that the colloquial and idiomatic nature of dialect makes it a very effective medium for humour. Compulsory military service has done a good deal to reduce the number of speakers of pure dialect free from the influence of Standard English, but it has also made many speakers of

Standard English and of dialect realize that there are varieties of English different from their own.

With monotonous regularity writers on dialect say that dialects are passing out of use and that it will soon be too late to record them, but if dialects are dying they are, like King Charles II, taking an unconscionable time about it. There is a revived interest in dialect research: the dialects of England are being surveyed by investigators from the University of Leeds, and those of Scotland from the University of Edinburgh. During the later part of the nineteenth century the English Dialect Society did a good deal of work in publishing grammars and glossaries which formed the basis of Joseph Wright's great *English Dialect Dictionary* (1896-1905). With the publication of Wright's *Dictionary* the English Dialect Society ceased to exist on the grounds that its work was finished. This decision was based on a rather narrow view of the purpose of a dialect society, since a dictionary, however good, is never definitive. Dialect research at the present day is concerned especially with establishing the boundaries between various dialect features, and the county dialect societies, which flourish especially in the North of England, are concerned with encouraging the use of dialect as well as with its study.

As we have seen, English dialects are now not merely regional but are also social. Class dialects are much harder to study than are local dialects. Nowadays people move from place to place so freely that it is becoming increasingly difficult to find speakers of unmixed local dialect; but the place where a man lives can be the subject of an objective statement, and statements of this kind do not as a rule cause offence. Social classes, on the other hand, are hard to define and are constantly changing, and any discussion of their speech habits is liable to be tinged with snobbishness or to seem to be so to the hypersensitive. It is, however, possible to notice certain broad distinctions, both in pronunciation and in choice of words, which may be said to be features of class dialect. In the North of England the long *a* sound in words like *pass*, *path* and *laugh* tends to have social as well as regional significance. Advertisers are quick to seize upon linguistic features which have snob value. For example, it is perhaps possible to say that the expression 'Dear lady' is less often met with in real life than in a certain type of advertisement, where it is used to build up an atmosphere of what the same advertisements would describe as 'gracious living'. On the other hand, there are certain widespread developments of meaning which can be described as vulgarisms: *chronic* in the sense 'bad', *mental* in the sense 'mentally deficient', and *saucy* in the sense 'impudent' are examples. Some words tend to become shibboleths, and then cease to be so regarded when their nature becomes widely known or when taboos are deliberately disregarded by speakers who resent the undue importance attached to trifles. Such pairs are *serviette* and *table napkin, couch* and *sofa, port wine* and *port*. A similar distinction applies to certain pronunciations, such as the pronunciation of *garage* to rhyme with *carriage* or the omission of the final *t* in *valet*. Certain words are used more often by men than by women and *vice versa*, although conventions of this kind are not so strong in English as in some other languages. The words *person, nice,* and *common* (in the sense 'vulgar') are perhaps used more often by women, while *chap* and *fellow* are perhaps used more often by men. Sometimes the distinction is one of age rather than of sex, and examples of this kind are particularly interesting to the student of language because they show linguistic changes in process. Pronouncing dictionaries and historical grammars tend to lag behind the facts of contemporary speech, and they record the pronunciation of older rather than of younger speakers. Pronouncing dictionaries still sometimes record *off* and *coffee* as having long vowels, but probably most younger speakers of today pronounce the vowels short. Other tendencies may be observed in the pronunciation of diphthongs. Books on English pronunciation describe the first element of the diphthong in *gay* as close *e* and the first element of the diphthong in *go* as close *o*, but very many speakers today use open *e* in *gay* and a central vowel in *go*, and among such speakers young people predominate.

It is possible to make a distinction between class dialects and levels of speech. The former vary from one speaker to another; the latter depend upon the occasion rather than the speaker. Most speakers use different varieties of speech in different environments, and these varieties generally represent different degrees of formality. The differences between one level and another may be differences of pronunciation, syntax or vocabulary. Pronunciation may vary in the extent of reduction of the vowels of lightly stressed syllables; syntax may be modified by the informal use of constructions which would be avoided on formal occasions; vocabulary may be modified by the admission of varying amounts of slang. One of the attributes of a good speaker is skill in the choice of level. If he chooses too high a level he is liable to sound stilted; if too low he is apt to sound slangy or to be suspected of talking down to his hearers. An example of variation of level may be quoted. An examination candidate had filled a page with solid though conventional criticism showing clearly the influence of some text-book or editor's introduction. He had then been struck by the absurdity of it all and added a sentence in what was clearly his natural colloquial style: 'It's all right me writing a mouthful like this about Chaucer, but these statements have to be proved'. He then resumed the style of conventional literary criticism.

One of the most important aspects of the choice of the right linguistic level is the use of slang. A distinction has to be made between slang and dialect, though both are felt by some people to be below the level of standard educated speech. Perhaps the most important difference between the two is that slang has always an air of novelty about it whereas dialect has its roots in the past as firmly as has Standard English. During the last few decades there has been a marked increase in the use of slang in England. In an attempt to secure informality, it is used today on many occasions where its use would have sounded inappropriate fifty years ago. The Stock Exchange has always had its own slang, and some slang words from this source, such as *bulls*, *bears* and *stags*, have passed into general use. Other slang terms describe the shares of particular companies, and are usually either curtailments, such as *Imps* for *The Imperial Tobacco Company* (*of Great Britain and Ireland*) *Ltd.*, or made up of initials like *Gussies* for *The Great Universal Stores Ltd.* It is, however, a comparatively recent development to find slang from other spheres used in technical discussions, with the result that a financial journalist describes a share as possessing 'plenty of oomph'.

Many people attribute the increased use of slang to the influence of the cinema and especially of American films, and this influence has often been blamed for 'debasing' the English language. There is some truth in these charges, but they make a number of questionable assumptions. One such assumption is the view that the introduction of slang necessarily debases a language. The permanent influence of slang on a language is not as a rule great. Since novelty is one of the chief sources of their appeal, slang words have a comparatively short life. A few of them, such as *skyscraper*, satisfy a need and pass into the standard language, but the introduction of such words does not involve any debasement of the language. Another questionable assumption is that slang is necessarily of American origin. Many of the slang expressions current in England today are borrowed from America, but many are of native origin. Some debasement of the language undoubtedly does take place as a result of the influence of American films, but in this connexion it is important to remember the existence of different levels of speech in both England and America. Many of the examples of illiterate speech that are quoted are from gangster films and are as offensive to an educated American as to an educated Englishman.

Apart from variations of this kind, it is undoubtedly true that there are differences between British and American English. These differences have been fully discussed in such works as H. L. Mencken's *The American Language*, and the length of that work, which, with its two supplements, extends to more than two thousand pages, is evidence that the divergences are considerable. It is natural that there should be many differences between the languages of the two countries, since it can often be noticed in the history of languages that divergent development results from geographical division. But to get those differences into their correct perspective, it is well to notice that the points of resemblance vastly outnumber the points of difference, and British and American English can more properly be regarded as dialects of the same language than as different languages.

Differences between the American and British varieties of English are to be found in pronunciation, spelling, syntax, and vocabulary, and some words have had a different semantic development in the two countries. Contact between Englishmen and Americans has made some of the differences less clear-cut than they might have been: we find some distinctly American linguistic features occasionally used in England as a result either of imitation, conscious or unconscious, or of independent development in the two countries. Some so-called Americanisms, like the use of *to guess* in the sense 'to think' or *sick* in the sense 'ill', are simply survivals of older English expressions that have become archaic or restricted in use in England. Whether a linguistic feature is to be considered as an Americanism or not therefore depends on the relative frequency with which it is found in the two countries. A few instances of the various types of Americanism may be mentioned. In pronunciation there is the tendency to use [æ] or [æ:] where Standard English has [ɑ:] before [f], [s], and [θ], as in *laugh, glass, path*, and before [n] in French loan-words, as in *dance*. It will be noticed that in this respect the American pronunciation resembles Northern English more closely than Southern English. Other features of American pronunciation are the unrounding of [ɒ] to [ɑ] in words like *hot* and the use of [u:] instead of [ju:] in words like *tune* and *duke*. Examples of American spellings are *plow, honor, traveler, program*, and *theater*. In syntax the use of *to* with the infinitive instead of *at* followed by a verbal noun after the verb *to aim* is generally thought of as an Americanism, although examples are fairly frequent in England. A less frequently noticed syntactic feature involves word-order. In sentences containing an adverb and an auxiliary verb, American usage puts the adverb first whereas in England the adverb separates the auxiliary verb from the following infinitive or participle. An American book contains the sentence *Groups of satellite cities frequently have been developed*; the usual word-order in British English would be *have frequently been developed*. Differences of vocabulary are not very important, since any word that satisfies a real need is liable to be borrowed, but there are many examples, such as *fall* beside *autumn, sidewalk* beside *pavement, elevator* beside *lift*, and *mimeographed* beside *cyclostyled*. The words that cause most confusion are those which are used in different senses in the two countries. An Englishman is liable to be startled if he is told that it is illegal to drive a car without a muffler, but that is only because he is accustomed to call a *muffler* a *silencer*.

Other parts of the world in which English is spoken have developed special characteristics, and these may be expected to grow in number in the future. In Canadian English there are two influences at work: those of Great Britain and the United States, with the latter influence vastly predominating. To an even greater extent than in the United States, there are in Canada considerable minorities who speak languages other than English; in Quebec speakers of French are in a majority. In the Union of South Africa English and Afrikaans are approximately equally widespread, English being more common in towns and Afrikaans in country districts; bilingualism is common. It is natural that the English spoken in South Africa should include a large number of loan-words from Afrikaans, such as *aardvark, trek, voortrekker, inspan*, and *veldt*. In pronunciation there is a tendency to round the [ɑ:] in words like *pass* to a sound approaching [ɔ:] and a tendency to lower [i] to a sound approaching [e] in words like *pin*. In Australian English there are a few loan-words from the languages of the aborigines, of which the best-known are *kangaroo* and *boomerang*. Many of the early settlers in Australia came from London and other large cities, and it has often been pointed out that there are several resemblances between Australian and Cockney pronunciation. Many of the early settlers in New Zealand came from Scotland, and their influence is sometimes to be found on the form of English spoken there, but there are also resemblances between the Australian and the New Zealand varieties of English.

One question which must occur to anyone who studies the history of the English language is how much further the trends which have been noticeable in the past may be carried into the future. We have seen that sound-changes are taking place at the present time, and there seems to be no good reason for supposing that they will ever cease to take place. As a result of sound-changes certain sounds are falling together and the number of homophones in the language is tending to increase. This tendency is more marked in the South than in the North. Few speakers of Southern English make any distinction between *which* and *witch* or between *when* and *wen*, and some speakers make no distinction between *moor* and *more*, *our* and *are*, or *fire* and *far*. Changes of meaning are constantly taking place and will continue to do so. The extension of our vocabulary as a result of the increased influence of science in everyday life may be expected to continue at an increased rate. Changes of all kinds will probably meet with stubborn resistance. We are familiar with the use of nouns as verbs, as when we speak of *tabling* an amendment, but a cry of pain still goes up from prescriptive grammarians when abstract nouns, like *sabotage* and *contact*, are used as verbs. Another change in syntax which is taking place at the present time is the use of *due to* with the meaning 'because of'. This construction causes pain to many people, including the present writer, but objection to it cannot very well be maintained on historical grounds. The simplification of English accidence has already gone a long way and could go further without any lessening of the efficiency of the language, but it is doubtful whether many further changes of this kind will be tolerated. Examples of irregularities of accidence which could be smoothed out are the plural demonstrative adjectives *these* and *those*, which are probably kept alive by their use as pronouns, where the distinction in form serves a useful purpose, whereas when they are used adjectivally the ending of the noun is sufficient to indicate plurality. Another anomaly is the distinction between the singular *was* and the plural *were*. Strong verbs are now so heavily outnumbered by weak that they must be regarded as irregular, but the surviving strong verbs are in such frequent use that it is unlikely that they will all become weak. On the other hand, the few remaining vestiges of the subjunctive may well disappear.

One question which is full of interest for speakers of English is whether their language is likely to spread until it becomes a world language. English is already one of the world's most important languages, judged by the test of the number of speakers, and it is pre-eminent in the wide distribution of its speakers over the face of the earth. Many Englishmen have welcomed the invention of Basic English, a form of English with a vocabulary deliberately restricted to 850 words, with the addition of a small number of technical words for special purposes. One point about Basic English which is often overlooked, however, is that an Englishman who wishes to speak or write it has the difficult task of remembering which of the

English words that he knows are included in the Basic word-list. A more serious objection to Basic English is that it distorts English syntax. Only eighteen Basic English words are verbs, and Mr G. M. Young[1] points out that Basic English, which exaggerates the part of the noun at the expense of the verb, is in a peculiar degree a deformation of English speech, since the strength of English lies in the verb. Moreover, the limited vocabulary of Basic English is a deliberate impoverishment of the language, which has the inevitable consequence that many subtle shades of meaning cannot be adequately expressed in Basic English. On the other hand, in a few limited fields, such as business communication, where a large vocabulary is not needed, Basic English may well prove to be useful. It is well to remember also that, although an Englishman has to memorize the Basic word-list before he can speak or write in Basic, he can understand Basic without making any special effort.

Any attempt to impose an artificial restriction on the vocabulary for pedagogic purposes raises two questions: what is the total extent of the English vocabulary and what part of this vocabulary is understood by those who speak the language? On such subjects no precision is possible; all that one can hope to do is to obtain some idea of the order of magnitude. New words are being borrowed every day, and new words are constantly being formed from existing elements to meet new needs, especially those resulting from scientific inventions; one may instance such words as *television* and *broadcast*. Once these words have passed into general use, other words can be formed from them. It is a matter of indifference to most speakers of English whether they have previously seen such derivatives as *broadcaster* or *broadcasting*; their meaning is clear because the suffixes they contain are still 'living', that is to say that they are used in the formation of new words. Apart from the difficulty of deciding what constitutes a separate word, there is the difficulty of deciding when foreign words are to be considered as assimilated into English as loan-words and how far obsolete or dialectal words should be included. A very rough idea of the extent of the English vocabulary may be gained from the fact that NED, excluding its Supple-

[1] *Last Essays*, p. 94.

ment, records about 240,000 main words, or about 415,000 if we include derivatives and compounds. These numbers include, of course, many words which are now obsolete.

Many of the estimates that have been made of the extent of the vocabulary of individual users of English are far too low. Too much has been made of the remark quoted by Max Müller that some country labourers have a vocabulary of less than 300 words. Müller quotes the remark on the authority of 'a country clergyman' speaking of some of the labourers in his parish.[1] The estimate has no pretensions to scientific accuracy and is comparable with the reported comment of a young woman on the 850 words of the Basic English vocabulary that she did not know that there were so many words. The vocabulary of most adults is to be reckoned in thousands or tens of thousands, not in hundreds. Any reader can gain an approximate idea of the extent of his own vocabulary by taking a number of pages of a dictionary at random and counting how many of the words he can define. A proportion sum then gives the approximate extent of the experimenter's vocabulary. Experiments of this kind have shown that extensive vocabularies of 50,000 words or so are quite common and that there is less variation than might be expected in the vocabularies of different persons.[2] The difference between a master of language and an average well-read man generally depends less upon the number of words known than upon what is known about each word: the expert recognizes subtle shades of meaning of which the average man is unconscious.

At first sight there may seem to be some contradiction between the average well-read man's vocabulary of 50,000 or so words and the vocabulary of Shakespeare's plays, which concordances show to have consisted of about 20,000 different words. The difference does not in the main arise from new words absorbed into the language since the time of Shakespeare, but from differences in the methods of computing vocabulary. As Jespersen has pointed out[3] there is a considerable difference between the number of words known and the number of words used. Within

---

[1] *Lectures on the Science of Language,* eighth edition, 1875, I. 308.

[2] Jespersen, *Growth and Structure of the English Language,* § 215.

[3] op. cit. § 216.

the large group of words which any one person would claim to understand, there are two smaller overlapping groups of words which he would use in writing and in speech respectively. Shakespeare's recorded vocabulary is unusually large when compared with that of other poets, but the figures derived from a concordance give a very misleading idea of what we may assume to have been his total vocabulary.

There is plenty of evidence of popular interest in linguistic problems at the present time. There are flourishing societies, such as the Philological Society, the English Place-Name Society, and the Linguistic Society of America. The Society for Pure English published many interesting pamphlets on matters of linguistic interest, and when it ceased to exist the reason was not lack of public support but a shortage of papers suitable for publication. This fact provides a pointer to what is needed in English linguistic studies today. There is plenty of work to be done; the greatest need is for trained scholars. In the nineteenth century a good deal was achieved by enthusiastic workers in such fields as the editing of early texts and the collection of dialect words. Some of their work, such as Sir Frederic Madden's edition of Layamon's *Brut* or Joseph Wright's *Grammar of the Dialect of Windhill*, is excellent even when judged by the more rigorous standards of today, but the emphasis today is on the need for training. The editing of early texts is not a mere matter of transcription; it calls for the application of linguistic knowledge. The study of contemporary English dialects needs trained fieldworkers who are able to detect very slight variations in pronunciation. There are branches of linguistic study which are badly neglected in England. Much has been written during the present century on English syntax, but, apart from elementary books, very little of it has been written by native English speakers.

One form which an interest in the English language sometimes takes is a desire to reform it or to prevent its degeneration. Such anxiety finds expression at many different levels. There are frequent angry letters to the press protesting about such normal linguistic events as the introduction of new slang terms or American loan-words, the use of nouns as verbs, and the spread of dialectal pronunciations. The man who says that he 'does not know anything about art but he knows what he likes' has his counterpart in linguistic matters, and such enthusiasts become troublesome only when they attach undue importance to their preferences. There are welcome signs of a desire to base linguistic preferences upon a sound knowledge of the history and nature of language, and the last few decades have seen the publication of a large number of prescriptive books on language by authors who possess such knowledge. Prescriptive grammar is, of course, no new thing; most of the English grammars written before the middle of the nineteenth century were of this type, and writers like Swift were fond of prescribing which kinds of writing were to be encouraged and which were not. During the present century well-known men of letters have emphasized the shortcomings of English and have proposed reforms. Robert Bridges and Bernard Shaw were convinced of the importance of the thorough reform of English spelling, and both writers introduced mild spelling reforms into their published works. One conclusion that can be drawn from the study of the history of the English language, however, is that both the hopes and the fears of the reformers are greatly exaggerated. Such hopes and fears do not sufficiently recognize how tough and robust a language is, in comparison with the activities of an individual. The habits of speech and writing acquired by the millions of people who speak English are too firmly held to be noticeably influenced by the exhortations of a few reformers, however influential, and Bridges and Shaw are unlikely to have any more lasting effect on the development of the English language than earlier reformers. On the other hand, fears that the English language is going to the dogs need not be taken too seriously. Some current developments seem to interfere with the efficiency of the language, and it is reasonable to resist them, but a language can stand a lot of inefficiency and the English language would not have continued to exist for so long if its users had been unable to devise ways of overcoming and counteracting degeneration when it attained serious proportions. The English language will continue to change, and the changes which it undergoes will continue to be a fascinating subject of study, but the object of such study should be to understand the language, not to change it.

Bibliography

THE books recommended here represent only a selection from a much larger number of useful books and articles. In particular, books in foreign languages are included only when they are of outstanding importance. Fuller information may be found in A. G. Kennedy, *A Bibliography of Writings on the English Language from the Beginning of Printing to the end of 1922* (Cambridge, Mass., 1927) and in volume I of the *Cambridge Bibliography of English Literature* (Cambridge, 1940). More up-to-date information may be found in the annual publications *The Year's Work in English Studies* published by the Oxford University Press for the English Association and the *Annual Bibliography of English Language and Literature* now published by the Cambridge University Press for the Modern Humanities Research Association.

The Bibliography is arranged on the same pattern as the book as a whole. The classification of books under the various chapter-headings cannot be rigid, since many books deal with the subject-matter of more than one chapter. The choice of heading for such books has been determined by what seems to be the most important aspect of the book in question. The date given is usually that of the latest edition containing important revision. The place of publication is London unless otherwise stated.

I. THE NATURE OF LANGUAGE

Perhaps the best introduction to the general principles of language study is E. Sapir, *Language, An Introduction to the Study of Speech* (1922). A fuller treatment of the same subject is Leonard Bloomfield, *Language* (1933). Both of these are standard works. Otto Jespersen's *Language, its Nature, Development and Origin* (1922) is readable and stimulating, but the first hundred pages, dealing with the history of linguistic scholarship in the nineteenth century, do not form an indispensable part of the book. The chief theories of the origin of language are summarized and discussed by G. Révész in the earlier chapters of *The Origins and Prehistory of Language*, translated from the German by J. Butler

(1956). One of the most important and influential books on general linguistics published during the present century is Ferdinand de Saussure, *Cours de linguistique générale publié par Charles Bally et Albert Sechehaye* (Lausanne, 1916). Sir Alan Gardiner, *The Theory of Speech and Language* (Oxford, second edition, 1951) deals with similar problems. An investigation of spoken English which shows how radically it differs from the written language is Randolph Quirk's 'Colloquial English and Communication' in *Studies in Communication* by A. J. Ayer and others (1955). L. R. Palmer's *An Introduction to Modern Linguistics* (1936) is particularly valuable for its chapter on linguistic geography. Louis H. Gray's *Foundations of Language* (New York, 1939) contains much valuable material, but the last three chapters, packed as they are with bibliographical information, are useful chiefly for reference. A good textbook of descriptive linguistics, illustrating an approach to language different from that adopted in the present book, is H. A. Gleason, *An Introduction to Descriptive Linguistics* (New York, 1956). Readable books dealing with general linguistics are J. R. Firth, *The Tongues of Men* (1937), Margaret Schlauch, *The Gift of Tongues* (London edition, 1943) and Mario Pei, *The Story of Language* (New York, 1949). A number of books deal with the general principles of language study with special reference to the English language; of these, H. C. Wyld's *The Historical Study of the Mother Tongue, An Introduction to Philological Method* (1906) and Eric Partridge's *The World of Words* (1938) may be recommended.

2. THE DEVELOPMENT OF ENGLISH

A work of outstanding importance is *The New English Dictionary on Historical Principles* edited by J. A. H. Murray, Henry Bradley, W. A. Craigie and C. T. Onions (Oxford, 1884–1928). A corrected re-issue in twelve volumes and one Supplement was published in 1933 with the title *The Oxford English Dictionary*. There have been many outline histories of the English language. Two of the older histories which may be strongly recommended are Henry Sweet, *A New English Grammar, Logical and Historical* (2 vols, Oxford, 1892–8) and Henry Bradley, *The Making of English* (1904). Albert C. Baugh, *A History of the English Language*

(New York, 1935, London edition, 1951) is an admirable survey, which pays attention to the relation of linguistic development to political and social history. More recent introductory surveys are C. L. Wrenn, *The English Language* (1949) and Simeon Potter, *Our Language* (Pelican Books, 1950). Logan Pearsall Smith's volume *The English Language* in the Home University Library (1912) has been re-issued with an Epilogue by R. W. Chapman (Oxford, 1952), and Ernest Weekley's *The English Language*, originally published in Benn's Sixpenny Library (1928), has been re-issued with a chapter on the history of American English by John W. Clark (The Language Library, 1952). There is a brief and lucid essay on 'The English Language' by C. T. Onions in *The Character of England* edited by Sir Ernest Barker (Oxford, 1947). Margaret M. Bryant, *Modern English and Its Heritage* (New York, 1948) is a comprehensive introduction to many different aspects of the history of the English language. A fuller treatment is contained in Karl Brunner, *Die englische Sprache, ihre Geschichtliche Entwicklung* (Halle, 2 vols, 1950–51). E. Classen, *Outlines of the History of the English Language* (1919) is a well-balanced comprehensive survey, but T. N. Toller's book with the same title (Cambridge, 1900) is chiefly concerned with Old English. H. C. Wyld, *A Short History of English* (third edition, 1927) deals mainly with phonology and accidence. Otto Jespersen's excellent *Growth and Structure of the English Language* (sixth edition, 1930) is in some ways complementary to Wyld; it deals mainly with vocabulary, but Chapter VIII deals lucidly with some frequently discussed features of English accidence and syntax. Albert H. Marckwardt, *Introduction to the English Language* (Oxford, 1942), adopts the unusual plan of working backwards from Modern English to Old English. J. A. Sheard, *The Words We Use* (The Language Library, 1954) deals mainly with vocabulary, and Mary S. Serjeantson, *A History of Foreign Words in English* (1935) is a study of the various strata of loan-words. There are separate studies of the English debt to various single languages; of these special mention may be made of Erik Björkman, *Scandinavian Loan-Words in Middle English* (Halle, 1900–1902) and Mario Praz, 'The Italian Element in English' in *Essays and Studies by Members of the English Association*, vol. XV (1929). A convenient

introduction to the study of Indo-European philology is pro-
vided by Antoine Meillet, *Introduction à l'étude comparative des
langues Indo-européennes* (Paris, eighth edition, 1937) and T.
Hudson-Williams, *A Short Introduction to the Study of Comparative
Grammar (Indo-European)* (Cardiff, 1935). The fullest account of
Common Germanic written in English is Edward Prokosch,
A Comparative Germanic Grammar (Philadelphia, 1939), a book
suitable only for advanced students. The first three chapters of
W. E. Collinson and R. Priebsch, *The German Language* (second
edition, 1946) are of value to students of English as well as to
students of German. G. L. Brook, *An Introduction to Old English*
(Manchester, 1955) contains an outline of grammar and ex-
tracts from Old English prose. *An Old English Grammar* (1955) by
Randolph Quirk and C. L. Wrenn contains a valuable chapter
on syntax and suggestions for further reading. The best full
account of Old English phonology and accidence is *Altenglische
Grammatik nach der angelsächsischen Grammatik von Eduard Sievers
neubearbeitet von Karl Brunner* (Halle, second edition, 1951). There
is much valuable information about the historical background
of Old English in Sir Frank Stenton, *Anglo-Saxon England* (Oxford, second edition, 1947), R. H. Hodgkin, *A History of the
Anglo-Saxons* (2 vols, Oxford, third edition, 1952), and Peter
Hunter Blair, *An Introduction to Anglo-Saxon England* (Cambridge,
1956). A more elementary treatment of the subject is Dorothy
Whitelock, *The Beginnings of English Society* (Pelican Books,
1952). Joseph and Elizabeth Mary Wright, *An Elementary Middle
English Grammar* (Oxford, 1932) provides a systematic treatment of Middle English phonology and accidence, and there is
an admirable essay on the English Language in the Fourteenth
Century in Kenneth Sisam, *Fourteenth Century Verse and Prose*
(Oxford, 1921). A good brief account of Anglo-Norman is
contained in Johan Vising, *Anglo-Norman Language and Literature*
(Oxford, 1923), and there is a study of the relative importance
of English and French during the early Middle English period
by R. M. Wilson, 'English and French in England 1100–1300'
in *History* 28 (1943) 37–60. The continuity of the tradition of
English prose from Anglo-Saxon times is emphasized by R. W.
Chambers in his essay *On the Continuity of English Prose from Alfred
to More and his School.* This forms part of the Introduction to

Nicholas Harpsfield's *Life of Sir Thomas More* (Early English Text Society, Oxford, 1932) and has also been published separately.

Two sound and readable surveys of the development of Modern English are G. H. McKnight and Bert Emsley, *Modern English in the Making* (New York, 1928) and Stuart Robertson, *The Development of Modern English* (New York, 1936). A more detailed study is H. C. Wyld, *A History of Modern Colloquial English* (Oxford, third edition, 1936). Joseph and E. M. Wright, *An Elementary Historical New English Grammar* (Oxford, 1924) deals systematically with the spelling, phonology and accidence of the modern period. A brief but valuable essay on Shakespeare's English by Henry Bradley is contained in *Shakespeare's England* (Oxford, 2 vols, 1916). A much fuller treatment of the same subject is Wilhelm Franz, *Die Sprache Shakespeares in Vers und Prosa* (Halle, 1939), which constitutes the fourth edition of his *Shakespeare-Grammatik*. Richard Foster Jones, *The Triumph of the English Language* (Oxford, 1953) is a very thorough and well-documented 'survey of opinions concerning the vernacular from the introduction of printing to the Restoration'.

3. THE SOUNDS OF SPEECH

There are many studies of phonetics with special reference to English, of which Daniel Jones, *An Outline of English Phonetics* (Cambridge, eighth edition, 1956) and Ida C. Ward, *The Phonetics of English* (Cambridge, fourth edition, 1945) are among the best. J. R. Firth, *Speech* (1930) is a useful introduction to the subject. A comprehensive treatment of phonetic principles is provided by Maurice Grammont, *Traité ae Phonétique* (Paris, troisième édition revue, 1946). A good pronouncing dictionary is that of Daniel Jones, now called *Everyman's English Pronouncing Dictionary* (eleventh edition, 1956). A comparison of the pronunciations recorded in the earliest editions with those in the later editions provides an interesting commentary on the way in which pronunciation is constantly changing. The best study of English intonation is L. Armstrong and I. C. Ward, *Handbook of English Intonation* (Cambridge, second edition, 1952). On the phoneme see Daniel Jones, *The Phoneme, its Nature and Use*

(Cambridge, 1950). The phonetic symbols of the International Phonetic Association are revised from time to time and are printed in the periodical *Le Maître Phonétique*. A. Lloyd James, *The Broadcast Word* (1935) is an interesting collection of essays on various aspects of contemporary English speech.

4. PHONOLOGY

The fullest survey of English phonology from the Old English period to the present day is K. Luick's monumental but incomplete *Historische Grammatik der englischen Sprache* (Leipzig, 1914–40). L. F. Brosnahan, *Some Old English Sound Changes*: *An Analysis in the Light of Modern Phonetics* (Cambridge, 1953) pays special attention to the phonetic implications of sound-changes. The Old and Middle English grammars mentioned in connexion with Chapter II pay a good deal of attention to phonology. The first volume of Otto Jespersen, *A Modern English Grammar on Historical Principles* (1909) is a study of the phonology and spelling of the Modern English period. Recent outstanding studies of Modern English phonology are Helge Kökeritz, *Shakespeare's Pronunciation* (New Haven, 1953), Wilhelm Horn and Martin Lehnert, *Laut und Leben: Englische Lautgeschichte der neueren Zeit* (1400–1950) (2 vols, Berlin, 1954), and E. J. Dobson, *English Pronunciation* 1500–1700 (2 vols, Oxford, 1957).

5. SPELLING

There is a general survey of English spelling by G. H. Vallins, *Spelling*, with a chapter on American spelling by John W. Clark (The Language Library, 1954). Sir William A. Craigie, *Some Anomalies of Spelling* (SPE Tract No. 59, 1942) is a shorter study. An important analysis of the problems underlying the study of spelling and spelling reform is Henry Bradley's lecture 'On the Relations between Spoken and Written Language with special Reference to English', printed in the *Proceedings of the British Academy* 1913–1914, and included in the *Collected Papers of Henry Bradley* edited by Robert Bridges (Oxford, 1928). Works on spelling reform include T. R. Lounsbury, *English Spelling and Spelling Reform* (New York, 1909), R. E. Zachrisson, '400 Years of English Spelling Reform' in *Studia Neophilologica* 4 (1931–2) and Sir William A. Craigie, *Problems of Spelling Reform* (SPE Tract No. 63, 1944).

6. ACCIDENCE

A concise survey of the development of English accidence from the Old English period to the present day is contained in the last chapter of H. C. Wyld, *A Short History of English* (third edition, 1927). A fuller treatment of some aspects of the subject is in George O. Curme, *A Grammar of the English Language*, Volume II, *Parts of Speech and Accidence* (New York, 1935). A comprehensive survey of the history of English accidence and syntax is included in the second volume of Karl Brunner, *Die Englische Sprache* (Halle, 1950–51). For the Modern English period see Part 6 of Otto Jespersen, *A Modern English Grammar* (1946). Among the studies of special problems may be mentioned H. Lindkvist, 'On the Origin of the English Pronoun *she*' in *Anglia* 45 (1921) 1–50, Mary McDonald Long, *The English Strong Verb from Chaucer to Caxton* (Menasha, Wis., 1944), H. T. Price, *A History of Ablaut in the Strong Verbs from Caxton to the end of the Elizabethan Period* (Bonn, 1910), and Erik Holmqvist, *On the History of the English Present Inflections, particularly -th and -s* (Heidelberg, 1922).

7. SYNTAX

C. T. Onions, *An Advanced English Syntax* (1904) is a useful survey of Modern English syntax which, in spite of its title, can be used as an introductory manual. H. W. and F. G. Fowler in *The King's English* (Oxford, third edition, 1930) discuss many problems of syntax from the point of view of the prescriptive grammarian. R. W. Zandvoort, *A Handbook of English Grammar* (revised London edition, 1957) is valuable. Leon Kellner, *Historical Outlines of English Syntax* (1892) briefly covers the whole history of English syntax. G. O. Curme, *A Grammar of the English Language*, Volume III, *Syntax* (1931) and Otto Jespersen, *A Modern English Grammar* (Parts 2, 3, 4, 5, and 7, Heidelberg, London and Copenhagen, 1909–49) deal mainly with the syntax of the Modern English period. Jespersen's rather individual approach to English syntax is represented more concisely in

Essentials of English Grammar (1933) and with fuller discussion of the general linguistic problems involved in *The Philosophy of Grammar* (1924). Among the many studies of special problems may be mentioned Samuel Moore, 'Grammatical and Natural Gender in Middle English', PMLA 36 (1921) 79–103, G. O. Curme, 'A History of the English Relative Constructions', JEGP 11 (1912) 10–29, 180–204, 355–380, C. A. Bodelsen, 'The Expanded Tenses in Modern English' *Englische Studien* 71 (1936–7) 220–238, and Alvar Ellegård, *The Auxiliary Do: The Establishment and Regulation of its Use in English* (Stockholm, 1953).

8. SEMANTICS

Of the many books dealing with the general principles of semantics two of the best-known are C. K. Ogden and I. A. Richards, *The Meaning of Meaning* (eighth edition, 1946) and S. Ullmann, *The Principles of Semantics* (Glasgow, 1951). The latter book has a full bibliography which shows how this branch of linguistic study has developed during the present century. Of articles on the subject mention may be made of J. R. Firth, 'The Technique of Semantics', *Transactions of the Philological Society* (1935) 36–72. Michel Bréal, *Essai de Sémantique* (Paris, 1897) was a pioneer work which can still be read with advantage. There is an English translation by Mrs Henry Cust with the title *Semantics: Studies in the Science of Meaning* (1900). An important book, which is not easy to read, is Gustaf Stern, *Meaning and Change of Meaning with Special Reference to the English Language* (Göteborg, 1931). Two readable books which give English illustrations of the chief types of semantic change are J. B. Greenough and G. L. Kittredge, *Words and their Ways in English Speech* (New York, 1901) and G. H. McKnight, *English Words and their Background* (New York, 1923). Logan Pearsall Smith's 'Four Words: Romantic, Originality, Creative, Genius', SPE Tract No. 17, later reproduced as Chapter III of *Words and Idioms, Studies in the English Language* (1925), is an example of the use of semantics as an aid to literary criticism. Another work belonging to the borderland between linguistics and literary criticism is William Empson, *The Structure of Complex Words* (1951). Two books which deal with the relation between semantics and social history are Owen Barfield, *History in English Words* (second edition, 1933) and Bernard Groom, *A Short History of English Words* (1934). Studies of special types of semantic development include G. A. Van Dongen, *Amelioratives in English* (Rotterdam, 1933) and H. Schreuder, *Pejorative Sense Development in English* (Groningen, 1929). There is an essay on 'Euphemism and Euphemisms' in Eric Partridge, *Here, There and Everywhere* (1950).

9. PRESENT-DAY TRENDS

General studies of the English language at the present day include W. E. Collinson, *Contemporary English* (Berlin, 1927) and Ernst Leisi, *Das Heutige Englisch* (Heidelberg, 1955). The standard work on dialect vocabulary is Joseph Wright, *English Dialect Dictionary* (6 vols, 1898–1905). *The English Dialect Grammar*, which forms part of Volume VI, was published separately (Oxford, 1905). More recent research is described by Angus McIntosh in *An Introduction to a Survey of Scottish Dialects* (Edinburgh, 1952) and by Harold Orton in 'A New Survey of Dialectal English' in *The Journal of the Lancashire Dialect Society*, 2 (1952) 5–13. A survey of dialect research and a list of monographs on separate dialects is provided by Eugen Dieth in 'A New Survey of English Dialects' (*Essays and Studies by Members of the English Association*, 32 (1946) 74–104). The best studies of English slang are Eric Partridge, *Slang Today and Yesterday* (third edition, 1950) and *A Dictionary of Slang and Unconventional English from the Fifteenth Century to the Present Day* (fourth edition, 1951). There is a study of American English by G. P. Krapp, *The English Language in America* (2 vols, New York, 1925), and a considerable body of material has been collected by H. L. Mencken in *The American Language* (fourth edition, New York, 1936); Supplement One (1945) and Supplement Two (1948) are substantial works. A more concise treatment of the subject is Thomas Pyles, *Words and Ways of American English* (New York, 1952; London edition 1954). H. W. Horwill, *A Dictionary of Modern American Usage* (Oxford, 1935) aims at describing some of the chief differences between the American and British varieties of English, and J. S. Kenyon and T. A. Knott, *A Pronouncing Dictionary of American English* (Springfield, Mass.,

1944) aims at recording American pronunciation. Studies of English as spoken in the Dominions are included in *A History of British and American English since 1900* edited by Eric Partridge and J. W. Clark (1951). Sidney J. Baker, *The Australian Language* (Sydney, 1945) contains much useful material. The future trends of the English language are discussed by J. Hubert Jagger in *English in the Future* (1940). There is an account of Basic English by one of its inventors in I. A. Richards, *Basic English and Its Uses* (1943), and a discussion of some of its drawbacks by G. M. Young in *Basic* (SPE Tract No. 62, 1943), reprinted in his *Last Essays* (1950). The Philological Society publishes an annual volume of *Transactions* and the Lakeland, Lancashire and Yorkshire Dialect Societies publish annual volumes of original work in dialect and studies of various aspects of dialect. There is an account of the work of the Society for Pure English in *Retrospect* by R. W. Chapman (SPE Tract No. 66, 1948). The English Place-Name Society has published more than twenty-five volumes since 1924. Volume I Part I of its publications is a useful *Introduction to the Survey of English Place-Names* edited by A. Mawer and F. M. Stenton (Cambridge, 1924). Volume I Part II is a dictionary of the chief elements used in English place-names, but this has been superseded by a later publication of the Society, A. H. Smith, *English Place-Name Elements* (2 vols, Cambridge, 1956). A compendious reference work is Eilert Ekwall, *The Concise Oxford Dictionary of English Place-Names* (third edition, Oxford, 1947). There is an important work on British surnames by P. H. Reaney, *A Dictionary of British Surnames* (1958). Perhaps the most influential of the prescriptive books on the use of English published during the present century has been H. W. Fowler, *A Dictionary of Modern English Usage* (Oxford, 1926). More recent books with a similar aim are Eric Partridge, *Usage and Abusage: A Guide to Good English* (fifth edition, 1957) and *The Concise Usage and Abusage* (1954). Sir Ernest Gowers wrote his *Plain Words: A Guide to the Use of English* (1948) and *A B C of Plain Words* (1951) primarily for the instruction of his fellow civil servants, but they have had a wide and salutary influence on other writers of English.

Index

This index does not include words used as illustrative examples and it contains no references to the Bibliography.